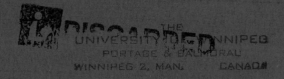

TWAYNE'S
RULERS AND STATESMEN OF THE WORLD
SERIES

Hans L. Trefousse, Brooklyn College
General Editor

CAMILLO di CAVOUR

(TROW 24)

Camillo di Cavour

By FRANK J. COPPA

St. John's University

Twayne Publishers, Inc. : : New York

ISBN 0-8057-3018-4
MANUFACTURED IN THE UNITED STATES OF AMERICA

Preface

THIS BOOK DOES NOT PRETEND TO BE A DEFINITIVE BIOGRAPHY OF Cavour, a duplication in English of what Rosario Romeo is doing in Italian. Such an enterprise would require not one but several volumes, each many times the number of pages allotted for works in the Rulers and Statesmen of the World Series. The present study, while examining the Count's life and policies, seeks to concentrate upon those aspects of his career and character not generally stressed in English accounts. At the same time, by utilizing some of the recent historiographical findings and conclusions, it aims to provide an updated and objective analysis of this maker of modern Italy. The notes and references, it will be seen, have been kept to a minimum.

In the course of writing this book I had recourse to the facilities of a number of libraries, archives, and institutes in Italy and this country and am particularly indebted to the gracious and helpful staffs of the Library of the Chamber of Deputies, the Vatican Archives, the Library of Congress, and the New York Public Library. This project was encouraged and assisted by a number of individuals. I should especially like to acknowledge the aid of Miss Cipriana Scelba of the American Commission for Cultural Exchange with Italy. Her letters of introduction opened many doors in Italy and facilitated my research. Other figures provided inspiration and advice, including John Zeender of the Catholic University of America, Rosario Romeo of the University of Rome, Robert Trisco, Editor of the *Catholic Historical Review,* and Hans Trefousse of Brooklyn College. The shortcomings of this volume are, of course, my own. Finally, this work would not have been written but for the patience and assistance of my wife, Rosina.

Contents

Chronology

1810 Birth of Camillo di Cavour.

1814 Savoyard monarchy restored in Piedmont.

1820 Camillo enrolled in the Military Academy of Turin.

1821 Abortive attempt to convert Piedmont into a constitutional state.

1824 Camillo appointed as a page to Carlo Alberto.

1826 Cavour commissioned as a second lieutenant.

1827 Cavour is assigned to the Corps of Engineers at Turin.

1828– He is assigned to a series of remote frontier posts.
1829

1830 The July Revolution in Paris upsets conservative Europe.

1831 Carlo Alberto assumes the throne of Piedmont.

1831 Count Cavour obtains an honorable discharge from the army; devotes himself to agriculture.

1835 Cavour visits France and England.

1846 The accession of Pius IX ushers in a reform movement in Italy.

1847 Cavour, in conjunction with others, establishes a newspaper called *Il Risorgimento.*

1848 Cavour adds his voice to the call for a constitution and Carlo Alberto grants one.

1848 Outbreak of revolution in Italy which ends with the restoration of 1849.

1849 Carlo Alberto abdicates as King of Piedmont and his son Vittorio Emanuele assumes the throne. Massimo D'Azeglio serves as his Prime Minister.

1850 Cavour's support of the Siccardi Laws bring him popular support and political power.

1850 Cavour enters the cabinet as Minister of Agriculture, Industry, and Commerce.

1852 Cavour concludes *connubio* agreement uniting his center-right coalition with the center-left bloc of Urbano Rattazzi.

1852 Cavour becomes President of the Council of Ministers.

1855   Cavour ranges Piedmont alongside England and France in the Crimean War.

1855   Cavour resigns as Prime Minister over differences with the King on the Law of Convents, but is recalled to power that same year.

1856   Cavour presents the Italian case at the Congress of Paris and makes the Italian problem a European one.

1857   Cavour comes to an understanding with the National Society.

1858   The Orsini attempt to assassinate Louis Napoleon.

1858   Meeting of Napoleon and Cavour at Plombières. The two plan a joint war against Austria with the aim of reordering the Italian peninsula.

1859   France and Piedmont declare war against Austria. Napoleon abruptly truncates the conflict soon after the allies have won Lombardy but before they have freed Venetia.

1859   Cavour resigns rather than accept the Franco-Austrian armistice. His cabinet is replaced by the La Marmora-Rattazzi Ministry.

1859   Tuscany, Modena, and the Romagna press for union with Piedmont, but Napoleon imposes a veto.

1860   Cavour returns to power, signs a new agreement with Napoleon, promising to turn over Nice and Savoy to France in return for French support of his annexation of Central Italy.

1860   Pius IX issues a bull of excommunication which collectively condemns all those who conspired to deprive the Pope of his possessions.

1860   Garibaldi and his Red Shirts conquer Sicily and then cross the straits and capture Naples.

1860   On the pretext of preventing Garibaldi from invading Rome, Cavour has his forces cross the papal frontier and deprives Pius IX of the bulk of his territory.

1861   Vittorio Emanuele II proclaimed King of Italy and Cavour becomes the first Prime Minister of the new Kingdom.

1861   Death of Cavour.

Introduction

THE NINETEENTH CENTURY PRODUCED A SERIES OF OUTSTANDING statesmen whose activity impinged upon and altered the course of world events. Metternich of Austria, Louis Napoleon of France. Bismarck of Prussia, and Lincoln of the United States all played a prominent part in shaping the policies of their respective countries, and had a profound impact upon the international plane as well. Count Camillo di Cavour of Piedmont-Sardinia, the man who forged modern Italy, occupies a position of honor in this gallery, a virtual giant among great men. His biography, more than that of any other figure, is inextricably intertwined with the story of the formation of the Italian state.

In less than a decade his courage and cunning lifted the prostrate monarchy of Piedmont to the rank of a serious contender for the control of all of Italy. His impact on the Church was no less crucial. Whatever his intentions, next to Pope Pius IX, Cavour did the most to mold the nature of the modern Papacy. "The work he accomplished belongs in that order of mind which has created nations, changed history, and consolidated new eras of social and political life," wrote one of his North American admirers.[1] By the time of his premature death in 1861, after he had served as Prime Minister for eight years, his accomplishments earned him the admiration of all of liberal Europe.

A brilliant pragmatist and experienced parliamentarian, Cavour's consummate skill, extraordinary mental capacity, consuming ambition, and iron will enabled him to accomplish feats more proportionate to the great powers than tiny Piedmont. For this reason Gladstone evaluated Cavour's performance as greater than Bismarck's, the other nation maker he admired, for he accomplished as much with far smaller means. Aware of the impracticality of Carlo Alberto's pronouncement *l'Italia farà da se* (Italy will do it alone) and suspicious of Giuseppe Mazzini's call to revolution in the name of *Dio e Il Popolo* (God and the People), Cavour looked to French backing and bayonets to remove the Austrian presence in northern Italy.

United Italy is the greatest testament to his success. His achievement is also attested to by the fact that even his bitter opponents, such as Pope Pius IX, who launched an excommunication against Cavour and his colleagues for depriving him of his territory, acknowledged that the Piedmontese statesman was a great patriot and a first-rate political manipulator. "That country has the good fortune of being led by a great minister," the Pope observed on one occasion. "If I had such a minister, I, too, would be a constitutionalist." Critical contemporaries as well as friends marveled at the audacity and accomplishments of the man, and found in him the proper balance of prudence and intrepidity characteristic of a great statesman.

Napoleon III esteemed Cavour and held his opinion in high regard, to the point of consulting him even in matters and problems extraneous to the Italian political scene. When others lamented that it was unfortunate that the Count did not have a wider scope for his talents, the Emperor commented that it was a formidable task to make a great state out of a small one and required a genius of Cavour's caliber. Only one man had an influence upon Napoleon, his last minister, Émile Ollivier, noted in his diary, and that was Cavour. Indeed, having disappointed the Count in the Italian campaign of 1859, he was to end that venture afraid of his alleged ally. From across the Atlantic President Buchanan inquired about Cavour, whose work he appreciated. Throughout the New World, in fact, the educated classes considered Cavour Italy's man of promise, and his performance fulfilled their expectations.[2]

Few would contest that the Count played a decisive if not the dominant role in destroying the old political status quo and ushering in a new age of nationalism in Central Europe. As the old but still perceptive Metternich watched the Machiavellian minister systematically undermine the system he had fabricated over the past half century, he commented, "There is now only one statesman in Europe, but, unhappily he is against us; this man is Cavour." [3] In an age of *Realpolitik* it was he who introduced into modern diplomacy the ruse of holding responsible for a war the adversary one provoked into declaring it. In 1859 the Emperor of the French was to share in the use of this technique when Cavour employed it against the Habsburgs; later Napoleon was to fall victim to the same strategy at the hands of Bismarck. Cavour sanctioned this and other irregular, or if you will, immoral means in order to attain his ends.

Undeniably the conception of Italian unity is indebted to impassioned thinkers such as Manin, Mazzini, and Gioberti who early upheld the traditions of the Italian people. But what for them was an inspiration, an enthusiasm, a cherished dream was to be realized by the Count. Even though it is true that Cavour more than Giuseppe Garibaldi or Vittorio Emanuele II made and shaped unitary Italy, devised the ecclesiastical policy of the new state, and imposed economic liberalism upon the new nation, why is another study of the Count necessary or desirable? After all, as the father of his country Cavour is one of the most studied protagonists of the *Risorgimento*.

Unfortunately, much of the scholarly work on this historical subject was produced in the half century following his death. Written at a time when liberals were euphoric over unification, while conscientious Catholics were confronted with the excommunication of all those who were responsible for the creation of the new state, objectivity was not the hallmark of Cavourian studies. Then, too, all the sources were not available. Some material was considered too confidential and was bypassed to avoid embarrassing those contemporaries who outlived the Count. In other cases, certain archives remained closed for years, so that important aspects of Cavour's activities could not be properly explored. Thus, the motivation for his legislation dealing with the Church and Rome has not been impartially studied. Indeed, the role played by ideological convictions, religious factors, and political expedients in the evolution of Cavour's policy has not been weighed.

Whatever the Count's intentions his domestic and foreign policies unquestionably provoked a bitter conflict with the Curia and the Church. In persuance of this course Vittorio Emanuele wrote the Pope in 1860 asking him to renounce the Romagna, and the Marches and Umbria as well. Shocked and scandalized, the Pontiff refused, calling the suggestion unworthy of a Catholic sovereign of the House of Savoy. "The Pope has lost his mind," the King told his guard. "I wrote him a nice letter and he responds with insolence and threats." [4] Pius IX did more than that, responding to the Cavour-inspired plebiscite in the Romagna, which favored union with Piedmont, by issuing a major excommunication against the authors, counselors, and adherents of the rebellion, invasion, and usurpation of his provinces. He repeated the censure following the Sardinian invasion and annexation of the Papal Marches and Umbria in September, 1860. In this fashion Rome excommunicated Cavour's work, creating a conflict of conscience for Catholics who were also patriots.

The Pontiff and conservative Catholics were not alone in their opposition to the Count. The federalist Carlo Cattaneo complained that Cavour's centralization did not respect the contribution of Italy's various provinces and peoples; when elected to the Chamber of Deputies from Milan, he refused to attend its sessions. Other federalists, unreconciled figures of the Party of Action, and of course Garibaldi and Mazzini, noting the flaws in the edifice he created, all criticized Cavour's role in the *Risorgimento*. Mazzini had little confidence in Cavour or the monarchy he served, denouncing their work as contaminated by the French alliance and lacking all moral mission.

Garibaldi, the son of a sailor, was no less outspoken and did not forget the obstacles the Piedmontese aristocrat placed in his path to prevent his conquest of the Italian South. Cavour's connivance in the Red Shirts' invasion of the Neapolitan kingdom, the manner in which he aided, used, and finally overcame Garibaldi was not only proof of his political aptitude but the turning point in the destiny of the democrats and the nation. Such an appropriation of democratic and republican energies for his own ends was understandably resented by the radicals. He had long used foreign fear of these same radicals to promote his own policy, and on more than one occasion had warned the English and French that they had to choose between Cavour and Mazzini, confident that their dread of the latter would make his solution for Italy more palatable. This opportunism, deemed brilliant statesmanship by the moderate camp he served, was considered treachery by the Party of Action.

Furthermore, the old Mazzinian and republican criticism of Cavour and the state he inspired, though shunted aside after 1861, was never permanently silenced or totally submerged. It found a new form and expression after World War I and even more so after the Fascist years and World War II. "The conquest of liberty was not bound in Italy with any mass movement capable of playing its role as myth and precursor," Carlo Roselli wrote in 1929. "The masses were absent." [5] If the unification of Italy was a great event from the point of view of the national tradition, observed the historian and sociologist Guglielmo Ferrero, it was from the social point of view a victory of the middle and upper classes. Cavour's accomplishment worked to the advantage of the possessing classes who obtained control of the constitutional state, he claimed, to the detriment of the lower classes who lost the protection provided them by the former "absolutist" regimes.

The publication of Antonio Gramsci's prison meditations, *Quaderni dal Carcere* in the post-World War II period represented an even more serious challenge to the traditional interpretation of the unification as the triumph of liberalism and moderate nationalism and somewhat deflated the figure of Cavour, the hero of Benedetto Croce's *History of Europe in the Nineteenth Century*. Gramsci, one of the founders of the Italian Communist Party, criticized the Count's part in producing a passive revolution of position and maneuver, as against Mazzini's call for a war of popular initiative and momentum. The triumph of the former over the latter, in the Communist leader's view, played a part in preventing the passage of real reform in the peninsula.[6]

Cavour, in Gramsci's writing, emerges as the creature of the landowning, aristocratic classes, transforming what might have evolved into a true revolutionary movement into a conservative conquest. There was thus no social and economic revolution to parallel the political alteration. Within this framework the *Risorgimento* has been seen as a *rivoluzione mancata* or missed revolution with Cavour still the protagonist, but more of a villain than a hero. "The expedition of the Thousand could have been the awaited surgical intervention, the peasant rising of the South. Garibaldi's plebeian spontaneity could have made him into the real head of a southern republic and perhaps of the Italian republic, the Italian Washington," wrote the Communist Ruggero Grieco, who further developed the Marxist interpretation of the *Risorgimento*. "But Garibaldi himself, who was the least tied to the programs of the Action Party, had become enmeshed in treacherous diplomacy, which clipped his wings. . . ."[7] In this view of the momentous events of 1860–1861, it was Cavour who wove the web which trapped the leader of the red shirts and ruined the prospect of meaningful reform.

The continuing controversy about the *Risorgimento* and its central figure, a century after unification, makes an updated biography of this fascinating personality long overdue. The passage of time, the postwar polemic, the finding of new papers, the declassification of others, and the opening of the Vatican Archives for the pontificate of Pius IX contribute to make a new biography of Cavour not only desirable but feasible.

CHAPTER I

Childhood and Youth

ALTHOUGH CAVOUR'S ROLE IN THE RISORGIMENTO IS STILL ENVELOPED in controversy, some things about him are clearly ascertained and accepted by all. Camillo, the second son of the Marquis Michele Antonio Benso di Cavour and Adèle de Sellon, was born in the summer of 1810 in what proved to be a lull before a new storm. Ever since Napoleon had swept into the peninsula, Italy had been in almost constant turmoil. Within a few short years the Austrians had been pushed out, old dynasties overturned, and Italian territory reorganized according to the will and whim of the "Italian" general who governed France and dominated all of Western Europe.

The aristocratic Cavours of Piedmont suffered as a result of the heavy contributions they were forced to make to the French victors, the upsetting of the national currency, and the abolition of feudal rights which seriously imperiled the family patrimony. So long as the republicans prevailed in Paris there seemed to be no relief in sight for the conservative classes in Piedmont. Small wonder that the Cavours developed a deepseated suspicion of republicanism, and it was later transmitted to Camillo.

In large measure it was Filippina de Sales, Camillo's grandmother, who helped the family survive in this time of trouble. Called Marina by her grandchildren, this dynamic woman was to occupy a central position in the Casa Cavour for years afterwards. It was she who, in the summer of 1801, suggested that her son turn his attention to business affairs—a suggestion Michele willingly accepted in light of an uncertain military future in the precarious political situation. As fiercely antirevolutionary as the rest of the family, the Marchesa Cavour was also a realist and considered Piedmont's union with France preferable to an autonomous state under republican control. She and her relatives accepted the decree of annexation and justified it as the means of avoiding revolutionary extremes.

With the passage of time their position toward the French moved from toleration to collaboration. This was facilitated by the fact that the Empire opened new opportunities for the Cavour family, which had endured one crisis after another in the 1790's. Presented with the prospect of holding higher office and position than those enjoyed while a subject of the Savoyards, Michele did not hesitate to compromise with the new order. When his friend Prince Camille Borghese, who had married one of Napoleon's sisters, was made governor of the recently incorporated territory of Piedmont, he served as his chamberlain while his mother served as a lady of honor to Pauline, his wife. So intimate was their relationship with the regime that when Michele had his second son, the Prince and his wife agreed to serve as sponsors at the baptism of the boy. In this fashion the young child was baptized by Pauline Bonaparte, whose brother had declared war against the traditional establishment. Camillo, in fact, was named after Napoleon's brother-in-law.

The very year that Camillo was born, his father was confirmed as a Baron of the Empire. Like so many other favors, it resulted from his friendship with the Prince and his Bonapartist connections. This was an unusual alliance produced by unsettled times. In some ways it was a portent of things to come, for within half a century a second extraordinary understanding between a Bonaparte and a Cavour would produce a spectacular change in the destiny of the Italian peninsula and the European balance of power. The ability to compromise and improvise—which later made it possible for Camillo Cavour to conclude the French alliance—had long been a family tradition, enabling it to preserve its power and prestige through the centuries.

The Bensos of Cavour were of an old and illustrious lineage. Since the middle of the seventeenth century the head of the household held the title of Marquis while the younger brother enjoyed the title of Count. In the eighteenth, the head of the family, Giuseppe Filippo di Cavour, had married Josephte Françoise de Sales, whose family had provided one of the greatest saints of the Catholic reformation. At the beginning of the following century, Don Michele had married the second daughter of Count Jean de Sellon of Geneva, also of a substantial family. This marriage was considered and contracted with material interests in mind and did indeed improve the financial situation of the Cavour family. In 1806 their first son, Gustavo, Marquis of Cavour, was born. Descended from Huguenot refugees, the De Sellons had been ennobled by Joseph II and were both liberal and Protestant. It was not until 1811, the year after Camillo's birth, that his mother abjured her Calvinist faith and entered the

Catholic Church. The De Sellons with their relatives and contacts in France and Switzerland were to rescue the two brothers from the dangers of Piedmontese provincialism.

By a quirk of history, their second son, Camillo, was born and brought into the Church as a French citizen and a special ward of the Bonapartes. The extraordinary chain of events which had produced this situation was soon to be reversed. For some time the imperial system had suffered a series of reverses in the Iberian peninsula—Napoleon's famed Spanish ulcer. This was but a prelude to the outright disaster of the Russian campaign 1812–1813), setting the stage for the war of liberation (1813–1814) which ended French domination in Europe. Since the Cavours had befriended and served the French administration, they trembled at the thought of a restoration and preferred to see their country governed by the Turks than the Savoyards. However, the fund of realism which had so often served the family well came to the fore, and the family disassociated itself from the French.[1]

The Cavours of Piedmont were not alone in their reversal of allegiance. In the rest of Italy, as well, there were those who welcomed the change. In some areas, in fact, the population had tired of Gallic excesses and applauded the Austrians, but soon learned that they preferred to play the part of new masters and that their liberation meant restoration and reaction. Early in 1815 a group of Italian patriots, which included Pellegrino Rossi, appealed to the exiled Napoleon to reconquer Italy, converting it into an independent constitutional state. Such a feat could have been accomplished by Napoleon at the apogee of his career; it was beyond his power if not his will following his fall. Thus the fate of Italy was determined by Austria and her allies.

The formal reconstruction of the peninsula and the entire state system was undertaken at the Congress of Vienna (1815) where the underlying aim was to create a new balance of power and restore stability to Europe. To attain this objective, Austria was confirmed in her commanding position in Italy, with the express mission of keeping the French out. In order to fulfill this obligation, she was allowed to absorb not only Lombardy but Venetia as well. Meanwhile Habsburg influence in Tuscany, Parma, and Modena was exercised through junior members of the family. Finally, the papal government which was restored to Central Italy, and the Bourbons, who were returned to the southern Kingdom of the Two Sicilies, found themselves indebted to the House of Austria. Everywhere national sentiment was ignored; sometimes it was foolishly irritated.

In 1815 Camillo was but a boy of five, unaware of the grave political issues of the day. Indeed the youngster did not hear too much criticism of the settlement because the Turin government did its best to discourage attacks upon the Congress to which it owed its life. Even within the walls of the Palazzo Cavour, few words were heard against the restoration government with which the Marquis Cavour desired to make peace. Hoping to be forgiven for the indiscretion of collaboration with the enemy, his father emerged as a devoted servant of the Savoy dynasty, anxious to prove his loyalty and orthodoxy to an ultra conservative regime.

Undeniably, of the eight states of the restoration peninsula, Piedmont displayed the greatest independence of Austria. Nevertheless, it was far from enlightened. On the contrary, within its borders reaction reached its high point in the post-Vienna world. In May, 1814, Vittorio Emanuele I returned from Sardinia where he had anxiously awaited the restoration. In his trail came an entourage arrayed in eighteenth-century garb, clinging desperately to old customs, presenting the spectacle of an outmoded world restored. The King flaunted his contempt for the new lifestyle and displayed his preference for the old ways by continuing to wear his powdered wig, but one of the many symbols of the *ancien régime* to which he clung. While he did not pursue personal vendettas, he did dismiss most of the officials appointed by the French. The Cavours who had compromised themselves by participating in the Imperial administration quite naturally aroused the suspicions of the restored regime. At court they were treated coldly and had their activities closely watched.[2]

Integral to the monarchy's conception of a return to stability and sanity was the full restoration of the privileges of the Catholic Church. Consequently, the Church calendar was reintroduced, clerical control of education restored, special ecclesiastical courts reestablished, and the clergy's general supervision of the moral and intellectual life of the country resumed. Civil marriages and divorce were again prohibited, and the religious toleration that had marked the French period was terminated. For these reasons liberals shunned Piedmont as a priest-ridden, authoritarian state dominated by narrow-minded aristocrats, the army, and the Society of Jesus, which the Pope had been quick to reconstitute following his return to Rome.

This aspect of the restoration did not unduly upset Camillo's parents who seemed to have anticipated the development. Since the latter part of the Imperial period, the Cavours had ostenta-

tiously displayed a renewed appreciation of the traditional religion, departing from the rationalism that had been in vogue and
which they had pursued in the last two or three decades. Conveniently this religiosity reached a high point in 1815, and during
the hundred days the Marquis Michele urged his wife to go on
retreat to think about eternal things and to invoke divine assistance against the renewed peril. At the same time the family
showed a new pride and domestic devotion to the family Saint,
Francis de Sales. Undoubtedly this public profession of Catholicism and appreciation of the Jesuits, on the part of the family
and the Marquis Michele in particular, were tied to their attempt
to win the goodwill of the successor to the throne, Carlo Alberto.

Not only did the Cavours share the restoration's return to the
old religion, they also valued the maintenance of law and order
and the preservation of most of their privileges, so they found it
both agreeable and advantageous to make their peace with the
monarchy. In the Casa Cavour this spectacular reversion to conservative principles was justified by the argument that the family
had always served the cause of social order, irrespective of the
political vicissitudes of the moment. Later, too, no matter how
much the family dabbled in liberal principles, its devotion to
social stability was always to prevail.

The family having returned to the conservative fold, the children of the household, Gustavo and Camillo, were inculcated
with a respect for the two most important institutions in Piedmont after the monarchy—the army and the Church. In accordance with custom, the first tutor of the boys was a cleric, the Abbé
Giovanni Frézet. Whereas Gustavo was serious and studious, his
brother was fun-loving and, though bright, did all he could to
avoid his lessons. "Study bores me," he frequently admitted.
"What can I do? It is not my fault." [3] Quite possibly he did not
apply himself because it would have been difficult, if not impossible, to outshine his older brother, and from the very beginning
Camillo found it distressing not to outperform all others. Whatever the reason, the young Camillo proved ingenious in his de-
vices to avoid his lessons. He treatened to kill himself with a
knife or throw himself out of one of the upper-story windows of
his house, according to his whim.

In part, the family was to blame for these tantrums, for
Camillo was pampered and permitted to have an exaggerated
notion of his own importance. At the age of six he demanded
that those who came for him be accompanied by at least two or
three domestics and adorned with diamonds and rubies. That

same year, 1816, when he was brought to Geneva, he complained of the coach service. The official who supervised it ought to be fired for providing poor horses, he insisted. When informed by his hosts, the De La Rives, that only the mayor could take such a step, he requested an interview. This was arranged as a joke, but Camillo seriously sought the removal of the official and repeated his complaints to the mayor directly. He was only satisfied when the latter promised to follow his instructions. This vanity and sense of self-importance, so hilarious in a child of six, was not so amusing in an adolescent, who according to his parents, showed a similar preoccupation with his own aims and a callous disregard for other persons and things.

Camillo was aware that his behavior left much to be desired. In one of his very first letters, most likely written at the preco-cious age of five, he informed his maternal Aunt Victoria that he had gone to Turin with his mother to torment all who were there. He informed this same aunt in other early letters that he had taken part in benediction services and prayed for her. The young Camillo was close to the Prior of Santena and confided always to this favorite aunt in Paris how well he had been treated by the good priest.[4] Unhappily this prelate could not teach the youngster humility, and this is already apparent in his earliest correspondence. The letters of the pre-adolescent Cavour reveal a young aristocrat, perhaps more haughty and strong-willed than others of his station, but otherwise fully accepting the values of his class and conscious of his privileged position.

Meanwhile, the family's manifestations of adherence to con-servative and Catholic principles produced the desired effect at Court for at the beginning of 1816 Camillo's mother and paternal grandmother were admitted into the circle of Queen Maria Teresa. His father, Michele, was permitted to resume his public career by being named to the communal council of Turin. He was also employed in the prefecture of police—a post which gave him a good deal of influence at court and throughout the capital. Thus a short six years after Camillo's birth, the political climate of his country and family had shifted radically.

Under the restoration, Camillo as the second son of a noble-man, was earmarked for a career in the army. Whereas the first son could expect a position in the administration or the diplo-matic corps, a second son had generally to look to the military, no matter what his inclination. Not surprisingly, on August 26, 1820, at the age of ten, Camillo was enrolled in the recently opened military Academy of Turin. Only then did the family realize the danger of its son's strong will, as he refused to submit to dictation and military discipline. At the Academy the superiors showed themselves remarkably tolerant of the boy's arrogant attitude, in large measure because of their friendship for his father.

Camillo's teachers found him quick-witted and clearheaded, but independent and not easily controlled. He did well in his study of French, which was the formal language of his household, but not as well in Italian which always remained for him a language that he had learned in school and never mastered. The confidential reports sent to his father in the years 1823–1824 graded him better than mediocre in Italian and Latin, excellent in French, mathematics, and philosophy, but unsatisfactory in his conduct.

Not long after his entry into the military school, a revolution of sorts erupted in Piedmont. Inspired by army leaders and some of the outstanding members of the country's aristocracy, the demands presented in 1821 called not only for the Piedmontese government to move from absolutism to constitutionalism, but to substitute opposition for the policy of friendship with Austria. The revolutionists placed their hopes upon the heir to the throne, Carlo Alberto, who temporarily assumed power as regent while the new monarch, Carlo Felice, was away in Modena. At first the Prince did not disappoint them. He conditionally accepted the constitution the insurgents had drawn up, pending the approval of his uncle, the King. This consent never came. Trusting to Austrian arms rather than the nebulous notion of harmony between people and prince achieved through representative institutions, Carlo Felice asked Metternich to intervene and forcefully restore the *ancien régime* in his territory.

Many factors contributed to the failure of this revolution. Without a doubt the upper classes were divided in their attitude, while the lower classes were not involved, so the movement lacked mass support. The Habsburgs, moreover, even if they had not been invited to intervene, would not have remained idle while revolution flared on their doorstep. Finally, the part played by the Prince of Carignano was less than praiseworthy; he was accused of having encouraged the venture but drawing back in the face of the determined opposition of Carlo Felice. Despised and distrusted by liberals and conservatives alike, the Prince was barely able to retain his right of eventual succession to the throne. He did so only at the price of promising, should he ever inherit the throne, to maintain the government precisely as he found it upon his accession. The abortive revolution impressed the young Camillo, who was a distant relative of Santorre di Santarosa, the hero of 1821. From this moment, Cavour had a strong antipathy towards Carlo Alberto and did little to hide this sentiment.

In this, and most other matters the young cadet followed his own inclinations. Pride, the desire to excel, the need to assert himself, already visible in the child, developed steadily in the youth and these were translated into all too frequent refusals to obey, a spirit of contradiction, and constant acts of insubordination. He asserted his autonomy and self-reliance in various ways. When his instructors and relatives advised him to study mathematics, a most useful subject for one in the officers corps and one in which the cadet excelled, the fourteen-year-old shocked parents and teachers alike by announcing, "The world moves; nowadays, one must study political economy instead of mathematics." Then making matters worse, he continued, "I hope to see my country under a constitutional government. Who knows if someday I might not be a cabinet minister?" [5]

This response was inopportune. It was deemed inappropriate not only because it revealed a lack of deference for his elders but also because it called into question the validity of the political regime his father served. Such audacity was immediately reported to Carlo Felice, who had succeeded Vittorio Emanuele I following the recent abortive coup. The ultraconservative monarch could not forget that precisely this type of constitutional talk among his young, noble officers had precipitated the outburst of 1821. More than anything else, it had been such liberal sentiment in the military that had encouraged his enigmatic nephew to grant a constitution. Only the armed intervention of Austria had enabled him to retract that disastrous concession and restore his full authority. To call for a constitution was serious, indeed subversive business. If Carlo Felice had not had complete confidence in the Marquis Cavour, his son's "dangerous" talk might have seriously compromised his future.

The headstrong Camillo, however, did not seem to appreciate his father's efforts on his behalf. Thus he was far from grateful in the summer of the same year, 1824, when the Marquis secured his appointment as one of the pages to the Prince of Carignano. Camillo was not happy about having to serve at court, displayed an aversion to the atmosphere in the royal household, and complained that "it was a great nuisance to have to wear that livery." [6] Carlo Alberto, always perceptive though never comprehensible, soon learned of Camillo's attitude and duly complained to his uncle, the King. Once again the intervention of the father saved the son and Camillo was retained at court, thus obtaining a second chance to secure a position for himself. Unhappily, Camillo continued to antagonize rather than appease the man he served.

Cavour's parents were irritated by the conduct of their younger son, convinced that the frequent punishments he received at the Academy were merited and provoked by irresponsible actions on his part. Complaining that he had disregarded all her recommendations, his mother was not sympathetic to his pleas for understanding. In an angry letter written in 1825, the usually even-tempered Marchesa branded the strong will and radical independence of her fifteen-year-old son as childish and not befitting a young man and future officer. Equally puerile, in her estimation, was his dream of governing the country and his illusion that he might be called upon to make national decisions. Even prior to his sixteenth birthday the young Count envisioned himself as the King's chief minister and relished the thought.[7] All this his mother regarded as folly and called upon her son to return to the realm of reason and reality.

At the same time the Marchesa condemned Camillo's analytical attitude, which accepted nothing on authority, as inappropriate if not dangerous to his military career. In his profession blind obedience rather than critical analysis was of the utmost importance. Even more frightening for her was the thought that this questioning approach might lead to an overriding skepticism which would undermine his faith. "Above all," she cautioned her son with the ardor of a convert, "be a good Christian, for the very future of your immortal soul is at stake." Mincing no words, she warned that she would rather see him locked in a fortress for a year than have him make some foolish move. His favorite aunt, Victoria, also urged him to moderate his vanity and to abandon his pretense of stoicism.[8] Apparently their words were wasted.

Both his parents were disturbed by his friendship in the Academy with Severino Cassio, who seemed to personify all that they condemned. Three years older than Camillo, Cassio also found himself at odds with his family, and a strong bond developed between the two adolescents. Having a wider literary background and a far more Italian outlook than Camillo, Cassio played an important role in the formation of the young Count's character. Most important of all, he recognized in his schoolmate the potential for a dynamic, Italian political leader and encouraged him to dream of playing an important part in the affairs of the peninsula. Since Cassio verbalized sentiments that Cavour still stored in his mind, he believed Cassio to be the first to understand rather than reject him.

The Marquis and the Marchesa became livid with rage when they suspected that the young Baron's political views might prove detrimental to the well-being of their son and very likely ruin his career. Frightened by this prospect, in 1825 his father took decisive action and criticized Camillo's liberal views, inordinate pride, his unwillingness to ask pardon from his superiors, and the train of trouble which he had brought the family. In an angry mood, he warned his son that he would allow him to die of hunger in America unless he changed his ways and terminated his relationship with Cassio. Confronted with the threat of being disowned, Camillo submitted. However, he soon repented of the decision which led him to sacrifice friendship for base interests. Within a year he was to beg forgiveness from Cassio, but his relations with his parents remained strained. Camillo emerged from this crisis more than ever attached to his ambitions, more autonomous than before, and far more mature.

In the summer of 1826, by the time he celebrated his sixteenth birthday, Camillo had passed his final examinations at the Academy, had been awarded his comission as second lieutenant, and ceased to be a page. On the last occasion he served in that capacity he revealed his relief that his service was nearing an end. This embittered the sensitive and punctilious Prince who determined to punish the disrespectful Count. "The young Cavour played the part of a jacobin," he confided to his squire, "and I showed him to the door." [9] Carlo Alberto wished to do more than turn the Count out of his court and sought to take away his commission. Carlo Felice, however, did not honor this request. Nonetheless the Cavour family was scandalized, for it was an error of no small magnitude for the ambitious youth to antagonize the future King. They hoped that his action would not lead to a deterioration of their relations with the Prince, whose protection had served them well in the past.

Cast out of the court and a possible position of power, Camillo now had only the army and his family as possible avenues to satisfy his ambitions. At the beginning of 1827 when Cavour had recovered from an illness and the repercussions of his last tempestuous episode, he was assigned to the corps of engineers at Turin, his own city. Cavour was thus able to live at home while serving in the military. Critics spread the rumor that the influence of the Marquis had produced this choice appointment. Actually it was less than ideal. After years of separation, Camillo found it difficult to readjust to life in the Palazzo Cavour, and his family had to face the fact that he did not share their enthusiasm for the principles of the old regime. He found the liberal views of his maternal relatives in Geneva, whom he visited in 1827, more congenial.

At home Camillo was able to establish a meeting of minds and a sense of affection only with his brother. Gustavo, who in these years also held some liberal views, was both the confidant and supporter of his younger brother. Sharing his passion for the political journals, his milder temperament and less aggressive attitude spared him the violent confrontations that Camillo had with the rest of the family. At the end of 1828, when a mutual toleration if not understanding was developing between Camillo and his family, he was transferred to a series of remote frontier posts. In October, 1828, he was sent to Ventimiglia to supervise work of the fortifications there. At the beginning of 1829 he was instructed to participate in the completion of the forts of Exilles, and in May he was transferred to Lesseillon, where the government of Carlo Felice was reinforcing its frontier fortifications on the French border in accordance with its treaty commitments to the allies.

He did not find peace in this romantic solitude but became increasingly embittered, giving vent to outbursts of anger, condemnations of life, fits of despair and depression, and even threats of suicide. His old teacher Frézet suggested that a good dose of religious philosophy might alleviate the Count's unrest and enable him to cope better with his trying situation. This advice was to no avail. Camillo's problems were both personal and political, but in his mind they were merged together and he blamed many of his difficulties on the repressive political system that did not permit him the freedom of choice he deemed essential. Dogmatism, whether of the official Church or the absolutist state, became his chief enemy.

Cavour's father made it clear that he did not oppose liberal institutions so much on principle as out of practical considerations, regarding them as dangerous to the upper classes in general and to his own family in particular. "I know that you will have a future if there is no revolution," he wrote to his eighteen-year-old son, adding that he could not foresee the consequences if a revolution did erupt. This argument proved no more effective with Camillo than the others, and at the end of November he explained his position to his brother. "Certainly all personal considerations—the probable political and material advantages—invited me to fight under the banner of absolutism. But," he continued, "an innate sentiment of self-respect, which I have always preserved with care, has repelled me from a course in which the first essential was that I should deny my own convictions and no longer see or believe except with the eyes and understanding of other men." [10]

The lonely life the young lieutenant experienced during these difficult months finally led him to a quiet acceptance of things which his Aunt Victoria termed "a superb system of stoicism." Not really resigned to his unhappy state, Cavour was simply tired. Hence by the summer of 1829 he welcomed his first furlough, which he spent by visiting his relatives in Geneva. This Swiss city was still a vibrant center of European intellectual life, and this was the secret of its fascination for Camillo. He found the intellectual freedom of Geneva exhilarating and the religious toleration of the various sects admirable. So impressed was he that he thought of making it his permanent residence, but he was restrained by the belief that he could be of greater service in Turin than in a city that was already overflowing with talent.

For some time, and most markedly since his last visit to the De Sellons in 1827, Camillo had fallen under the influence of his mother's brother. Humane and cultivated, Jean Jacques de Sellon championed a number of worthy causes and almost alone organized the Peace Society. Camillo found his uncle's views liberal, enlightened, tolerant, and a welcome contrast to those adhered to within the walls of the Palazzo Cavour in Turin. His two visits to the De Sellons, following his graduation from the academy, had a marked impact upon his future development. Reading François René Chateaubriand, David Hume, Adam Smith, and Benjamin Constant had made him painfully aware of the fragile basis of his religious beliefs.[11]

During Camillo's years of inner turmoil and search for a new principle of authority, the opinions of Jean Jacques de Sellon were most important to him. His impact was paramount upon his nephew from 1828 to 1833. Within the family circle his council was most respected and listened to by the young Count. Nevertheless, even his influence was far from absolute and he confided as much to his Aunt Cecile de Sellon, admitting that while his manner of thinking could be modified it could never be changed. Hence, despite the advice he received from various quarters, he found it impossible to remain for long in the service of a regime

which violated his principles. He felt that his uncle would understand how he felt in this matter, if other relatives did not.

In 1829, as Camillo thought of resigning from the army, his
uncle published his *Lettres et discours en faveur du principe de
l'inviolabilité de la vie et l'homme,* and almost immediately a
new dialogue opened between the author and his nephew. All the
courageous efforts one puts forth on behalf of a higher cause
against restrictive privileges, his uncle wrote him, well aware of
his personal antipathy for the present system in Turin, actually
perfects the individual who consecrates himself to the task of
advancing the common good. Camillo concurred entirely, asserting that the march of civilization was as dear to him as the next
man and he would gladly devote his entire life to make it progress by one single step. He differed with his uncle only as regards
the best means of achieving the end which they both sought.[12]
Already the young Cavour questioned the efficacy of purely
pacific means and the traditional faith to effect the changes he
deemed absolutely necessary.

Certainly Cavour was still religious, if one means by this that
he believed in providence, in higher laws that governed the uni-
verse, and assumed the existence of some unknowable higher
being. He also continued to recognize the value of Christianity
and appreciated the role the Church played in the formulation of
man's moral conduct. His writings in the years from 1828 to 1835
reveal that he was open to new religious ideas as he sought a
substitute for Catholicism, which did not satisfy the needs of his
soul. Little pleased with the defenders of natural law who he
found long-winded and intolerant, he never assumed, as did some
others, that man could discard all thought of the divinity and
pursue a purely secular moral code.[13]

Still, he was unable to accept a religious system founded only
upon revelation and the truths of the Gospels. No intelligent
man, he insisted, could interpret the Bible literally, some recourse
to special interpretation was absolutely essential. Unfortunately
these issued not in unanimity but in an alarming number of
answers. Not rejecting the truths of the Bible, Cavour called for
a better means of interpreting them and determined that pragmatism provided the most perfect mechanism. So convinced was he
of the orthodoxy of the principle of utility, that he defied anyone
to find in Scripture anything in opposition to the common sense
of Jeremy Bentham.

Envisioning a new Christianity, purged by positivism so it
would contain a greater emphasis on virtue and less upon dogma,

Cavour also found himself attracted to the works of Benjamin Constant. He found his approach appealing because it was at once dominated by religious sentiments, but not dulled by forms, symbols, and dogmas. Revelation, Cavour believed, could be reconciled with this system. After all, he insisted, religion and skepticism shared one common belief—that reason alone could not achieve reality. According to Camillo, skepticism renounced the attempt, while religion provided a supernatural explanation.[14]

After this period Cavour rarely discussed matters of religious belief or practice. Once when in the mountains with his friend Michelangelo Castelli, the beauty of the setting led him to speculate about the prospect of other worlds, the nature of God, as well as the origin of the world and man. However, his practical mind and positivist philosophy prevented him from accepting too many assumptions he could not verify, and he finished by saying *que sais je?* Camillo preferred to treat matters that were within his range of reason and subject to his control. He thus convinced himself that agricultural improvement, industrial development, expansion of transportation, and the adoption of free trade were far more important than philosophical or ideological speculation.

In concentrating upon agriculture and business he was not far afield from his forebears who had played a key role in the formation of a company to introduce the cultivation of Merino sheep in Piedmont. Later his father had shown skill in the acquisition of the estate at Leri and great wisdom in its direction, emphasizing the need for capital investment in the land, the value of agricultural education, and technical innovations. Michele also played a part in the effort to bring steamship service to Lakes Maggiore and Como—all of which undoubtedly influenced the development of his son as an agriculturalist and man of affairs. Thus, the Marquis who was to become increasingly conservative in political matters was progressive in agriculture and business, expert in financial matters, and prepared to assume calculated risks to increase the family patrimony. In economic matters he differed from his son in his conviction that the country was not yet prepared for industrialization. Finally, Michele's concerns were almost always Piedmontese.

Camillo, too, initially thought only in terms of Piedmont, but by 1830 made his first reference to the plight of Italy in his correspondence. Writing to his favorite uncle, he observed that Greece had managed to acquire its independence, but not so unhappy Italy.[15] Dissatisfied with his own condition in life, the young Count found it easy and convenient to relate this to the sad state of the peninsula. The winter of 1829–1830, which he spent in Turin, seemed endless to Cavour, whose future seemed as bleak as that of Italy.

CHAPTER II

The Count and the Marchesa

IN MARCH, 1830, CAVOUR WAS DELIGHTED TO LEARN OF HIS appointment to the staff of engineers at Genoa, especially since Severino Cassio, his school companion, was also to be sent. After the oppressive atmosphere of the capital and the solitary confinement in the mountains, he found the port city exhilarating. A seaport open to the products and ideas of the entire world, Genoa had preserved its intellectual tradition and something of a political life. For these reasons Cavour gladly abandoned the stifling ambience of Turin for the freer air of Genoa.

Incorporated into Piedmont by article eighty-six of the Treaty of Vienna, the inhabitants of the former republic had not as yet reconciled themselves to their new and subordinate status and openly displayed their contempt for the bureaucratic and dynastic traditions of the Piedmontese. The Genoese nobility and the bourgeoisie had more deeply absorbed national and liberal ideas and stubbornly clung to them, especially in intellectual circles, despite the Savoyard attempts to suppress such sentiments. Even a part of the masses in Genoa had been affected by democratic notions and the dream of unification; thus, the city proved a fertile ground for secret societies of all sorts—from the *Carbonari* to the Mazzinians. Accustomed to the stolid resignation of the people of Turin, Cavour found Genoese criticism of the regime refreshing. Assisted by friends and relatives, the second lieutenant soon established a broad base of interesting acquaintances, finding ready acceptance in the most fashionable salons in Genoa.

Cavour, who liked discussions and seldom retreated from an argument, found the exchange of ideas profitable. He was convinced that even in the company of men who held diametrically opposed views, one could always learn something. For this reason he favored maintaining a dialogue with men of all parties, something one could easily accomplish in the parlors of Genoa. This was the case in the salon of the Marchesa Anna Schiaffino-Giustiniani, wife of the President of the Board of Health of Genoa. The Marchesa, who excelled in her use of French and also knew English and German, attracted the most interesting people and encouraged the most stimulating conversations. Her likes were as varied as the guests in her salon in the Piazza San Siro, and she displayed a vivid interest in music, literature, and most of all, politics. Curious by nature and rebellious by temperament, she early found herself at war with the world around her. Even before she met Camillo she had been driven by two conflicting desires: to assert herself on the one hand, and to cease her struggle and seek the solace of death on the other.

Recognizing her as a kindred spirit, the young lieutenant was initially attracted by her restive mind and tenacious will. As he continued to frequent her house, Cavour found himself falling in love with the witty and vivacious hostess. The Marchesa did not discourage his advances, but welcomed them as she had others. Among the many factors which drew the two together was a similar sense of frustration and spirit of rebellion against the disappointing aspects of their respective lives. Camillo, who was then at a low point in his own career, readily sympathized with her plight and seconded her polemic against the present state of affairs. They also shared a religious affinity for in her adolescence the Marchesa had rejected the religion of her father as she decried "the absurdities of Catholicism." She did not, however, move toward positivism but adopted a vague mysticism which apparently left her dissatisfied, for like Camillo she thought frequently about death and contemplated suicide.

Though she was three years his senior—she was twenty-three when he was twenty—and married with two children, Cavour could not conceal that he found the Marchesa personally, politically, and physically attractive. While radical in her political views, the young woman upon whom he showered his attentions, came from one of the best families of the area. The daughter of the Baron and Baroness Schiaffino-Corvetto of Genoa, Anna, or Nina as her friends called her, had been born in Paris and had spent her early years there. She was married at the age of nineteen to the Marquis Stefano Giustiniani, who was seven years older than she, and rumor early spread that the marriage was a total failure. The reasons for the failure were not only political— he upheld absolutism while she was democratic in her tendencies —but personal as well, for while he was reserved and rigid, she was passionate and tolerant. The Marchesa found some relief and diversion in the soirées she held and in the stimulating atmosphere of her salon, where she made the acquaintance of Cavour.[1]

A striking if not a beautiful blonde, Nina was at the same time gentle and understanding and far superior in culture and education to most women of her class in Piedmont. This combination appealed to Camillo, who was also attracted by her progressive political position. Given her French training, her liberal outlook, her excitable temperament, and her sense of intellectual independence, she was inclined to support the most radical tendencies of the time and provided a haven for a brilliant group of young intellectuals. Cavour, too, sought refuge in her salon.

Within this exciting atmosphere and under the spell of Nina, Cavour gave vent to his most extreme views. His drift to the left was accentuated by the presence of Cassio whose republicanism was bound to leave some mark upon his friend. It was under his wing, in fact, that Camillo studied English in the summer of 1830, in order to better follow the foreign press. Inebriated by the freer air he found in Genoa, the young second lieutenant showed himself as indiscreet as Nina. When news reached them of the July Revolution in Paris, he was heard shouting from the pavilion of the Engineering Corps, "Long live the revolution!" "Long live the Republic!" and "Down with all tyrants!" [2] Although Cavour later insisted that he had never entered any secret society, he most likely had contact with members of the *Carboneria* and other sects.

Delighted by the news of the revolution of 1830 in France, the young aristocrat was equally elated to hear from England of the downfall of the Tory ministry which had sympathized with, if not supported, the Holy Alliance. The collapse of conservative regimes elsewhere made Cavour all the more conscious of Italy's plight. During this tumultuous period he lamented to an English friend that, while the rest of Europe was marching steadily along the road of progress, unfortunate Italy remained beneath the same system of political and religious oppression. Afflicted both by sorrow and indignation, Cavour insisted that Italians, too, were worthy of liberty. The triumph of the revolution in France, he hoped, would pave the way for the regeneration of Italy. Already a liberal, Camillo was now profoundly influenced by the nationalist sentiments of Nina.

She, in turn, fell beneath the spell of Cavour's personal fascination, indomitable will, and undeniable genius. Like Cassio, she foresaw that the young lieutenant who frequented her parlor would play an important role in Italian affairs. "I am certain," she assured him, "that one day your talent will be seen by all." No better able to hide her feelings from him than her political views, rumor soon spread of her attachment to the soldier. Such gossip agitated her family and her husband. Since word of their liaison spread outside the city, Cavour decided that his visits to the Marchesa had to cease. This decision was opportune, for at the same time Nina's parents forbade her to see or write to Cavour again.

Political problems also intervened to complicate and prematurely truncate their relationship. The July Revolution brusquely broke the torpid atmosphere prevailing in Piedmont and threw the conservative classes into a state of convulsive fear. Alarmed by the news from Paris and the reports he received from his phalanx of spies in the port city, Carlo Felice determined to crack down upon his unruly subjects on the Ligurian coast. The University of Genoa was closed for the academic year 1830–1831, and students were constrained to pursue their studies elsewhere. A long list of political suspects was compiled and on it were almost all the officers stationed in Genoa. Among these Cavour and his companion Cassio were signaled out as worthy of special surveillance.

Knowing that the authorities considered him suspect, Cavour ceased his criticism of the regime and curtailed his correspondence. At the end of October he wrote his uncle Jean describing the situation in Genoa and his own particular predicament.

The city is full of spies. There are actually lists of suspects, and (I know not by what fatal coincidence) nearly all the members of the honourable Corps of Engineers have been entered on these lists. Hence it has come out that for a month all our words, and, I believe, all our thoughts, have been the subject of reports. You will understand that it would have been imprudent on my part to run the risk of furnishing incriminating evidence to those who watched me, so I have refrained from writing to you—in spite of my desire to do so.[3]

Unfortunately the damage had already been done, as against him were launched the most serious charges. He was even shunned by some of his fellow officers who feared that his company would compromise their own careers. Despite these difficulties, the Count was duly appointed lieutenant first class at the end of November. Small consolation for the outraged Cavour.

At the beginning of December Camillo wrote to his father that the accusations of the ultraconservatives against him continued, indeed reached a high point, making his life in Genoa unbearable. He failed to mention that being so close to the Marchesa, but unable to see her, was equally distressing. Rather he emphasized that given his liberal sentiments, he could no longer in good conscience remain in the service. Pleading for his father's permission to leave the army, he disclosed that he was prepared to devote himself to agriculture.

Just before Christmas 1830 Cavour was recalled to Turin together with his friend Cassio. There is no proof that his indiscreet relationship with Nina was responsible for this move, but it was known that both his and her parents were determined to put an end to the affair. Warned by her parents not to write, Nina obeyed except for an occasional note which she sent to Cavour in desperation. She confessed that her most ardent prayer was that things would turn out as Camillo desired.

After Cavour left Genoa at the end of 1830, Nina sent three letters without receiving a response. The man to whom she poured out her innermost thoughts was preoccupied with other matters and feared political reprisals. While away, however, he thought of her and her memory became all the more meaningful with the passage of time. His departure from Genoa and Nina closed one stage in his life and career. The impact of this interlude is immeasurable. Years later when Cavour had moderated his views, the recollection of his own youth led him to view radical behavior among the young with sympathy and understanding. He always recalled with pleasure the days he spent in Genoa and retained a special affection for the port city and its people.[4]

Following their separation things did not go well either for the Marchesa or the Count. To his dismay, Cavour found that the reactionaries in the capital continued the harassment initiated in Genoa. Possibly this was because they suspected the motivation behind his suggestion that the directing classes frankly adopt the reformist approach. Evidently they did not share his conclusion that only such a daring course would channelize the drive for change so that rather than being overturned by it, they could give it leadership and direction. The Piedmontese aristocracy, according to Cavour, in refusing to pursue this path showed themselves intransigent and insensitive to the needs of the moment. They disagreed to the point of calling for his imprisonment in the fortress of Fenestrelle, reserved for political prisoners. He was saved from this fate by the powerful contacts of his father. Early in March, 1831, he was sent instead to Bard in the Val d'Aosta where the army was supposed to construct fortifications, far from the clamor of the conservatives. To complicate matters, the monarch's death the following month brought Carlo Alberto, no friend of Cavour, to the throne.

The situation of the Marchesa was little better. Her conduct at the time of Carlo Felice's death had caused such commotion as to warrant an official censure. Shortly after the death of the King, the Marchesa went to the theater with a number of other aristocratic ladies, all gaily dressed, all failing to observe in their wardrobe the prescribed regulations governing the official mourning. This "scandalous" action was duly reported to the Turin government which interpreted it as disloyal to the dynasty. What was worse, when the Marchesa was questioned on that occasion, she reportedly uttered words that were disrespectful to the late King. To prevent their daughter from provoking further punishment, her parents all but confined her to their summer home for a number of weeks.

For the moment the two were silenced; neither, however, accepted this situation: Cavour, meditating in the isolation of his new assignment, resolved to leave the army at the first opportune moment. Nina, once freed from her house confinement, became an ardent admirer of Mazzini and one of the earliest supporters of his "Young Italy."

During the eight months of his rustic life in Bard, where Cavour complained he found neither work to execute nor workers to supervise, he had ample time for reflection. In discussing his future with his father, Cavour indicated that he could not envision a life that would be purely speculative. Moreover, he was convinced that he could not realize his potential in the army. Consequently, he again wrote his father for permission to leave the service. The previous year he had not pressed the issue because there had been talk of war and he feared that under these circumstances his resignation might have been misconstrued as an act of cowardice. Now that no such rumors disturbed the peace, he wanted to leave.

This time his request was granted and a decree of November 12, 1831 accorded Cavour an honorable discharge. Upon his return to Turin and private life, his father proposed that he administer the family farm at Grinzane, some forty kilometers outside the capital. Having no resources of his own, Camillo gladly accepted the offer and for the next three years played the part of the gentleman farmer—and did so surprisingly well. Despite his discharge, the year ended sadly for Cavour. The July Revolution had not broken the conservative hold upon Europe and the hoped-for changes in Italy had not materialized. In fact, the outburst in the Duchies and the Legations had only provoked Austria's intervention and renewed reaction so that by March,

1831, matters were worse than they had been before. The call to arms issued by Giovanni Berchet in his poem commemorating the revolution went unheeded. People in the peninsula were still separated by seven boundaries and faced seven different destinies.

Domestic difficulties served to aggravate Cavour's dissatisfaction with the existing political situation. For one thing, he continued to depend upon his family for the allowance which permitted him to live in the style of the class he so often criticized. Furthermore, his political views continued to clash with those of most others in the Casa Cavour, giving rise to heated arguments that degenerated into violent scenes. Even his relations with his brother deteriorated, in part because of too close an association after years of separation, in part because Camillo resented the love and attention the family showered on Gustavo's first son, Augusto, born in 1828. On one occasion when Camillo corrected his young nephew, the two brothers fell into a violent confrontation that ended with the usually tranquil Gustavo hurling a chair at the head of his younger, and in his opinion, meddling brother.[5]

Then, to make matters worse, his great-uncle and uncle died in succession in 1831, the latter after a great deal of suffering. Cavour remained by his uncle's bedside for two entire days, but the attending clergymen forced him to leave at the moment of death—a fact which he never forgot or forgave. At the end of this disastrous year he wrote his favorite uncle that the recent tragedies had impressed upon him the vanity of worldly ambitions and he had resolved to renounce the dream of making a name for himself. This was not a promise, but idle talk.

Although Cavour had not in fact abandoned his aspirations, the political climate in Italy was discouraging. In his own state of Piedmont, little was expected of Carlo Alberto, who assumed the throne in April, 1831. Mazzini in a published letter to the King had invited him to assume the leadership of the national movement. "If you do not act," he warned," others will—without you and against you." These words had little noticeable effect upon the mysterious monarch. Word quickly spread that, though the King had earlier shown some liberal sentiments, he had long since thrust these aside, and had become a convinced conservative.

In a hundred ways Carlo Alberto earned the label. A devoted son of the Church, he abstained from rich food, kept long fasts, and reportedly wore a hairshirt; he restored the ecclesiastical courts and relied upon the Jesuits to supervise higher education in his state. Half-friar, half-knight, clerical influences were seen to guide his political conscience, and he opposed any move he

considered a menace to his throne or the Church. No sooner
was he in power than he made common cause with Metternichian
Austria by concluding a military alliance.

Like other members of his dynasty he looked forward to expansion in Italy and recalled Emanuele Filiberto's advice that
Italy was like an artichoke that had to be eaten leaf by leaf. Even
this gradualist approach called for a well-trained army which he
was prepared to support. In this matter he parted with Carlo
Felice who liked to exclaim, "What need have I of my own army
when Austria offers me an excellent one without cost?" [6] Nevertheless, there was not the slightest indication that Carlo Alberto
would undertake any action to liberate the peninsula.

Further south conditions seemed even more deplorable. The
mismanagement and insensitivity of the papal government led to
open rebellion in the Legations. Although the revolt barely lasted
three weeks, it had far-reaching repercussions. In the first place,
a nephew of the more famous Bonaparte, Prince Louis Napoleon,
who had been a student at the University of Rome, participated
in the fighting and his brother was killed in the process; this
undoubtedly colored his attitude and action toward the papal
regime. Secondly, Austrian intervention on behalf of the Pope
once again showed that Metternich's state was the real enemy of
liberalism and nationalism in the peninsula. Then, too, the collapse of this carbonarist insurrection against papal misrule
opened the door for the doctrines preached by Mazzini, and his
Young Italy now became the focus of nationalist attention.
Finally, the French, disturbed by this latest Habsburg intrusion
into Italy, took two steps to remedy the situation. They garrisoned Ancona to counteract the Austrian presence at Bologna,
and also insisted that the major powers suggest reforms to the
papal government.

Meeting in Rome, the representatives of France, Austria,
Prussia, Russia, and Britain recognized the weakness in the papal
administration and called for changes. Among other things their
Memorandum of 1831 suggested a secularization of the bureaucracy and an end to the clerical monopoly in the judiciary.
Gregory XVI, not interested in political and administrative problems, largely ignored these proposals. Looking to the past,
Gregory considered many of their innovations dangerous and refused to accept their definition of progress. Regarding even the
railroad as an "invention of the devil," he sought to spare his
subjects from it, rather than foster its development.

Disturbed by the revolution and subsequent repression in the

Romagna, Cavour noted that the major powers had not succeeded in imposing reforms upon the papal government. He complained to his English friend William Brockedon in April, 1832, that the half-measures of the intervening states had only aggravated the situation. Even the intervention of France, he observed, was insufficient to extract the most moderate concessions from the Pontiff. There was no improvement in the Italian situation. "Confronted on the one side by Austrian bayonets, and on the other by the Pope's furious excommunications," Cavour lamented, "every manifestation of independent thought, every generous sentiment is suppressed as a sacrilege or a crime against the state. . . ." [7] The condition of Italy, of Europe, and his own country was for him the source of deepest sorrow. Initially the July Revolution in France had engendered new hopes and aspirations, but these were premature, the restoration settlement prevailed, producing in him and others of like mind a deeper depression than existed before. The Count's disappointment was obvious, and this rendered him suspect to the police who continued to consider him "a very dangerous man."

Cavour perceived the struggle of the restoration world as one between the forces of light and darkness. On the one side he saw ranged the defenders of civilization, progress, humanity while on the other the partisans of ignorance, absolutism, and obscurantism. Although the proponents of reaction seemed everywhere to be in the ascendancy, he consoled himself with the thought that their victory was temporary, that the march of progress could not be permanently halted, and that the reformers would eventually triumph. He did not abandon his dreams or his principles. "I shall always remain faithful to my ideas," he wrote to his cousin Cecile de Sellon in 1832, "for these ideas are bound up with my existence. I shall profess and endeavor to promote them as long as I breathe." [8] During the reign of Carlo Alberto these ideas hindered rather than helped the ambitious Count who remained out of the capital and active political life.

Fortunately his father's influence was once again applied, so that Cavour was appointed syndic or mayor of the commune of Grinzane. Having dreamed for years of serving as a minister under the King, Cavour was far from satisfied with his lot as administrator of a commune which as late as 1848 had only 350 inhabitants. He could not help but contrast his actual role with what he felt he ought to be. At the risk of being ridiculed, he confessed to the Marquis di Borolo in 1832 that he had earlier believed that nothing was impossible for him. In fact, he revealed that there was a time when he thought it quite natural that one day he would awaken and find himself the Prime Minister of the kingdom of Italy. The wish to preside over a nonexistent kingdom called into question his mental stability.

Realistic men realized that under Carlo Alberto loyal servants of the *ancien régime* such as his father, rather than those seeking far-reaching constitutional changes, were likely to advance. Indeed, the Marquis Cavour was appointed mayor of Turin and continued to enjoy an influential position at court. From his country estate his son still hoped for change, but did not sanction the republican conspiracy concocted in the ranks of the noncommissioned officers. Resolved to act before the revolution could strike, Carlo Alberto reacted energetically to the threat of a Mazzinian insurrection. He established a special military commission and between May 22 and July 22, 1833, twelve men were condemned to death and publicly executed for their part in the plot. Cavour was convinced that such confused plots conceived by confused individuals served only to reinforce the government's repression and bring it closer to Metternichian Austria. Consequently he condemned not only the reactionaries but also the revolutionaries who sought to remake the state and society. Labeling their solutions simplistic and dangerous, Cavour championed a *juste milieu* between the extremes.

Although Cavour ostensibly led a tranquil life at Grinzane, he was burdened by a consuming ambition and a sense of squandered potential. Frustrated in romance and prohibited from participating in politics, Cavour found no consolation in the traditional religion. "We others," he confessed, "who do not have religious faith must devote all our tenderness of soul to the service of mankind." His close friend Pietro di Santarosa remained tied to the Church, and the Count looked upon him as a link with the religious world. "God preserve him for my old age," Cavour wrote, "so that his living faith can overcome the barrenness that the years and skepticism have produced in my heart." [9]

Skepticism, separation from Nina, and the scant chance of success led Cavour to the depths of depression. "I had but one remaining illusion—a faith in friendship," he explained, "but now this too has passed like the other delusions of grandeur." He found few outlets for his restless energy. Piedmontese society bored him, and he might well have shunned it but for the romantic opportunities it provided. "We pass our time in discussing common, dull things," he complained, "deploring our fate, criticizing the social order and a hundred such miserable matters."

The situation at home contributed to his unhappiness. An independent spirit, Cavour was chagrined by the fact that he was the most dependent of men, a son of the family in the full sense of the term. At the end of 1833 his sister-in-law, of whom he was very fond, died, compounding Cavour's sense of isolation and pessimism. "We do not love one another any longer," he wrote of his brother and he indicated that as regards his mother he was more of an obstacle than a means for her happiness, while his father found greater consolation in his grandchildren. Having evaluated his situation, Cavour found no strong link that attached him to life.

At the beginning of 1834 the despondent Count could see no relief in sight. On the contrary, the future threatened a progressive aggravation of his problems and boredom. "What shall I be when I am thirty? A son of the family as I have been until this hour? I would rather be dead. Oh! if only I did not have any lingering doubts about the morality of suicide," he wrote in his diary, "I would free myself from this troublesome existence. However, I cannot justify such a step, even employing the logic of Bentham." [10] Nonetheless, in the winter of 1834 both he and the Marchesa contemplated suicide.

The summer of that year brought relief if not hope. On June 22 he received a letter which he immediately recognized as written by Anna. Trembling, Cavour opened the letter and learned that she was only forty kilometers away in Turin and desired to see him. Abandoning all his assigned projects, he decided to leave for the capital immediately, traveling beneath the scorching sun, for he was too impatient to wait for sundown. Arriving in Turin that evening after a forced ride, he bathed, changed clothes, and hurried to the Hotel Feder to discover to his disappointment that the Marchesa had left for the opera. Without a moment's hesitation, without regard for the gossip that he knew would ensue, he followed her there. Scanning the boxes, he spotted the Marchesa dressed in black, her face showing the lines of what for her had been a long and cruel separation. He ran to her crowded box and waited for the others to leave so they could talk.

When they were finally alone, the two who had so much to say to one another remained silent. Finally, Nina confessed that she had suffered the past four years while away from him. Rarely sentimental, never maudlin, Cavour was since youth struck by a generous act and his eyes would tear, as they did now. He responded that he too had been troubled by the separation. Later he wrote in his diary that he was proud of, and invigorated by, such a pure and constant love. When he thought of his conduct toward Nina, when he considered the terrible ordeal she had endured on his account, he accused himself of cruelty if not infamy.[11] Seeing the Marchesa again brought back all his old feelings for her and a determination to spare her further heartache.

Having made the decision to redeem himself and rescue Nina, Cavour decided to go to Santena, the family villa located some thirteen miles outside Turin, to discuss the matter with his father. Enthused and excited by the thoughts and memories that flashed through his mind, Cavour forgot to hail a carriage and unconsciously began the long walk to Santena. It was midnight and as he strolled along the bank of the Po, the moonlight played upon the ripples in the river, producing a warm glow that harmonized perfectly with his inner feelings. For the moment he knew the meaning of peace. Halfway to Santena, he found a cab which carried him the rest of the way, allowing him to dream all the more freely. Arriving at three in the morning, he had perforce to wait until daybreak to tell his father the full story and his decision. He found a sympathetic listener in his father, but one who cautioned him about the Marchesa's delicate situation.

The Marquis's sound advice did not stop his son from returning to Turin and Nina's hotel that evening. Unfortunately he arrived just in time to be seen by her husband who was going out for a walk. Undaunted, Cavour entered Nina's room. During their second rendezvous, Cavour asked if she had forgiven him for his neglect in the past years. Impetuous as ever, the Marchesa responded with an embrace that revealed her innermost thoughts. Deeply moved, Cavour made a promise to himself, "Ah, I swear it, I shall never, ever forget; I shall never abandon that celestial woman. My existence," he vowed, "shall be consecrated to her, she will be the end of my life, the only object of my dreams and my efforts."

While Cavour made vague if sincere promises, the Marquis Giustiniani made concrete plans to leave the capital. He had brought his ailing wife there to consult with the well-known Doctor Rossi about her health. When this specialist suggested baths, the Marquis immediately complied by taking his wife to the Baths of Vinadio at the end of June. No sooner had the Giustiniani carriage left the city than Cavour wrote Nina an ardent letter reaffirming his eternal love. Her departure, however, did not produce sufficient sorrow to prevent Cavour from beginning another affair with the Marchesa Clementina Guasco **di**

Castelletto only a week later. Perhaps this was the only means he had of momentarily forgetting Anna.

At the beginning of July, Nina wrote Camillo that she did not know what more to ask of God after he had brought her his love. The letter never reached him; the Marchesa's husband intercepted it and discreetly placed it among his own papers. Knowing Nina's feelings, Cavour was certain that she would respond. In fact she had written him yet another letter in which she poured out her innermost feelings. "After God," she wrote on the verge of blasphemy, "you are my God, you are what my senses conceive the divinity to be." [12] This letter, too, was intercepted by her husband, so Cavour was left without hearing a word. He was plagued by the thought that the Marchesa was forcibly prevented from writing and thus suffered once again on his account. So upset was the myopic Count that he considered it his duty to fight a duel with her husband. Fortunately he decided otherwise. Nina, he recognized, was bound to another by matrimony and had certain responsibilities toward her children. Furthermore, religious tradition, state practice, and his father's opposition dictated against a normalization of their relationship.

The Marchesa could not as readily give up her hope for happiness with Camillo. Thus in the summer of 1835 when Nina proposed abandoning her family for Cavour and actually left for Turin, the Count found himself in a dilemma. Luckily she was detained at Asti by the quarantine imposed in the face of the cholera epidemic raging in the peninsula. Cavour therefore had time to dissuade the passionate Marchesa and did so by his letter of August 1, 1835. In that letter he argued that he could not join her because he was detained in Turin assisting his father coordinate the campaign against the cholera in Turin—an obvious pretext. More to the point, he urged Nina to reconcile herself with the family she had left for him and practice the virtue of resignation. This rejection momentarily cooled the Marchesa's ardor and played a part in her suicide attempt at the end of the month. Unsuccessful, she tried again to take her life at the beginning of 1836, and made several attempts thereafter; the melancholy Marchesa finally succeeded in April, 1841, when she threw herself out of an upper-story window. After six days of painful agony she died at the early age of thirty-four.[13]

Disillusionment and depression caused by the tragic life of the woman who was so devoted to him, her love and then her death all played a part in his decision to remain single. He still sought the company and affection of women, but he practiced the resignation he had suggested to her by refusing to marry. He would have liked to transfer his energies into politics but did not find the means to do so. The political situation in Piedmont offered him few opportunities to display his talents. Nonetheless, this was the last avenue available to the Count. Unable to find happiness with Anna, Cavour more than ever tied his future to that of his country, determined to fulfill the role she had predicted for him.

CHAPTER III

Obscure Citizen of Piedmont

FRUSTRATED IN HIS ASPIRATIONS, CAVOUR BECAME HYPERCRITICAL of life in Piedmont. He cried out against the ignorance and prejudice that prevailed and served as an obstacle to knowledge and progress. He particularly despised the dull social life, the repressive climate, the lack of intellectual stimulation, and the superstitious base of religious life. "I took part in a procession at Voltri in honor of some Virgin or other," he commented in his diary on September 8, 1834. "Nothing in the world is more ridiculous." [1] Despite his dissatisfaction with the establishment, Cavour did not approve of the conspiracies of Mazzini, such as Young Italy planned for Piedmont in 1834. These radical and futile solutions, he concluded, rendered the work of reasonable reformers all the more difficult. Proof positive could be found in the renewed repression in Piedmont and the appointment in 1835 of Solaro della Margarita, a frank conservative in politics as well as religion. His attitude was reflected in the Albertine Penal Code which punished offenses against the Church with the same severity as offenses against the crown and its government.

In 1835 the Count found an escape of sorts by scheduling a series of trips abroad to improve his mind and leave his problems behind. During the course of his visit to France, where he made the acquaintance of Madame de Circourt, some of his friends urged him to settle permanently in Paris, assuring him that he would soon establish a reputation. Cavour categorically refused, observing that flight was no solution to his or Piedmont's problems. A realist in the tradition of his family, Cavour also was aware of the flood of émigrés that poured into cities like Paris and knew that precious few managed to make a name for themselves.

Unfortunately his trip to Paris did not permit him to forget how little he had accomplished following his resignation from the Sardinian army. In the French capital he felt ignored by all the really important people, such as the historian François Guizot. "One has to be a celebrity of sorts to attract the attention of these great men," he lamented in his letter of March 31, 1835, to his cousin, "and I, alas, am only an obscure citizen of Piedmont who has done nothing to warrant recognition outside of the limits of the small commune over which I preside as mayor. Thus," he continued, "I cannot reasonably expect to frequent the society of those shining lights of the political world." [2]

On the other hand, the Count had no problem in making the acquaintance of some of the most extreme revolutionaries who called Paris home. He was frightened, indeed horrified, by the strength of the revolutionary colony in the French capital. While there he reaffirmed his conviction that to avert catastrophe, moderate men of good-will had somehow to steal the thunder of the radicals. He shared his thoughts on this problem with the same Swiss cousin, Augusto de La Rive:

We are all rushing fast towards democracy. Is it for good? Is it for evil? Anyhow it is an inevitable fact and we are bound to promote it, since it accords with the laws of progress. Could you imagine any possible and practical plan for the reconstruction of any species of aristocratic government? All we can do is to embark upon the advancing flood of democracy while opening a free channel for it. How can the uneducated masses, who will assuredly come into power, be trained in the traditions and experience required for the direction of a new state of society that has not hitherto been seen in Europe? [3]

These questions haunted Cavour as he left the Continent for England in the company of his friend Pietro di Santarosa. Undoubtedly he hoped to find some of the answers in the island kingdom which he believed had already achieved an equilibrium between change and conservation. Britain, in his opinion, was the most progressive as well as the most traditional state in the world. Hence his desire to study its institutions first-hand and to be introduced to the country's leading figures who could facilitate his political inquiries and economic analyses.

Cavour had for some time thought of making a trip throughout Italy, realizing that such a journey was even more important than a visit to France or England. He recognized Italy as his *patria* and saw the flaw in visiting other lands while he remained unfamiliar with his own. Unfortunately for one reason or another, Cavour postponed the trip which was never made. As a result he always knew and understood the major powers of Western Europe better than he did his own peninsula. Since 1832 he had desired to tour the nearby provinces of Lombardy and Venetia but had not been welcomed by the Austrian administration, though it was well known that he belonged to one of the most respected families in Piedmont and his father was held in high esteem by the court party. Only in 1836, when gossip about the Count had subsided and a new ambassador appointed to Turin, was he permitted through Lombardy-Venetia on his way to Villach. Even then he was stopped at the frontier and his letters were opened and read by the police. There was little he could do in protest. For the moment Austrian control of the provinces, with all of its humiliations, was inevitable. He did not lose hope, however, and his travel abroad contributed to his conclusion that the Italian question had to be settled on a European plane.[4]

Cavour's trips also played a decisive role in the evolution of his thought and personality. He frankly admitted that prior to leaving Piedmont for France, Switzerland, and England, he ingenuously believed that as an aristocrat he was naturally superior to those who belonged to the bourgeoisie. In effect, he nourished the traditional class prejudices endemic to men of his station. In his case, Cavour developed new attitudes and he always attributed this to his travels which introduced him to other people, facts, and modes of thought. Abroad, he learned to respect a man for his worth as well as his class or position. Not unexpectedly, when he returned to Turin he was more than ever at odds with the Piedmontese establishment and questioned its sterile social attitudes as well as political and religious practices. He did not attack the country's population which he deemed second to none. The weakness lay in her institutions, not in her people; properly directed they too could accomplish great things. "Were I the chief minister of Carlo Alberto," Cavour prophesied, "Austria would tremble and the world would be astonished." [5]

In the summer of 1835 this aspiration seemed an impossible dream. His father, however, remained in the King's favor and on June 27 was nominated *Vicario* of the city of Turin, a post which gave him access to Carlo Alberto's ear as well as supervision of the special security forces. Such a position did little to endear the Cavour family to liberal or even moderate elements and suspicion of the father cast yet another shadow upon the future of his son. Nevertheless, the Marquis's new position indirectly provided some compensation for Camillo. More than ever bound to the capital, his father turned over to him the family estates at Leri in addition to the farm which he already held at Grinzane. Frustrated in so many other areas, Cavour turned his talent to farming and made a good deal of money. From this moment until the eve of the revolutionary outburst of 1848, management of these estates was his principal occupation, though entry into the political life of the country remained a constant preoccupation. Participation in the government was prohibited by the political climate of the regime and the views of the reigning monarch.

Carlo Alberto, though Catholic and conservative, was not averse to some limited reforms under the aegis of the monarchy. Thus customs duties were relaxed in 1835 while Solaro della Margarita concluded a series of commercial agreements. Though they were steps in the right direction, Cavour considered these changes as too little, coming too late. For this reason he continued to criticize the political atmosphere of Turin, which he found oppressive. For him political repression was intolerably intensified by clerical censorship. Outraged that the priestly reviewers did not find his brother's work sufficiently Catholic, he believed that they provided sufficient proof of the real attitude of the Catholic party toward liberty of speech and progressive education. On more than one occasion Cavour termed Turin an inferno for intellectuals.

A new wind appeared to sweep over Italy in 1839. That year the first Italian railroad was built and commenced, in Massimo D'Azeglio's words, stitching up the boot. Beginning with the Congress of 1839 held in Pisa, annual scientific congresses were called in the various Italian states to disseminate knowledge and exchange ideas. Even Carlo Alberto could not remain indifferent to the new current. Aloof from liberal circles since the fiasco of 1821, the King returned to the road of reform and entertained expansionist if not patriotic ideas. Cavour's disappointment with the pace of progress aside, Carlo Alberto genuinely sought to enlighten his administration. He aimed, he observed in his reform memorial of 1839, to establish a strong government upon just and equal laws, to facilitate every type of industry and reward merit in whatever class it appeared.[6] Cavour approved of these changes, but he found them insufficient because they made no mention of establishing a constitutional government.

Unable to translate his need to participate into political action, the Count saw other opportunities in the economic expansion that was taking place in his homeland. Though an aristocrat, Cavour enthusiastically supported the economic liberalism of the middle classes and welcomed the economic transformation which ensued. Following his father, he personally took part in the trend toward modernization by applying the latest agricultural techniques to the family estates and looked forward to the development of industry and the railways in his native province. The increased use of coal and iron, the dawn of the railroad age, and the extraordinary accumulation of capital were without precedent in Piedmont and offered new horizons to the enterprising. Even cynics and skeptics acknowledged the noteworthy though gradual increase of wealth and the spreading popularity of the principles of economic liberalism. Cavour was quick to grasp the close connection among agriculture, industry, and commerce and was one of the first to call for a sound credit structure to support the unusual boom.

Underlying the economic expansion was a steady rise in the value of land, which in turn depended upon the changes in agronomy and proprietary arrangements which approximated an agricultural revolution. Between 1832 and 1840 the remaining feudal privileges of the landlords were abolished, and more important, many large property holders now transformed their holdings into modern enterprises depending upon a market economy. This brought about a new concentration of capital, improved agricultural techniques, and even the introduction of farm machinery from England. The results were spectacular. While the population of Piedmont increased by 50 percent in the century from 1750 to 1850, the production of cereals jumped 200 percent, while that of forage sky-rocketed 1000 percent. In 1842 an agricultural association was formed in Piedmont to promote the well-being of the country by the dissemination of information on the utilization of rural resources. Cavour was a founder and a leading figure of the organization which soon became a vehicle for political as well as economic expression. It was both a product and a progenitor of Piedmont's increasing prosperity.

Meanwhile the monarch's new commercial policy, which moved in the direction of free trade, opened the subalpine state to the impact of international commerce. Even Cavour could find no major cause for complaint against the twenty-six navigation and commercial treaties concluded between 1832 and 1846.[7] In 1842 a new and more liberal commercial code was elaborated and the next year Genoa was revived by making it a free port. To further the accumulation and dispersal of capital, the government chartered a bank of issue in the port city in 1843, a move which was warmly supported by Count Cavour. That same year the Turin government concluded with France a new treaty of commerce which lowered their respective tariff walls.

Having read and approved the work of the French physiocrats and the economic liberals of England, Cavour could not but applaud the application of their principles in Piedmont. His correspondence in 1843 showed broad support for the country's new commercial policy in general and the lowering of the tariff on sugar in particular. In his opinion the decision to sacrifice the exorbitant duties accorded this industry struck a mortal blow to the protectionist system and would serve as a precedent for future developments. Still removed from political life, Cavour considered the commercial question of the greatest importance and was delighted by the progress made by the principle of liberty in this area. Unfortunately, freedom of action was still excluded from too many other aspects of Piedmontese life.

As before, Cavour held the clerical party directly responsible for the repressive atmosphere in Turin and indirectly responsible for his own painful exclusion from political life. The increasing influence exercised by the Church upon his brother widened the chasm between the two and embittered Camillo; he deplored Gustavo's conversion from a liberal philosopher to a philosophical theologian and an ultra Catholic. He reluctantly watched the ties that had bound the two break.

The frequent complaints of the archbishops of the realm as well as the clerical determination to uphold their ecclesiastical courts vis-à-vis the state's regular tribunals earned his enmity. "When the Church and its ministers would adopt a true humility," he wrote to one of his close friends in March, 1843, "I shall probably become as devout a Catholic as you." No such change occured in his opinion, for he continued to view the Church and part of the clergy with suspicion. For this reason Cavour doubted the practicality of the program put forth by Vincenzo Gioberti in 1843 in his *Del primato morale e civile degli Italiani* (On the Moral and Civil Primacy of the Italians) .

Within its pages Gioberti specified not only that Italy had to regain its greatness as a nation, but that it could do so under the aegis of the Church. Published in Brussels where Gioberti had taken refuge from the repression of the early years of Carlo Alberto's reign, the book did much to help Italians develop a good self-image and assured them that some form of unity was then feasible. Gioberti proposed to prove that Italy contained within herself and above all, through religion, the conditions required for her national and political resurrection and that to bring about this *Risorgimento* she had no need of revolution within and still less of foreign invasion or intervention. He found the potential for union in an Italian breed, a common language, laws, institutions, sentiments, and especially a common religion —Catholicism.

Observing that there are two kinds of revolutions: one changing the state without violating its sovereignty, the other overturning its structure with the intent of establishing a new state upon its ruins, Gioberti considered the first legal and the second illegitimate. Consequently, he renounced the dream of creating a unitary state and advocated instead a confederation of the existing states under the leadership of the Pope. Piedmont, he proposed, would supply the military means to assure the continued existence of the confederation.

The *Primato* provided a moderate alternative to the "insanities" of the radicals while apparently satisfying national sentiments. The very moderation of its message as well as its praise of the Papacy and the princes saved the book from being prohibited. Permitted to circulate throughout the peninsula, the work was acclaimed by many liberals as providing the ideal solution for the Italian problem. Cavour, however, questioned the possibility of this approach.

He was not the sole skeptic. A year after the appearance of Gioberti's volume, there was published in Paris Count Cesare Balbo's *Delle speranze d'Italia* (On the Hopes of Italy). Although dedicated to Gioberti, and favoring the federal over the unitary solution as a principle of organization, Balbo did not believe the Papacy capable of providing effective leadership for the new Italy. Piedmont, alone, could provide the initiative once the Austrians were diverted to the Balkans as a result of the dissolution of the Ottoman Empire. The Pope was to be respected as head of the Church and a great moral force, he might even be accorded an honorary title, but could not be expected to govern the entire peninsula. Massimo D'Azeglio, painter, writer and future Prime Minister, concurred. In his pamphlet *Degli ultimi casi di Romagna* (On the Recents Events in the Romagna), written following the insurrection of 1845 there, he revealed in measured but unmistakably clear terms that the Pope was unsuccessful in governing his own state and, by implication, incapable of governing all of Italy.

Cavour placed even less faith than the Marquis D'Azeglio in the neo-Guelph dream of making the Pope the leading figure in the unification movement. In part this was due to the fact that the present Pontiff, Gregory XVI, responded less than enthusiastically to the praises heaped upon the Papacy and seemed little inclined to assume the role earmarked for him by the Piedmontese prelate. Cavour also opposed Gioberti's program because of his continuing suspicion of the clerical party in general and the Jesuits in particular. Even though he made few public comments on this matter, his correspondence was filled with criticism of the society. "They have learnt nothing, forgotten nothing, their spirit and their methods are the same as ever," he wrote soon after the publication of the *Primato*. "Woe to the country, woe to the class which shall entrust them exclusively with the education of its youth." [8]

Even when Cavour recognized talent and true devotion in a member of the order he considered it fruitless, indeed dangerous, for the country, and more to be feared than admired. Claiming that in their determination to achieve religious and spiritual ascendency the Jesuits sought political domination, he pointed to their activity in Piedmont to prove his point. He even suspected the motivation for their sacrifices, observing that they took pride in their misery and poverty, thus vitiating their good works. Furthermore, like the other orders, they lived in an isolated world without real sympathy for the forces which moved modern society. The secular clergy, on the other hand, Cavour observed, were forced by their functions to lead a more active life and to be somewhat more sensitive to the pressures of public opinion.[9] Nonetheless, his overall opinion of the secular clergy and especially its bureaucracy was not much better. He expected little from the Church in the reformation and reorganization of the peninsula.

Piedmont remained Italy's only hope, even though the Count continued to dislike and distrust her close-minded and mysterious monarch, whose course of action remained unknown even to his closest advisers. Years before, at a ball given by Cavour's Aunt Victoria, the Duchess of Clermont-Tonnere, Carlo Alberto had engaged Costanza Taparelli D'Azeglio in conversation. Eyeing the book of mottoes she was skimming through, he turned and asked her to choose an emblem that would suit him. The Marchesa sought to decline the unexpected invitation, but the Prince insisted and she nervously looked through the volume without success. The next morning, however, she sent two copies of an emblem her husband Roberto had designed. It portrayed a knight arrayed for battle and below was the caption "Je me ferai connaitre." Carlo Alberto was pleased with the sketches, and on the back of one had written "Country, victory, sincerity, perseverance" and returned it to the Marchesa.

Meanwhile, patriots from Sicily to the Alps waited for Carlo Alberto to make himself known. Once again he chose a D'Azeglio, this time Costanza's brother-in-law, Massimo, to convey his thoughts. In October, 1845, this moderate was granted an audience and D'Azeglio related his efforts to restrain liberals and nationalists from taking part in actions that would only provoke Austrian intervention and a new round of executions and exiles. "Let those gentlemen know that they should remain quiet and take no steps now, as nothing can be done at present," Carlo Alberto replied calmly and resolutely, "but they can rest assured that when the opportunity arises, my life, my children's lives, my arms, my treasure, my army, all shall be given in the cause of Italy." [10] Surprised, rather shocked, by the words he had not expected to hear, the Marquis was not certain he had understood correctly. To avoid confusion he asked if he should let those gentlemen know of the King's commitment, to which Carlo Alberto nodded his approval. Although taken aback by his monarch's remarks, and still suspicious of his unfathomable behavior, D'Azeglio lost little time in reporting his message thus regenerating the hope that the Savoyard dynasty would take the initiative in the national movement. Within a short while Carlo Alberto aroused even greater enthusiasm by revealing his displeasure with Austria's wine tariff in particular and her commercial policy in general, while the other states in the peninsula remained servile and silent.

Count Cavour, too, seeing no other reasonable recourse, joined the ranks of those who believed that Carlo Alberto was the most practical and responsible agent for progress in the peninsula. Thus he did his part to keep his monarch on the road of reform. Knowing the King's sensitivity to the Parisian press and its image of him, when Cavour wrote an article on the railways in Italy he sent it to the French capital for publication. Appearing in the *Nouvelle Revue* in 1846, it predicted the role the railways would play in the stimulation of Italian nationalism and the glory the line from Turin to Chambéry would bring to Carlo Alberto if he had the courage to build it. Dangling the prospect of acquiring a progressive reputation before his monarch, the author promised that this construction would bring him recognition not only in his own provinces but throughout the peninsula. The day of conspiracies had passed, liberation could not result from secret plots or surprise attacks, Cavour wrote to reassure the hesitant King. Rather it was the inevitable result of civil and economic progress as well as the spread of Christian civilization.

Economic and social reform rather than conflict and revolution, claimed Cavour, worked best to destroy petty provincialism and secure the triumph of Italian national aspirations. Such developments did not threaten the various rulers in the peninsula, hence he hoped they would contribute to rather than resist the program of peaceful change. To prove his point he referred to developments within his own state, implying that the Piedmontese dynasty would continue to enjoy power and prestige so long as it continued along a progressive path.

The Count's new public enthusiasm for the dynasty influenced his friend and later partner, Michelangelo Castelli. Originally sympathetic to Giuseppe Mazzini and his revolutionary *Giovane Italia,* Cavour had since convinced Castelli of the fantastic speculation and the political problems inherent in the Mazzinian approach. Having heard the opinions of men of the calibre of Cavour and Cesare Balbo, Castelli became one of the leading exponents of a moderate course. He concurred with them that to help the fatherland one had to support the national monarchs who had their roots in the peninsula and especially encourage the King of Piedmont.

The "revolutionary" princess, Christina Belgiojoso-Trivulzio, who founded the *Gazzetta d'Italia* in 1845, agreed with Cavour on the need for material regeneration to precede political redemption. She, too, stressed the need for agricultural reforms, savings banks, schools, scientific and other learned societies, and railroads. Internal progress combined with diffusion abroad of the Italian situation, she believed, then provided the best means of advancing the national cause. By 1846 the bulk of political publications came out against the radical changes called for by Young Italy and other groups of this stamp; they favored instead patience and moderation. That year Giacomo Durando, the Piedmontese general, writer, and politician, produced his *Della nazionalità italiana* (On Italian Nationality). This work, though opposed to the neo-Guelph program of having the Pope lead the nation, nevertheless favored a moderate federalist approach which would reconcile liberty with monarchy.[11]

Moderates north and south hoped that the ambitious King of Piedmont would take some step or that the European climate would change so as to provide a more advantageous situation for Italian aspirations. Carlo Alberto, however, provided no clear sign that he would champion reform, much less nationalism. Indeed, following Cavour's publication of the article on the railroads, it was rumored that his suspicious monarch had ordered him out of the country. Concluding that little could be expected of such a ruler, other patriots hoped that the Pontiff to succeed the aged and ill Gregory would prove to be more sensitive to the demands of the age. Gregory remained adamant to the end, though just before his death he sensed that there was a storm in the air and predicted a revolutionary upheaval. Within two years this prophecy came to pass.

On the morning of June 1, 1846, at the age of eighty-one, in the sixteenth year of his pontificate, Pope Gregory passed away. Less than two weeks later in the shortest conclave since the election of Gregory XIII in 1572, the fifty-four year old Giovanni Maria Mastai-Ferretti, Bishop of Imola, was elected Pope by more than two-thirds of the required majority. The new Pope, who took the name of Pius IX (Pio Nono) had not as yet a national reputation. In fact, Jerome Bonaparte had heard rumors that Mastai had been pushed by the Austrians and feared that he would be another Habsburg puppet. In Imola and Spoleto where he was known, however, he was reported to be a generous man, a dedicated priest, and not blindly opposed to all liberal aims. It was recalled that Gregory XVI had suspected his political principles and had allegedly asserted that in the Mastai household even the cat was a *carbonaro*.

True enough, the future Pope, though devoted to ecclesiastical discipline, in private criticized the political atmosphere in the Papal States. He could not understand the hostile attitude of the government toward the youth and progressives, when it was so easy to keep them happy and satisfied. Neither did Mastai-Ferretti comprehend Gregory's opposition to railroads, the illumination of city streets, the construction of suspension bridges, and the continuing prohibition against the meeting of scientific congresses. "Theology is not opposed to the development of science, art, and industry," he asserted, but humbly added, "I know nothing about politics, however, and perhaps I am mistaken." [12]

The election of Mastai as Pope followed by the formation of a liberal government in England on June 26, which brought the Italophile Viscount Palmerston to the foreign office, aroused the hope that a new age had dawned for Italy. Even skeptics were startled by the suggestion that the head of the Church, hitherto considered an enemy of the new current, should be instead one of its chief supporters. Massimo D'Azeglio was so delighted by the reports that the new Pope was a man of talent and understanding that he promised to attend mass to express his gratitude. Pius's election had brought about such startling changes that the *Gazzetta Torinese,* an official journal, could urge the Pope to continue on this forward course.

The mounting enthusiasm for Pio Nono reached a new peak

in mid-July when his amnesty was plastered on the walls of Rome. "All our subjects who are in prison for political crimes are to be pardoned, provided they make a solemn declaration in writing that on their word of honor they will not in any way or at any time abuse this our act of grace, but faithfully fulfill the duties of a good subject," read the first article of the amnesty.[13] As the crowds gathered round the placards the sultry summer evening of July 17, the excited Romans learned that more or less the same conditions applied to all repentant refugees. Within a short period more than two thousand captives and refugees accepted the clemency of the Pope. The appointment of Cardinal Pasquale Gizzi as Secretary of State provided further proof of Pius's determination to pursue a program of reforms. The masses cheered as their monarchs groaned.

Metternich particularly disapproved of Pius's amnesty of political prisoners and compared it to an invitation to thieves to set upon one's house. The Austrian Foreign Minister also disagreed with the Pope's disposition to make greater concessions in favor of the Legations than he thought prudent. When the Pope safeguarded, if he did not approve, the right of the citizenry of Ravenna to cry out "Down with the Germans!" Prince Metternich lamented that he had made plans for everything except for a liberal Pope. His opposition made the Pontiff all the more popular.

In Cavour's Piedmont, Carlo Alberto was not unaffected by the upsurge of enthusiasm that had followed the election of Pius. The evening following the proclamation of the Pope's amnesty, when the palace of the Austrian ambassador in Rome was dark and closed, the palace of the Piedmontese representative remained open and was splendidly illuminated. Given the new political situation the Sardinian monarch allowed the Congress of scientists meeting in Genoa in September, 1846, to issue a series of patriotic pronouncements. Carlo Alberto did little to restrain the ardor of the Congress whose members all but acclaimed him as a co-leader of Italy. To further annoy Metternich, the people of Genoa were permitted to hold a solemn celebration in commemoration of the centenary of their expulsion of the Austrians. Milan, too, joined the movement when at the end of 1846 the Lombards took advantage of the death of Count Federico Confalonieri, one of their heroes who had been imprisoned in the Spielberg, to express their national sentiments. Meanwhile the populations of Ancona and Ravenna greeted even the slightest concession by the Pope with

cries of "Viva l'Italia!" "Down with Austria!" "Death to Metternich!" [14]

Without a specific plan, Pius was shaping opinion in the peninsula and day by day assumed the moral leadership in the fight for
Italian liberation and unification. Cavour was not alone in won-
dering where all this would lead and how it would end.

CHAPTER IV

Il Risorgimento *and Revolution*

FOR THE ITALIANS, EXCITED BY DEVELOPMENTS IN ROME, THE NEW year, 1847, opened with demonstrations and displays of understanding between people and princes in Rome, Tuscany, and Piedmont. This reformist and national current was resisted by the Dukes of Parma and Modena, by the King of the Two Sicilies, and of course, Austria. "Italy is a geographical expression," Metternich wrote to his ambassador in London. "The Italian peninsula is composed of sovereign and mutually independent sovereign states recognized by international law and this is the system which the Emperor is determined to uphold." [1] The English liberal reformer Richard Cobden, who happened to be traveling in Italy in 1848, concurred. Though he considered the idea of Italy becoming one empire under one sovereignty "a child's dream," he was nonetheless impressed by a number of Italians and especially by Count Cavour whom he labeled the ablest man he had ever met.

Cavour, who corresponded with friends in England and read the English journals, knew that, though their government did not favor or foresee the unification of the peninsula, both public opinion and the liberal cabinet were sympathetic to the reform movement in Italy. It was known that to encourage reform and prevent Austrian intimidation, Palmerston had sent Lord Minto on a special mission to Italy in 1847. In Turin, Minto told Carlo Alberto that the British government sympathized with the progressive measures of the Sardinian state and regretted to hear reports of Austrian interference in its internal affairs. The Sardinian monarch, in turn, assured Minto that he planned to proceed with his reforms.

As if to confirm this, the cautious and conservative Solaro della Margarita, who had directed Piedmontese foreign policy for the last twelve years, was removed from office and replaced by the more moderate Count Asinari di San Marzano. At the end of October, Carlo Alberto issued a decree announcing a series of long-awaited reforms, including provisions for the free election of communal and provincial councillors, greater equality in the penal and juridical systems, and the removal of many of the restrictions on the press. This last provision encouraged political journalism; such journalism sprang into existence in Piedmont, as it had earlier mushroomed in the Papal States.

Nevertheless, Cavour remained far from political power. Following the change in the ministry he wrote to a friend in Savoy explaining his difficult situation. Convinced that he possessed sufficient skill and intelligence to hold office, he considered himself no more liberal than those who held the most important government posts. Others shared this view and, on a number of occasions, sought to bring him into the government, but met an invincible obstacle in the person of the King.

Shut out of the cabinet, Cavour was one of the first to take advantage of the revised press law. He and Cesare Balbo called a meeting of prospective contributors and stockholders in the Palazzo Cavour and suggested the establishment of a moderate, liberal daily. This newspaper, Cavour explained, would overcome the stagnation found on the right while avoiding the excesses of the left. The projected paper, to be called *Il Risorgimento* was to seek the golden mean between the extremes.

The task of persuading well-to-do moderates to lend their money and managerial assistance was not an easy one. Some of his invited guests distrusted the Cavour family because of the activities of his father, the *Vicario* of Turin. Others still thought of Camillo as no better than a *carbonaro* with whom collaboration was dangerous, for he had earned the enmity of the King. Consequently, almost all hesitated to associate their name with Cavour, even in a business venture. One by one they slipped out of the meeting as Cavour tried to overcome their reluctance by convincing them of the merits of the project. At length only Cavour, Balbo, and Castelli remained. The last, one of Camillo's closest friends, was also about to withdraw when Cavour walked over to him, grasped his arm and pleaded for him to remain.

Castelli did stay by Cavour's side, while a number of others reconsidered their positions. "I hear that Balbo and Cavour are beginning a new newspaper in Turin," Mazzini wrote to his mother in mid-November from his exile. "I regret this, as they are behind the times." [2] A month later the first issue of *Il Risorgimento* appeared. The paper was edited by Cavour and its board included Balbo, Pietro di Santarosa, and Luigi Franchi, among others. Balbo outlined the program of the paper which was to give voice to the sentiments of the moderate camp. Independence, the conciliation and cooperation of princes and people, and finally the creation of a league of Italian princes, were the main political aims of the men of the *Risorgimento*. Such reforms, Balbo cautioned, were to be attained in an orderly manner.

A second article in that first December issue announced the journal's economic policy. This, in accordance with Cavour's beliefs, supported free trade and favored full liberty of exchange. Recognizing that a country's political resurgence depended largely on its economic vitality, the journal favored not only an increase in production but an improvement in the lot of the working classes as well.[3] Cavour, who had dedicated himself to agricultural improvement and the building of railroads while helping to establish a discount bank, a fertilizer plant, and a rice mill, was especially interested in economic matters. He now had the means of expressing his liberal convictions.

From the beginning Cavour's *Risorgimento* came out in favor of curing the country's ills by liberty which it presented as something of a panacea. Paradoxically, the cure of liberty was not to be employed upon the Society of Jesus, rather restriction and repression were the remedies suggested. The Count justified this by branding the Jesuits the greatest foes of freedom and hence not qualified to claim its protection. The question of the religious orders, however, did not take up much space in the early issues of the journal. Most of the editorial comment in the early columns centered upon the changes produced in the peninsula since the accession of Pio Nono. In comparison to the stagnation of earlier years, the progress was spectacular.

Pope Pius, who initiated the reform movement, wanted, with gradual and moderate action, to eliminate the most outrageous abuses, reestablish finances, and reinvigorate the administration of his lands. Undoubtedly the Pontiff desired first and foremost to remove the unfortunate shadow which maladministration and mismanagement of the Papal States had cast upon the Papacy in particular and the clergy in general. He wished to arouse in his subjects attachment to their sovereign and in the people, faith and devotion to the Church. Seeking peace, he hoped to see a similar accord develop between princes and people in the rest of Italy. Since the present Pope's influence was extraordinary, his words carried great weight. From Montevideo Garibaldi hailed Pio Nono as the messiah of Italy and offered his services in the task of redemption. Without exaggeration, what happened in Rome had peninsular-wide repercussions.

When Pio Nono formed a Council of Ministers and armed the

population by permitting the formation of a civic guard, great pressure developed in the rest of Italy for equivalent reforms. Meanwhile the Pontiff's protest against an Austrian troop movement in Ferrara, aroused national sentiments from the Alps to Sicily and made the Pope a national hero. Metternich was distressed by these developments. "A revolution is made," he told the British representative, "when the Government of a State is deprived of all of its power, of all governmental action; and that is the case of Rome." [4] He deplored the fact that Central Italy had been given up to a revolutionary movement under the leadership of those sects that for years had undermined the tranquility of Italy.

As coachman of Europe during the restoration, Metternich feared and fought those changes which challenged his direction of the state system. Under the guise of favoring progress, he observed, those who applauded the Pope's reforms really aimed at the subversion of the existing legitimate order in the peninsula. What these men sought, the Prince warned, was a federation of states under one supreme power. For this reason he called into question the wisdom of the customs league formed among Rome, Tuscany, and Piedmont, interpreting it as the first step in the transformation of the Vienna settlement. His assessment was not inaccurate for the Pope looked upon this agreement as a means of moving closer to a political league. Few implications of this reformism were missed by the Austrian Minister who watched the excitement and expectation penetrate even the Lombard frontier. In 1847 the Milanese took advantage of the entry of the new Archbishop into their city, to publicly express their support of Pius's progressivism and the national cause.

The year 1848 opened with violence and bloodshed as a result of the popular boycott of cigars and the lottery in Milan. At the other end of Italy, the people of Palermo rose in revolt on January 12, igniting a spark which set the entire island of Sicily on fire. Despite the bombardment of their capital by the Neapolitan forces, the Sicilians remained steadfast in their demands. From their turbulent terrain the disruption spread to the mainland. Ferdinand II, frightened by the developments in Sicily and the disorder on the Continent, capitulated, and on January 28 decreed a constitution patterned on the French document of 1830, which the Parisians were soon to overturn. Success in the south encouraged militants from the Alps to the Tiber as an irresistible call for constitutionalism engulfed Italy.

Count Cavour, suffering from a defect common to most of the

Piedmontese aristocracy, knew England and France better than Italy. He did not seem to perceive the full purport of events in the *Mezzorgiorno* and did not dwell upon them at any great length in his columns or correspondence. With Piedmontese provincialism, Cavour concentrated upon the situation in his home state, and when he looked outside it was to London or Paris rather than to Naples or Palermo. Fascinated by English parliamentary life which he meticulously studied and closely followed, he believed that the legislation then before the House of Commons to liberate the Jews provided Piedmont with a wonderful example to emulate. Such a policy, he argued, served not only the cause of liberty but would win English public opinion for the Piedmontese and Italian cause. He did not consider the impact of such a course upon relations with Rome. Not surprisingly, within two weeks of the English action, Cavour's *Risorgimento* called for the emancipation of the Jews in Piedmont.

Although inclined to look across the Alps rather than the Appenines, Cavour could not ignore the spectacular news from the Papal States. His paper recognized the great debt that the resurrection of Italian liberty owed to Pio Nono and the example he had set in Rome.[5] There the year had opened with the ominous cry "Long live Pius IX alone!" Moderates such as the Count hoped that the Pope would proceed resolutely along the path of reform, but always within prescribed limits. Such advice was easier to give than to follow. The crowds in the eternal city wrung more and more from the politically inexperienced though well-meaning Pontiff by their applause or threats of disorder. Pius eventually recognized the predicament he had been placed in by the process of pressure by acclamation. "Do not make demands," he pleaded with the masses, "that I cannot, must not, and do not wish to permit."[6]

In Piedmont, too, pressure mounted for change, and, as before, the most vocal elements were to be found in Genoa. Since the celebration of the centenary of the expulsion of the Austrians, an air of excitement pervaded the port city. On January 3, 1848, some four to six thousand people paraded about the city which held so many memories for Cavour, crying, "Away with the Jesuits!" and "We want a civic guard!" Within hours, some 20,000 signatures were collected for a petition to the King, and to hasten his liberal moves they sent a deputation to Turin. On January 7, the journalists of the capital met at the Hotel Trombetta to determine how best to support the suggestions of the Genoese. To the surprise of those assembled, Cavour truncated the discussion of partial solutions, insisting they ask for something more—a constitution.

The proposal of the editor of *Il Risorgimento* provoked a debate and aroused suspicion. Almost immediately the rumor was born that Cavour had asked for so much to infuriate Carlo Alberto, thus impeding further progress. Others, however, recognized the logic of the Count's suggestion and therefore Roberto D'Azeglio, Pietro Santarosa, Angelo Brofferio, and Giacomo Durando all seconded it. Though Carlo Alberto believed firmly in his own right to rule and recognized the privileged position of the Church, he could not ignore the reforms in Sicily, Naples, and Tuscany and the disturbances in Lombardy and Venetia. He found it difficult to remain steadfast while his fellow sovereigns retreated. The need for action became critical following demonstrations in Genoa, Novara, and Turin in his own kingdom. Prudently shunting aside the declaration he had made in 1824, that he would not alter the fundamental law of the land, he promised a constitution and its principles were established by a decree of February 8, 1848.

The day before the King's proclamation Cavour once again called for a constitution. The example of the liberty already accorded to the Neapolitans and of that being prepared for Tuscany, he wrote in the pages of his journal, had increased the desire of the Piedmontese for similar benefits. When the King issued his statement promising a *Statuto,* Cavour's paper published it in a supplement. Carlo Alberto's belated resolve to adopt a fundamental statute establishing a representative form of government in Piedmont pleased the Count and his associates directing *Il Risorgimento.* "There are those who fear that the King by granting a constitution has diminished his force as the first custodian of national independence," an article of February 8 read. "Actually," the directors of the paper continued, "Carlo Alberto by so doing, has increased his influence in European politics as if he had doubled the size of his army. Now the head of a free people, the King was all the more to be feared by the enemies of liberty."

A fortnight following the proclamation of the *Statuto* a great demonstration was arranged in its honor by Roberto D'Azeglio. On that occasion an estimated 50,000 citizens of the capital, arranged according to their callings and trades, marched in procession before the King and his entourage, assembled before the royal palace. Cavour, like Angelo Brofferio whose views he opposed, marched in the journalists' section. That group's spirit, according to the Count, was far better than the voices in it, which he laughingly compared to "barking dogs." On that day gratitude if not talent abounded.

Very soon the euphoria following the King's proclamation vanished and the principles of the proposed *Statuto* were scrutinized. Cavour called for a system that would follow tried paths. Political experiments are always costly and often dangerous, he wrote, suggesting they follow forms sanctioned by time and experience. He could not consent, therefore, to the insistence of the radicals for universal suffrage. Such a system would be acceptable and applicable, the Count explained in his journal, in a republic which had long been educated in the school of liberty. It was not compatible, in his opinion, with the existing conditions of European society and with the principles of constitutional monarchy. "We are decisively opposed," he repeated, "to the fallacious doctrine which proclaims the right to participate in the goverance of society, a natural right." Cavour delineated the basic prerequisites for the privilege of suffrage: independence of the citizen so he could not be bribed, intelligence of a sufficient awareness to judge candidates and issues, and finally an interest in the preservation of the social order.[7]

Cavour refused to compromise on yet another issue. "I trust that our statute will sanction religious freedom," he wrote in mid-February, "otherwise I shall work against it even at the risk of alienating the clergy, who have been favorable to us so far, and might manage to ruin us if they joined with the Radicals." [8] This willingness to cross swords with the clergy revealed more than his attachment to liberal principles. It was also a reflection of Cavour's ingrained suspicion of the regular clergy and their "pretensions." In the privacy of his chamber, in his intimate correspondence, and above all in his diary, he riled against them.

Initially Cavour kept private his distaste for part of the clergy. Politically a liberal, he was by class and instinct socially conservative and appreciated the role played by religion in the inculcation of authority. Observing that the intellectual life of the masses moved within a rather limited range, he recognized the impact of religion to be even greater than the call of country or nationality. Furthermore, he felt the moment was not propitious for what might be construed as an attack upon the Church. Pio Nono was then the acknowledged initiator of the new reformism in Italy and without question the most popular political personality in the peninsula as well as spiritual leader of the slumbering masses.

Nonetheless, there was an anticlerical agitation in Piedmont as some claimed that certain clerical forces, and the Jesuits in particular, were attempting to restrain the liberal sentiments of the Pontiff. Cavour was alert if not responsive to this agitation, viewing the anger against the regular clergy with special interest. The clamor against the Society of Jesus evoked in him a sympathetic response not only because it echoed many of his own suspicions but also because it had already played an instrumental role in persuading his own King to grant a constitution. From time to time his newspaper published articles exposing clerical abuses; among such articles was one of February, 1848, which warned that the Piedmontese episcopacy resented the government's new press law and considered the prohibition of its duty to examine, revise, and supervise the press, a violation of its rights. Cavour and his colleagues disagreed, refusing to recognize the Church's claim to a right to maintain a watch upon the press. For the moment, however, they preferred to avoid a more serious confrontation with the Church.

On February 4, 1848, Cavour published an article which predicted that the Italian *Risorgimento* would not follow the path of the English, French, and Spanish revolutions because, unlike these, the Italian had the support of a clergy that was the true friend of liberty. Even the Jesuits were not a real menace. If the Italian *Risorgimento* should ever become hostile to the Church and anti-Christian like the French Revolution, Cavour prophesied, then the influence of that order would have to be feared. Since the Italian revolution was not at war with the established religion, the nation need not fear the opposition. Admitting that there were some misguided spirits in the Church, the Count warned that the new political order had to confront the prejudices, exaggerations, and apprehensions they aroused. However, the obstacles posed by such recalcitrants in Italy were negligible in comparison with the problems faced by other revolutions.

Within the columns of *Il Risorgimento* was now voiced criticism of special ecclesiastical courts, which alone could handle clerical cases. At the same time there was support for the introduction of a broad policy of religious toleration and the removal of disabilities from those who did not share the faith of the majority. At no time did the editorial policy of the paper favor discrimination against the Catholic clergy in their capacity as citizens. Rather, Cavour's journal indicated that as members of the body politic they were to be admitted to office and enjoy the right to vote on an equal basis with others.[9] These were the principles the Count wanted to see established in the forthcoming constitution whose arrival he anxiously awaited. Unfortunately on a number of key issues that document proved to be purposely vague. "The Roman Catholic Religion is the sole religion of state," read the first article of the *Statuto* published on March 4, and other religions were to be tolerated in conformity with the law. Precisely what this meant, no one was sure.

Other parts of that document seemed to imply that special privileges, including some enjoyed by the clergy, were to be abolished. Article twenty-four, for example, stipulated that inhabitants of the kingdom, regardless of rank or title, were equal before the law. When coupled with article sixty-eight, which asserted that justice was to be administered in the King's name by the judges whom he appoints, the legality and the future of special clerical tribunals were called into question. Perhaps it was this which led Monsignor Giacomo Filippo Fransoni, the Archbishop of Turin, to remain discreetly silent about the constitution in the pastoral letter he issued following its promulgation. Alarmed rather than assured by such progress and the pressure of current events, the Archbishop preferred to look backwards to the old, familiar world. Action, not contemplation, dominated the moment, however, and this suited Cavour if not the conservatives.

The fear of a renewed French outburst which had haunted the conservative classes, and most of the Cavour family since 1815, materialized in February, 1848. The government of Louis Philippe, which had sought to stifle opposition by prohibiting the political propaganda banquet scheduled for February 22, found its authority and its very existence threatened by the people of Paris, who poured into the streets in defiance of orders. True enough, the capital was much more radical than the rest of the country, but the French system was so centralized that Paris functioned as a fuse to detonate the entire country. Terrified, Louis Philippe found it necessary to follow in the footsteps of his predecesser, Charles X, to England and exile. Shortly afterwards the Second French Republic was proclaimed in Paris.

Word of these events was transmitted by telegraph to the rest of Europe, producing everywhere an air of excited expectation. The news sent shudders through Metternich, who recognized the vulnerability of the empire he served. His fears were not unjustified. In a matter of weeks, Central Europe tumbled into revolution. Within the borders of the Habsburg state the dissatisfied Magyars under the leadership of the dynamic Louis Kossuth in the early part of March demanded autonomy if not independence. By mid-month the revolution reached Vienna, the center of conservatism, the rock of absolutism, where a mob crying "Long live liberty!" precipitated the resignation of Metternich, the man who most symbolized the old, antinationalist order. This unexpected event threw Austria into the throes of revolution. The collapse of the colossus of Central Europe was the best proof that the settlement of 1815 had been smashed to pieces.

Word that the high priest of the status quo and stagnation had been put to flight, and that the revolution had reached Vienna as well as Berlin, aroused a new agitation in Italy and especially in its northern regions. The battle against the Austrians commenced in Venice, where the irate citizens secured the release of the recently incarcerated Daniele Manin and Nicolò Tommaseo. Upon receiving their freedom, these patriots assumed direction of the campaign against the hated *tedeschi*. A civic guard was hastily formed, and with practically no bloodshed they convinced the Austrians to abandon the formidable arsenal, making themselves masters of the city and the adjacent countryside. On March 22, under the leadership of Manin, the old republic was restored pending the formation of some new political entity.

Events in Vienna and Venice encouraged the people of Lombardy to challenge the authority of General Radetzky, and barricades were erected in the city of Milan on March 18. Patriots throughout the peninsula were moved when they learned that the people of Milan had spontaneously risen against the powerful Austrian force in their midst. Unaided from the outside, lacking formal training and regular supplies, they were breaking the yoke of Habsburg control. Such heroism inspired confidence and new enthusiasm. Volunteers rushed northward from all of Italy as peasants, aristocrats, and even princes pledged their support. Naturally the people of nearby Piedmont could not long remain indifferent to a movement which assumed the nature of a national crusade.

During these tumultuous times Piedmont was attempting to initiate its constitutional regime under the leadership of Cavour's friend and business associate, Cesare Balbo. It was his government which received the fervent requests for assistance from the parade of messengers sent from Milan. Individual Piedmontese had already responded by crossing the Ticino River to assist their brothers in Lombardy. No official decision, however, came from Carlo Alberto who pondered the course to pursue. He did permit General Franzini to issue orders placing the Sardinian army on a war footing. As the fighting in Milan became increasingly bitter, the cries for Sardinian participation increased. Moderates joined with radicals in clamoring for war and even Count Cavour joined the ranks of the war party.

On March 23, in a momentous article, Cavour called upon Carlo Alberto to go to war. Pointing to the heroism of the neighboring Lombards, he called upon his government to show equal resolution. "The supreme hour for the Piedmontese monarchy has struck," he warned, "the hour of firm decisions, the hour which will determine the fate of empires and peoples. In light of developments in Lombardy and Venetia, hesitation, doubt, delay are no longer permissible, these of all policies would be most calamitous," Cavour continued. "As men of cool judgment, accustomed to paying attention to the dictates of reason rather than the impulses of passion, we feel bound in conscience to declare, after carefully weighing our every word, that only one road is open to the nation, the government, the King. That path is war —immediately without delay." [10]

After five successive days of fighting the Milanese forced General Radetzky to abandon the capital and to seek refuge beyond the Mincio in the quadrilateral of fortresses: Peschiera, Mantua, Verona, and Legnago. In Turin Carlo Alberto finally put on the tricolor scarf sent to him by the people of Milan, indicating that he would fight alongside the Lombards. By coincidence, the very day that Cavour had published his impassioned plea, the King issued a proclamation to the peoples of Lombardy and Venetia promising his support. Adopting as his standard the revolutionary tricolor with the cross of Savoy upon it, Carlo Alberto led his troops into Lombardy.

The news rocked the length and breadth of the peninsula, pushing part of its people into a new stage of frenzied agitation. In the Eternal City the Habsburg coat of arms was lowered and burned in the Piazza del Popolo while the Antonelli Ministry decreed the formation of an army. Hastily Colonel Andrea Ferrari was made commander of the volunteer forces, while the Piedmontese General Giovanni Durando was selected as the supreme head of the regular papal forces. In countless other ways the Romans showed their sympathy and support for the national crusade. The religious orders and the Pope himself made rich donations, while 12,000 volunteers, including two nephews of the Pope, marched north. Pio Nono, in an apostolic benediction at the end of March, warned that the events of the last two months were not the work of man and cautioned all to heed the voice of God.

Despite his apparent support of the national movement, Pius had strong reservations. In the first place, he suspected the motives of Carlo Alberto who insisted upon the fusion of Lombardy and Venetia with Piedmont and refused to elaborate his other war aims. Secondly, he wondered how he, as spiritual leader of all Catholics, could wage war upon Catholic Austria. The Pope's reluctance to declare war seemed justified when he received word of the proclamation issued by General Durando in early April. "The Holy Father has blessed your swords," the General told his soldiers." Those swords, united with those of Carlo Alberto must exterminate the enemies of God and Italy, and those who abuse Pio Nono, profane the Churches of Mantua, assassinate our Lombard brothers, and who by their iniquity place themselves outside the pale of all law." [11] For this reason Durando called for the war cry, "God wills it!"

The Pope thought otherwise. As he read and reread Durando's proclamation he became increasingly furious. Not only were his troops passing the Po, contrary to his orders, he was being pushed forward as more than a participant, indeed as the principal author of the war. He resented even more the attempt to convert the war from a purely national one to a religious struggle, which made him fear a disastrous schism among the South Germans. Distressed, he complained that Durando wanted to play the part of Pontiff and threatened to raise his voice against the scandal which placed him in an impossible position. His cabinet urged restraint but realized that the prompt formation of the Italian League was the sole means of enabling the head of the Church to entrust his troops to others and thus escape the opprobrium of waging war. Unfortunately, the Sardinian ministry was not favorable to this plan. Moderates in Rome sought a solution for this perilous situation, but the time for compromise was slipping away.

In Piedmont, too, the day of the moderates was quickly passing. There the electoral law which Count Cavour had helped to draft called for general elections to be held April 17–26 and the convening of Parliament in early May. This plan met the determined opposition of the radicals and democrats, who resented the restricted suffrage which they claimed favored the aristocracy and the court party at the expense of the people. Consequently, they called for a postponement of the elections at least until such time as the Lombards and Venetians should by plebiscite join Piedmont in a new union.

Cavour fought this radical proposal and his call for immediate elections prevailed. However, the democrats wreaked their revenge, for the Count who had been nominated in four constituencies proved unsuccessful in all. Chagrined that he had been defeated while some with no reputations had been elected, he explained to his friend Castelli why his fellow citizens had not voted for him. "Many of them are motivated by such anti-aristocratic prejudices," he wrote in April, "that my belonging to one of the oldest families of the realm is a title for my exclusion that no personal merit on my part can overcome." This rationalization satisfied neither Castelli nor the Count, but it was a convenient explanation for the embarrassing fact that even though constitutionalism now prevailed in Piedmont, he was still excluded from a position of political power. Rejection by the electorate was far more devastating to Cavour's ego than his exclusion because of his conflict with Carlo Alberto. Visibly disturbed, he was not vanquished and vowed to continue to speak out on important issues. "Not being elected deputy will in no way diminish my devotion to the cause of liberty and progress," he promised Castelli. "I will not fight for them in Parliament, but shall fight in the journals, in which, thanks to the assistance of my friends and yours in particular, I have an arena that envy and hostility cannot close for me." [12] The events of the next few months provided Cavour, the journalist, with a good deal to write about.

On April 29, Pio Nono who had never explicitly announced his intention of declaring war upon Austria, denounced the notion that he do so. To the fervent requests of the nationalists for a declaration of war, he proclaimed that as Vicar of Peace, such a measure was unthinkable. This pronouncement, which was delivered against the unanimous recommendation of his Ministry, encouraged the withdrawal from the war of Ferdinand II of Naples and marked the beginning of the Italian defeat of 1848. Pius who had sown the wind had now to reap the whirlwind as overnight his popularity began to wane. Liberals and nationalists throughout the peninsula now realized that the dream of having the Pope unite Italy was dead and began to look elsewhere for the fulfillment of their ambitions. Naturally, attention focused on Piedmont, which alone carried on the struggle against Austria, while attempting to organize her liberal institutions at home.

On May 8, 1848, the first Piedmontese Chamber of Deputies

met in the Carignano Palace in Turin to consider the conduct of the war and the implementation of the constitutional order. Cavour was conspicuously absent, though his voice was heard through the pages of *Il Risorgimento*. This journal not only came into conflict with Pio Nono over the question of freeing non-Catholics, it also opposed papal policy in the national struggle against Austria. Nationality is the first need of every people, and Italy cannot grasp this without ejecting the foreigner, the men of *Il Risorgimento* announced, implying that if Rome did not help, the Italians would eventually conclude that nationality and the temporal power were incompatible.

While a war of words debated the Pope's policy, the campaign against the Austrians continued. Despite the defection of Pius and Ferdinand, the Piedmontese were optimistic at the end of May because they believed the fall of Peschiera, one of the fortresses of the quadrilateral, to be imminent. They did not expect Radetzky to leave the safety of Verona and attempt to break the siege of the city. When the Habsburg commander took this step, Carlo Alberto managed to move his forces to Goito, preventing the Austrian advance. Thus at the beginning of June, Turin celebrated a dual victory: the success at Goito and the fall of Peschiera.

Cavour was one of the few who could not enjoy the festivities, for in the fighting at Goito on May 30, 1848, his twenty-year-old nephew, the Marquis Augusto Cavour, to whom he had become attached, died on the field of battle. When his friend Castelli heard the news he went to see Camillo and found him in his room in total anguish, rolling on the carpet and crying unashamedly. Despite his many efforts, Castelli could not calm the Count or draw a single word out of him. More than ever Cavour was determined to help push the Austrians out of northern Italy. In fact, having received his nephew's uniform, which showed the traces of his mortal wound, he hung it in a cabinet in his room, thus having a constant reminder before him.[13]

June, which began so bleakly for the Count, was to end on a better note. Unable to obtain a seat in Parliament in the April contest, he won a seat in the by-elections of June 26. Before the Chamber opened, the duchies of Parma and Modena had voted for fusion with Piedmont (May 10, 1848); the plebiscite in Lombardy had produced a similar result (May 29, 1848); and even the Venetians had decided the first week in July to throw in their lot with the Piedmontese. A powerful northern Italian state was in the process of formation and radicals, moderates, and conservatives vied with one another to influence its evolution. Cavour could not help but become embroiled in the debate. His first speech in the Chamber of Deputies, which was on the question of the union of Lombardy and Venetia with Piedmont, was not well received. He concluded that such divisive issues as the final constitution of the enlarged state would best be concluded when the war had been won, calling attention to the almost forgotten fact that Austria had not yet been defeated.

Acute observers could not lose sight of the fact that Radetzky was receiving reinforcements while Carlo Alberto had to endure the loss of some 10,000 men. The balance of power was now in Austria's favor and Radetzky used this advantage to assume the offensive in mid-July. The Balbo Ministry, caught by surprise, fell, and the King appointed Count Gabrio Casati, President of the provisional government of Milan, as the new Prime Minister. Unfortunately on July 25, 1848, the same day the new cabinet assumed office, news reached Turin of Carlo Alberto's defeat at Custozza and the retreat of his forces. Confronted with this disaster, Casati resigned, Parliament was prorogued, and the King assumed emergency powers. Originally the besieged monarch sought to defend Milan, but finding this an impossible task, dispatched two of his generals to secure an armistice from the Austrians. Under its terms Milan had to be surrendered within twenty-four hours; the distraught Carlo Alberto abandoned the city amidst a chorus of complaints and charges of cowardice. "If he chooses to preserve his crown by dint of crime and cowardice," announced Garibaldi, "we will not abandon our sacred soil to the profanation of usurpers." [14]

Cavour, who had deplored the outbreak of violence in Paris in June, 1848, and had applauded General Cavaignac's suppression of that revolution, feared that revolution might erupt in Piedmont. Since the beginning of the year his paper had struck out against the democrats and radicals, opposing their republican and utopian dreams. The withdrawal of the Grand Duke from Tuscany and the flight of the Pope from Rome paved the way for two radical republics and talk of a constituent assembly to consolidate all of Italy into a republic. "A republic is possible in the peninsula," the readers of *Il Risorgimento* were warned, "and it is the best means of ruining Italy."

The Count's fears were not without foundation. In Turin as well as Milan, insinuations were made about the bravery and loyalty of the King, and the value of the monarchy itself was called into question. "The war of kings is over," phophesied

Mazzini, "and that of the people about to commence." Radicals in the capital looked to Gioberti for leadership, but Carlo Alberto to their disappointment called the Marquis Alfieri and the Count di Revel to office. Another serious division soon developed as those for and against renewal of the war sought to carry the day. To reopen the war without French help, Cavour wrote in late August, would be an act of virtual madness which he was prepared to prevent by every means at his disposal. He suggested moving as close as possible to France, in order to drag her into a war with Austria, if Austria did not show herself compliant in the negotiations that were about to open. To win such support, Cavour's paper suggested, Piedmont must show herself to be neither revolutionary nor disorderly. Rather, it was indispensable that she resist the rowdyism that reigned in Tuscany and Rome.

This sensible advice was not heeded as rhetoric triumphed over reason. Because he opposed the desire of the democrats to reopen the war with Austria, Cavour was booed from the gallery. Accustomed to criticism, he refused to be silenced by the reaction he provoked in the Chamber. "The uproar will not deter me," he replied on one occasion," for I shall continue even with this not very agreeable accompaniment." [15] The writers of the *Risorgimento* censured the irresponsible position of the radicals who called for war but said nothing about the means of conducting it, who claimed they had faith in the Piedmontese army, but based all their hope on the unlikely prospect of French intervention. In turn, Cavour's cautious position was little appreciated by the democrats who disparagingly referred to him as *Il Codino*, which derived from the pigtail plait of hair worn down the back by aristocrats, and was a term used to describe the members of the absolutist and clerical party.

Earlier the radicals had forced Cavour out of a position of leadership in the agricultural association he had helped to form by attacking his conservative connections and his backward political beliefs. The Count was so unpopular that the directors of the Infant Asylum Society had regretfully to ask for his resignation lest the opposition to his person hinder the work of the Society. Cavour's opposition to a renewal of the war did little to dispel his image as a reactionary.

Gioberti, in league with the radical National Political Club of Turin, called upon the government to show initiative, break the armistice, and renew the conflict with Austria. Finally in December, this patriotic prophet and ex-priest was called to power and had the opportunity to implement his program. One of the first things he did was to dissolve the Chamber and call for new elections. Not surprisingly, when this occurred, Count Cavour, who was accused of being cold to the Italian cause and maligned as an aristocrat, lost his seat to the extremist Pansoya.

Paradoxically, the moment that Gioberti was saddled with the responsibility of power, he saw the wisdom of the suggestions of Cavour and the crown prince Vittorio Emanuele, the Duke of Savoy. Fearful of outside intervention to restore the Pope to Rome following his flight in November, Gioberti concluded that the call to war, which he had earlier championed, was inopportune. Rather, he reasoned that Piedmont would do better to take steps to return the Grand Duke to Tuscany and Pio Nono to Rome, thus eliminating the pretext for foreign intervention. He therefore instructed Count Martini, the Sardinian envoy to Rome, quietly to offer his services to mediate between the rebels and the Pope. When in February, 1849, the radicals learned that the man they had called forth to reopen hostilities with the enemy planned instead to act against the recently formed Tuscan and Roman republics, they howled him out of office.

Gioberti's resignation paved the way for the entry of the bellicose democrats of the National Club under the leadership of General Chiodo and Urbano Rattazzi. Cavour still resolutely opposed renewal of the war. "Between the program of Carlo Alberto of March, 1848 and the proposals of the Rattazzi Ministry of March, 1849," ran one editorial in his paper, "one could see the difference between the sublime and the ridiculous. Italy could have 'gone it alone,' Piedmont by herself could not make Italy. Twenty-five million men who were of one mind could have achieved their objective, instead, energies were being dissipated in throwing out the Pope and the Archduke of Tuscany and creating divisive, squabbling republics." [16]

Nonetheless the new government refused to heed moderate advice and renew the armistice which expired on March 12, persuading their disheartened monarch to declare war on March 20. Within three days the Piedmontese learned that their army had been routed by the forces of General Radetzky at Novara and soon after Carlo Alberto, the Hamlet of Italian independence, to save his dynasty and country, decided to abdicate. The campaign that had opened with such high expectations ended with the Austrian occupation of Lomellina and Alessandria. The victors would have occupied much more but for the watchful position of France and England, who were determined to preserve Piedmont as a buffer. Following this defeat, Cesare Balbo, commenting on the need for peace, observed that Piedmont never concluded permanent peace with Austria, it only signed truces that lasted ten years. Cavour promised that the Piedmontese would learn from their errors and "do better next time."

CHAPTER V

A Powerful Parliamentary Figure

THE HOPES THAT THE REVOLUTION HAD RAISED THROUGHOUT ITALY were extinguished by the news of Novara. With Venice and Rome fallen and Piedmont broken, the dream of 1848 had led to the nightmare of 1849. Piedmont's situation was critical both at home and abroad: the army was defeated and demoralized, the treasury was empty, the administration was in chaos, and there was strong pressure from the extremists on both sides to undermine the constitutional system. One of the few positive results of the defeat was the calling of the writer, artist, soldier, and statesman Massimo D'Azeglio to power in May, 1849. He was well-known and respected in Piedmont and throughout the peninsula, and men such as Cavour were delighted by his selection, knowing full well that he would steer a middle course between the reactionary right and the revolutionary left in the crucial postwar period.

In view of the difficult situation confronting the government, Cavour considered himself fortunate that D'Azeglio had not invited him into the cabinet. Thus rather than strike out against those who kept him out of power, he promised to send them a note of gratitude. Despite the pretense that he preferred his simple, pastoral life to the maze of political machinations, Cavour actually resented the unjust criticism of him and riled against the invidious envy which kept him out of the government. He was disturbed by the fact that his name still provoked an outburst of passion and resentment, feelings which were counterproductive to the cause he sought to promote; for a time he even thought it best that he abandon direction of his paper. His enemies, he complained to Castelli, had succeeded beyond their wildest dreams in the campaign to discredit him. His friends, he continued, did nothing to rehabilitate his name—on the contrary, they accepted his unpopularity as a *fait accompli*. Like so many others, Cavour was dissatisfied with the present.[1]

Conservatives and liberals, clerics and anticlerics, focused their attention on the new monarch and wondered what path he would pursue. Various forces were seen to pull him in the direction of

Austria and absolutism. Not only was his mother a Habsburg but his wife also came from that formidable family. Furthermore, during his formative years, in fact until he reached the age of twenty-eight, Piedmont was an absolutist state, so that the crown prince had expected to succeed to a throne in which the royal will was all-important. Finally, the army was the state institution that most attracted his attention, and the military remained one of the pillars of conservatism in the country.

The education that Vittorio Emanuele received was poor, in part because of his lack of interest in most of the traditional disciplines and his disinclination to devote his energy to scholarly matters. Indeed, his teachers complained that he was "always asleep," "thoroughly bored," and that it took more than an hour to get him to comprehend even the most simple point. His political education was little better. Allowed no part at all in practical politics by his father, Vittorio Emanuele spent his time in the barracks, the bedroom, and hunting field rather than at his desk. Small wonder that he was coarse in his language and easily tired by the details of administration. These unfortunate features were balanced by an affability and simplicity of manner, a good nature, great physical courage, and a strong dose of common sense. These last characteristics were to prove invaluable in the difficult days ahead, for his first act as King was to negotiate an armistice with the Austrians.

Those who sought to make the new ruler a hero claimed that at Vignale Vittorio Emanuele vigorously defended Piedmont's constitution against the enemy's demand for its destruction. In reality the very reverse occurred, for Vittorio Emanuele privately assured Radetzky that he planned to destroy the liberal tendencies of the Piedmontese parliament and depart from his father's domestic and foreign policy. Calling for Austrian cooperation and generosity, he indicated that if the Austrians would help him by conceding reasonable terms, he would be able to restore part of the monarchical authority which his father and parliament had helped to undermine. Later he defended the reconstruction of the army in terms of his need to create a military regime which could defeat the democrats.[2]

Liberals feared that the "old fox" Radetzky, in conjunction with absolutist and clerical circles, would persuade the inexperi-enced King to emasculate the constitutional order. Thus when he confronted the people of Turin on March 27, there was a notice-able absence of enthusiasm and applause. The capital assumed a less hostile attitude two days later, when Vittorio Emanuele II swore to uphold the institutions which his father had conceded. Nonetheless, the suspicion prevailed that the King might alter his position, fold and put away the tricolor, and, caught in the momentum of reaction then sweeping over the peninsula, restore absolutism in Piedmont. Since the Pope was the most spectacular apostate from the national cause and constitutionalism, some surmised that the clerical camp would convince Vittorio Emanuele to follow in his steps. Hence the element that considered clericalism the vanguard of absolutism and the Pope the personification of Italian reaction called for action against them.

Cavour saw the wisdom in this course, but sensed the danger inherent in it as well. He did not consider the cause of Italian independence lost simply because Piedmont had suffered a military setback. To watch, wait, and prepare was his policy. As part of the preparation he and Castelli sought to keep alive the liberal and national spirit by discrediting the reactionary party as well as the radicals who had recently brought the country to the brink of ruin. Since the Papal Allocution (formal address or warning to the clergy) of April, articles in *Il Risorgimento* had assumed a more antagonistic tone towards the Papacy. Whereas the Pope had been previously depicted in Cavour's journal as the leader of the reform movement, he was now seen as the great stumbling block to unity. The temporal power itself was called into question and one writer for *Il Risorgimento* went so far as to predict that so long as it existed, attempts to achieve unification, even of a federal nature, were doomed to failure.[3]

Relations between Piedmont and the Papacy had been less than cordial even before Cavour's journal commenced its attacks upon the policies of the Court of Rome. For his part, Pius was deeply disturbed by the anticlerical manifestations that issued from that Catholic country. Unquestionably since the publication of Gioberti's vehement attack on the Jesuits in his *Gesuita moderna* (The Modern Jesuit) published in 1846, there had emerged a profound distrust of the order and undeniably some had become apprehensive of all clerics. To add to the Pope's consternation, at the close of 1847 the Ministry of Justice in Turin had already called into question the value and viability of special ecclesiastical courts and the whole idea of exempting the clergy from trials in the civil courts.

With the advent of the constitutional order and a free press, criticism of the Church and its ministers intensified both in tone and pace, distressing the Holy Father. Under this system attacks upon the religion of the state were launched in the very halls of

Parliament by Angelo Brofferio, Lorenzo Valerio, Riccardo Sineo, Agostino Depretis, Urbano Rattazzi, and others of the *sinistra ecclesiastica* or ecclesiastical left. While most of these men also belonged to the *sinistra* or simply the left, the ecclesiastical left included within its ranks moderates and even some otherwise conservative figures who took a radical position on the religious issue. Drawn principally, though not exclusively, from the bourgeoisie, these men clamored for the immediate and complete secularization of the state as the first step in the suppression of the prerogatives of the privileged.

The chief exponent of this group and the most demagogic of the democrats was the historian, journalist, and deputy in the Subalpine Parliament, Angelo Brofferio. Firm in his conviction and rigid in his attitude, he was a doctrinaire rather than a statesman; his panacea was the principle of democracy which he hoped to apply everywhere. Thus, in his ardor he sought to impose democracy upon the hierarchical, aristocratic Church. Contrary to the public position of Cavour who welcomed clerical participation in the country's life, Brofferio did not wish to see the Church take any part in politics. According to him, that institution could not begin its regeneration until it "had shorn itself of the scepter and crown which it should never have worn." [4]

Outside the Chamber Brofferio's views were upheld by a number of periodicals such as *L'Imparziale* and the *Voce della Libertà* of Turin and *La Maga* of Genoa. Another important journal of the left was *L'Opinione*, which was directed by Giacomo Durando. Commencing its career as a moderate journal which proclaimed its complete adherence to the Church, *L'Opinione* became progressively more radical. By 1849 it had clearly degenerated into an anticlerical organ whose editors declared Article I of the *Statuto* which pronounced Catholicism the state religion, and section one of Article XXXIII, which permitted admission of Bishops to the Senate, fatal mistakes. *La Concordia,* under the direction of Lorenzo Valerio, also upheld the tenets of the ecclesiastical left. This newspaper was greatly influenced by Vincenzo Gioberti; when this prelate turned against the Pope, so did *La Concordia.*

Their polemic strengthened the position of conservative Catholics who had all along asserted the absolute incompatibility of Catholicism with the liberal world. The Jesuits assumed the initiative in insisting that the divinely instituted Church not adapt itself to the present iniquities, but promote the restoration of a truly Catholic civilization. Perhaps the clearest spokesman of this persuasion was Father Taparelli D'Azeglio, the brother of the Piedmontese Prime Minister, who rejected outright the suggestion that the Church place itself at the service of a national philosophy. In opposition to those who spoke of national right and destiny, Father Taparelli pointed to the importance of the family, the commune, and the village in the formation of the individual, antagonizing moderates and radicals alike. These two groups differed, however, in their response to the "pretensions" of this "medieval" philosophy.

Long interested in the sensitive issue of relations between Church and state, Cavour could not help but become embroiled in the debate. As soon as the Subalpine Parliament opened its doors, members of the ecclesiastical left came into conflict with the Count. While he welcomed and supported Riccardo Sineo's law which provided for the emancipation of non-Catholics, he would not go along with Brofferio's more radical proposals. Hence in 1848, when the latter proposed that all convents be abolished, Cavour denounced the move as inexpedient. "I will not examine if these convents are or are not useful to the Catholic religion, if there be any that need to be reformed, or others that should be maintained," he asserted, "I will only observe that this reform disturbs opinions, the beliefs, and if you like, even the prejudices of a great part of the population, and I would almost say (at least for the population on this side of the Alps) of the great majority of the population." [5] In opposing Brofferio's proposal, Cavour revealed the pragmatic bent that was to permeate his approach to ecclesiastical questions throughout his career. The country, he concluded, was not yet prepared to accept the principle of separation between Church and state or pursue a policy in conformity with it.

At the moment only the left desired that the state affirm its rights even in ecclesiastical matters. It called for a revision of the concordat of 1841 with Rome, placing particular emphasis on eliminating the abuses which made the clergy a state within the state. Frightened by the anticlerical campaign of the radicals, the profoundly Catholic Balbo, Piedmont's first constitutional Prime Minister, asked the curia for some concessions to silence the criticism. Thus from 1848 onwards the Sardinian representatives in Rome called for a new agreement to regulate relations between Church and state. These negotiations were temporarily interrupted by the Pope's flight from his capital, only to be resumed when the Piedmontese pursued him to Gaeta. Anxious to continue the talks, Gioberti subsequently offered the Pope asylum in

Nice or some other city of the realm. Above all, Gioberti urged him to rely upon Italian rather than foreign intervention to restore him to Rome. Pius, however, was not prepared to place himself in the hands of the Piedmontese, whom he distrusted.

The perturbed Pontiff let it be known that the frequent changes in Turin's government did not inspire his confidence, and at any rate force, not talk, was needed for his return to Rome. After having invoked the help of all the princes, the Pope sought the special help of Austria, which had always been quick to defend the temporal power. Gioberti did not accept this decision gracefully, complaining that the appeal had purposely not been sent to constitutional Piedmont. Since the curia thought only of its own interests, Gioberti called upon the Sardinians to respond accordingly. Piedmont would always be devoted to the spiritual head of the Church, Gioberti said but insisted that it could not meekly accept the intervention of Austria in Italy— even if this were at the request of the Roman Pontiff.

Cavour early understood that, if antagonized, Pius could ruin the national program and therefore advised caution in treating with him. Circumstances conspired to make it difficult for the Count to follow his own advice. He strongly disapproved of the encyclical of January 1, 1849, *Ai nostri amatissimi sudditi* issued by the Pope from Gaeta to his "beloved subjects." In his letter Pius deplored the vile sacrileges against his followers, denounced the calling of a national general assembly to give political institutions to his state, and announced that he would not return to Rome until the excesses, frauds, and barbarisms ceased. At the same time he revealed that all those who prompted or even participated in the rebellion were excommunicated.[6] Cavour and his associates were disturbed that the Pope had used ecclesiastical fulminations in contending with political problems. Furthermore, the editorial board of *Il Risorgimento* was alarmed by the nature of the Pope's condemnation, it being critical not only of those who had forced him to flee but of democracy in general.

Pio Nono was as upset with the Piedmontese as they were with him. He believed that they sought to promote among the Catholic population of Italy an unrestrained license of thought and a willingness to dare and try anything, so long as it worked to the detriment of the Catholic religion. He was confirmed in this opinion when he received word that under the inspiration of Urbano Rattazzi the Piedmontese government was threatening the charitable institutions run by the clergy. To aggravate this already strained situation, the Pope judged Turin's candidate for the diocese of Piacenza to be infected with Jansenist and liberal principles.[7] Political and religious factors thus combined to render reconciliation between Piedmont and the Papacy difficult if not out of the question at the moment.

Nevertheless, D'Azeglio, soon after becoming Prime Minister in 1849, sent the scrupulously orthodox Count Balbo to Gaeta to combat the "dark forces" which had turned the Pope against constitutionalism. He sought also to improve the deteriorating relations between the royal court of Piedmont and the Holy See. This envoy found the acting Secretary of State, Cardinal Giacomo Antonelli, affable and amiable, but adamantly against the concessions asked by Turin, as was Pio Nono whose position he reflected. Realizing that his efforts were to no avail, Balbo asked to return home, citing poor health and an incompatible climate as his reasons. In September, 1849, he was succeeded by Count Giuseppe Siccardi, who was entrusted with a special mission to the Holy See.

Among other things Siccardi sought the removal of the unpopular and some thought impolitic Archbishop of Turin, Fransoni, as well as the Bishop of Asti. The latter had written to the Apostolic Nuncio at Turin explaining his plight. It was his contention that the opposition of a boisterous faction prevented him from living in his diocese and fulfilling his responsibilities. At the same time he denounced the actions of the Turin cabinet which for reasons of state and military strategy had ejected a number of religious from their convents. Naturally, the story told by Siccardi differed from that of the Bishops, but at any rate the Sardinian representative stressed the need to replace the Bishop not only for the religious interests of his state but also to restore friendly relations with the Holy See. Antonelli, who once again showed himself ingratiating as a person, remained intransigent in his support of the position taken by the Pope.

Pius was scandalized by recent events in Piedmont and the turn taken by the press there. In May, 1849, the Nuncio in the subalpine capital protested against the publication of an article in the republican *Messaggero Torinese* which maligned the Holy Father. Some of the articles in Cavour's *Risorgimento* were almost as offensive. Antonelli supported the Nuncio's protest, pointing out that where religion and its head were not respected, there could be neither peace nor tranquility. The Cardinal Secretary of State, displeased by the response of the government to the papal protest, sanctioned other steps.

When Vittorio Emanuele promised the Nuncio at Turin that

he would never permit a wrong to be done to the Church in his state, the latter utilized this opportunity to catalogue the complaints of the Court of Rome. He deplored the attitude of the press, which he termed insufferable, since it attacked the most sacred things and venerated institutions in the most infamous manner. The King responded that he knew all this and was also aware that the Nuncio had protested to the Foreign Minister. His government, the King continued, had already presented a bill to the Senate to curb the license of small publications and would soon present one to limit the excesses of the press. If the Chamber should prove recalcitrant in this matter, Vittorio Emanuele indicated that he would personally intervene and might be inclined to go so far as to close the Chamber.[8]

Such talk enraged Cavour and his colleagues on *Il Risorgimento* who were alarmed by the ominous rumors of an impending repression. "Do not touch the press!" warned a series of articles in his paper, which sought to save their sovereign from falling beneath the sway of the Pope or any other of the absolutist rulers in Italy. The continuation of the constitutional regime, they pleaded, was essential not only for the well-being of Piedmont but for Italian independence as well. The future of Italian liberalism was at stake, according to Cavour's journal. Piedmont, therefore, should in no way compromise its special mission of establishing a government which would serve as a showcase to the other states in the peninsula.

The situation in Piedmont was far from ideal as far as Cavour was concerned. In the elections of the summer of 1849, some sixty-seven democrats and irreconcilables were seated in contrast to the fifty-five who might be classified as moderates. Though the ultraliberals carried the day, Cavour did manage to win back his old seat. Unfortunately, as before, his counsel was little appreciated by the majority. When the Chamber reopened at the end of July, it chose the radical Marquis Pareto as President and soon showed itself unwilling to second the moderate course outlined by the Ministry. Cavour, in contrast, supported the government and its attempt to restore the country to normalcy by approving the peace treaty with Austria.

The inflexibility of the left created a critical situation for the country. Inebriated by their own rhetoric which distorted their vision of reality, these men refused to accept the terms imposed by Austria and some even suggested a renewal of the war. This placed the King in a most difficult position. While he wanted to preserve the *Statuto* and govern constitutionally, he realized that the terms of the Peace of Milan were not bad for a country that had been disastrously defeated and could not reopen the war in the near future. Cavour and *Il Risorgimento* concurred with Vittorio Emanuele, noting that those who irresponsibly plotted for war imperiled the safety of the *patria* as well as the experiment in parliamentary rule.

Cavour, like Massimo D'Azeglio, realized that there were those on the right who hoped that Vittorio Emanuele, confronted with the insanities of the radicals, would disband the Parliament and dismantle the constitution. In mid-November the King took the first step, but shied away from the second, calling instead for new elections. Encouraged by his Prime Minister, he issued a personal appeal to the nation known as the Proclamation of Moncalieri, which called for moderation and responsibility on the part of the electorate. In the ensuing elections more than peace with Austria was at stake; actually, the constitutional order was being put to the test and the leadership of Piedmont in the national movement was called into question. Cavour's journal considered the moment critical, for reaction had triumphed elsewhere and it was in the wings in Piedmont. The democrats and radicals, Cavour believed, helped rather than hindered the reaction.[9] For this and other reasons he defended the D'Azeglio Ministry against the polemic of the left.

Fortunately for the moderates, the elections of December brought forward a Chamber which Cavour felt had some understanding of the reality of the situation. Early in the new year it overwhelmingly approved the treaty of peace with Austria. The signing of the peace put an end to one phase of Piedmontese policy and ushered in another. Until that moment the national struggle had absorbed most of the energies of the country and Chamber. Now that it was clear that the war was over and Piedmont, alone, could not solve the national problem on the battlefield, some other means had to be found. The government was forced to look inward, and this finally paved the way for dealing with a host of internal issues that had been long neglected.

Clearly Turin's anti-Austrian attitude had to be moderated, had to be less direct and more subtle, for the Piedmontese could not meet the Austrians on the field until such time as they found a strong and reliable ally. Since Austria seemed to be removing every trace of Josephism while the Grand Duke and Ferdinand of Naples vied with one another in showing their submission to the Pope, Piedmont would have to chart a different course of action toward the Church in order to assert its independence. Such a tack was also suggested by the fact that since the fiasco of 1848–49, every national program had to be somewhat anticlerical as well as anti-Austrian, and in light of the intimacy between Vienna and Rome an attack on the latter was considered a means of striking at the former. It was the left, however, not Count Cavour or D'Azeglio, that originally outlined the plan to be put into action.

No sooner had the war ended than the radicals insisted that Piedmont's constitutional and parliamentary life had to be the instrument to effect the liberation and unification of Italy. The rising young men of the left, such as Agostino Depretis, were no longer satisfied with D'Azeglio's promise that his government would maintain the constitution—nothing more nor less. Depretis insisted upon the actualization of a broad program of reforms that would differentiate Piedmont from the absolutist states of the peninsula. Expecting little help from abroad, at least for the present, he pressed for internal innovations that would strengthen the regime in its resolve to confront Austria in the future. According to Depretis, the reforms could well commence by curbing the privileges and eliminating the abuses of the clergy. He thus proposed that the Ministry seriously consider the appropriation of ecclesiastical benefices, the suppression of some religious orders, the sequestration of convents, and the introduction of legislation to provide for civil matrimony. Since he believed that part of the clergy resolutely opposed the parliamentary regime, he considered it essential that the new order show its determination and strength by acting against it.[10]

The left, which found Depretis's suggestions sensible, embraced them, and besieged the Ministry with requests for ecclesiastical reform. This movement gained momentum from the intemperate response this call provoked from some bishops, priests, and brothers who insisted that the government could not unilaterally alter the position of the Church or its hierarchy in Piedmont. At the beginning of 1850 the demand for the abolition of the clergy's special ecclesiastical courts assumed a new urgency. The left considered such reform indispensable to illustrate to all the willingness of the King to implement the constitution which provided for equality under the law. His refusal to restrict clerical privileges, the left contended, would be interpreted as an unwillingness to operate within the constitutional framework. Moderates of Cavour's stamp were as anxious as the radicals to preserve the *Statuto*, but initially questioned the wisdom of an anticlerical campaign.

D'Azeglio, however, could not ignore the demands of the democrats who were not reassured by his promises that Vittorio Emanuele would remain loyal and true to the constitution. Gioberti had in fact warned that while Vittorio Emanuele was less astute than Carlo Alberto, the court was aristocratic and Jesuit to the core and hence against the constitutional order. For this and other reasons the democrats wanted actions, not words, and a series of concrete reforms to reveal the King's intentions. If the government did not take the initiative, the President of the Council later explained, the left would have taken it. To avoid this contingency the government decided to satisfy the left, quiet its outcry, and win the support of public opinion without threatening the social order by introducing some ecclesiastical reforms. D'Azeglio understood that every measure against the Church provided further proof that the nation would not submit to Austria and would not rescind one of its constitutional guarantees.

Despite the obvious advantages to be derived from curbing clerical abuses, D'Azeglio moved cautiously lest the conscience of Catholics throughout the country be aroused. Count Cavour, who was later intimately associated with the campaign to reorder Church-state relations, shared the Prime Minister's fears. For this reason he had supported the Balbo and Siccardi missions to seek reconciliation with Rome. In his newspaper he struck out against Brofferio and the extreme anticlerics whom he accused of blind impetuousness and of pandering to the crowd to increase their own popularity—even at the expense of the public interest. Although Cavour pressed for the removal of the unpopular and unpatriotic bishops of Turin and Asti, he did not wish to embitter the conflict between Church and state. Above all, he worried that the radicals would so frighten the clergy that they would strike back in defense of religion, converting a simple national program into a complex and explosive religious one.

In the Chamber Cavour assumed the same tack. He was not prepared to support the vindictive measures proposed by Brofferio and contested his call that all convents be abolished, viewing this as a declaration of war upon the Church and hence dangerous. "I confess frankly," Cavour announced in the Chamber, "that try as I might, I have not been able to see the distinction that he—Brofferio—has established between the spirit of the clerical party and the Church: if he had directed his severe criticism against the Jesuits and the Jesuit party," he continued, "I would have agreed with him, but his accusations, his words, were directed against all the cloisters, against all the sacristies." [11] In January, 1850, Cavour was not prepared to pursue such a course.

The following month Cavour reinforced his position in *Il Risorgimento*. The democratic party believes that to fulfill its mission it must sweep away all the religious beliefs of the people, ran one editorial, but it should have the foresight to recognize that the Catholic clergy will likewise seek to fulfill its own mission by resisting such attacks with its pastoral counterattack. The responsibility, Cavour insisted, would rest upon the shoulders of both groups, but it would be clear that the Church was acting in self-defense. Cavour and his colleagues were outraged by the abuses and indiscretions of certain clergymen, but they insisted that these individuals be fought and curbed quietly, without creating unnecessary rancor or giving the impression that the Church was being persecuted.

Admitting the arrogance of individual prelates, Cavour deplored the attempt on the part of some to utilize clerical abuses to attack religion. This, he felt, would pave the way for incredulity and indifference which were as injurious to the state as to the Church. He and his paper, determined to defend liberal institutions, sought at the same time to remain respectful toward the religion of state. The editorial writers of *Il Risorgimento* revealed their ecclesiastical policy by asserting that misunderstandings might in the future be averted by making distinct the realms of Church and state.

For the moment, however, Cavour did not personally endorse the separatist program. Rather, he seconded the Ministry in its attempt to bring the country's civil and penal codes into harmony with its fundamental law which provided for the equality of citizens. The fact that this necessitated the elimination of certain ecclesiastical privileges did not deter Cavour, though he did concur with the Prime Minister that negotiations with the Pontiff, rather than arbitrary unilateral action, provided the most prudent mode of procedure. This approach was employed and Giuseppe Siccardi was sent to deal with Pio Nono and Cardinal Antonelli. Like Balbo, he found the Pontiff and his Secretary of State most amiable, but adamantly opposed to Piedmont's proposals.

To the surprise and consternation of the Curia, Siccardi once home introduced legislation to alter his country's ecclesiastical jurisdiction so as to provide equal justice for all. With this end in mind, the Minister of Justice called for all cases, even ecclesiastical ones, to fall within the purview of the civilian jurisdiction and for clerics to be subject to the same penal laws to which the laity was subject. Thus only civilian courts were to impose punishment, save in aberrations of a purely spiritual nature, where the Church was permitted to discipline its own. The state's authority was so widened that even the Church's acquisition of property was to be regulated. In addition, provision was made for abolishing the Church's ancient right of asylum and for the abolition of legal penalties for the nonobservance of certain religious holidays. Finally, the first steps were to be taken for the state to recognize marriage as a civil contract. Taken together, the Siccardi Laws were hailed as the initial move to restore the full sovereignty of the state.

Discussion of the laws commenced in the Subalpine Parliament with Attorney General Siccardi's strong presentation in favor of the proposals. Though the clerical and conservative party rose in protest against the laws, and was followed by moderates such as Balbo, the following day Cavour spoke on behalf of the legislation in the Chamber. At this point Cavour was less than a popular figure. Having neither the good looks of Massimo D'Azeglio nor the silver tongue of Angelo Brofferio, his burning ambition was frustrated by his bulky appearance and his inadequate command of spoken Italian. He suffered from other handicaps as well. Unacceptable to part of the conservative establishment because of his business activity and his failure to pursue the army career for which he had been earmarked, the radicals considered him suspect because of his aristocratic background and the role his father had played in the restoration regime. In favoring the Siccardi Laws Cavour undoubtedly hoped to overcome these obstacles and win the support of the political center.

In championing this legislation, Cavour had his first chance to uphold a popular cause before the Chamber and the tribunal of public opinion. This was the long awaited opportunity to commence his rise toward the political preeminence he had dreamed of for years. He rose to the occasion. In a precise and pragmatic manner, the Count observed that the opposition to the bill revolved about two axes: one theological, the other practical. Citing his lack of background in theological matters, Cavour preferred to approach the problem from the practical point of view, especially since he was convinced as he had never been on any other measure, of the appropriateness and opportuneness of the Attorney General's suggestions. He explained that when reforms are recognized as intrinsically good—he maintained that even

Balbo and Di Revel recognized the present one to be so—then such reforms are expedient.

Before the Chamber Cavour reiterated the old maxim that an ounce of prevention is better than a pound of cure. "How can we avoid violent upheaval and profound dislocation?" he asked rhetorically. "The safest means is to grant reforms during peaceful periods," he answered, "to eliminate abuses before their elimination is imposed upon the government by the extremist parties." Then turning to the moderates, he advised, "If you want to reduce these extremists to impotence, or at least reduce the influence of these parties, your best means of doing so is to take away their most potent weapon, which is to demand the reform of abuses whose existence is recognized by all." [12] To disarm the extremists, immediate action on the part of the Ministry was necessary. Thus the Count rejected the suggestion that the government reopen negotiations with Rome before approving the pending legislation. In fact, he produced prolonged hilarity in the hall when he asserted that according to reports from Gaeta, the conservative Cardinal Lambruschini was the individual most amenable to change in the Curia.

Cavour then turned to the question of Piedmont's relations with the Papacy. Anxious not to say anything which might be construed to be disrespectful to the person of the Pope or the position of the Holy See, Cavour frankly admitted that he did not approve of the political policies of Rome and by implication its attitude toward constitutional Piedmont. Restating his reverence for the Pope as the head of the Church, he announced it would be impractical for the government to postpone its own business on the unlikely prospect that some new talks might alter the Curia's position. Having discarded the demands for new negotiations, the Count turned his attention to Di Revel's admonition that these laws would alienate part of the clergy and consequently the population under their influence. Cavour conceded this might occur if the projected laws violated Catholic principles. Not one speaker, he observed, had maintained that they would be detrimental to Church dogma. Since, in his opinion, it was sufficiently clear that Catholicism was not under attack, the clergy had no need to retaliate. Aware that some priests had ranged themselves alongside the enemies of the country's institutions, Cavour stressed that they were a minority. In any case the laws served a positive function, he insisted, for they worked to bring into the open their clandestine if not conspiratorial opposition.

While Cavour acknowledged that the passage of the Siccardi Laws might temporarily cause consternation in Rome, he expressed confidence that the Roman religion possessed sufficient resiliency to adjust quickly to the changes. This ability to adapt to the times, to bring its principles into harmony with the party that ruled society, could not but appeal to the Cavour family, which had in the past found it necessary to adjust to varied situations. The Count believed that the Church could do as much. When society rested on the basis of privilege, the Church knew how to obtain its share, and a large part at that, he announced: now that society called for equality under the law he was sure the clergy would find the means to adapt and see its influence grow.[13]

To the surprise of moderates and radicals alike, Cavour declared that the passage of the laws curtailing ecclesiastical privileges was necessary. He shared D'Azeglio's concern that should passage fail, the left might conclude that the existing constitutional structure was incapable of implementing those changes called for by the public and sanctioned by the needs of the times. Furthermore, he, too, was disturbed by the rumors circulating throughout the country that the King was not disposed to implement fully the constitutional system; he also feared that Vittorio Emanuele's reluctance on the religious issue was symptomatic of a new, reactionary trend. "I believe that this reform should clearly manifest what the real interests of the crown are and by whom it is counseled," Cavour said. "This factor is of such gravity for me, of so high an importance, that it would suffice to decide my vote even if there were no other considerations in favor of the proposed laws." [14]

From the beginning political considerations determined Cavour's position on the Siccardi Laws. He feared that if the Ministry did not demonstrate its intentions, did not continue its policy of reform in some area, the vital forces in the country would either revert to the extreme right or move toward the Jacobin left. Either step he adjudged disastrous, for both these groups were hostile to the constitutional order. Worst of all, the constitutional party, deprived of its thunder, would be reduced to a few educated men incapable of action and scorned as doctrinaires. At the end of his speech Cavour, who previously could not open his mouth in the Chamber without causing dissension, and who often had to have the galleries of the house cleared before he could continue speaking, was applauded by the Ministry, by the Parliament, and by the people. Congratulated by deputies from the right, center, and left, Cavour had achieved his first great success in public life. From that moment he assumed the moral leadership of the liberal party. He had correctly gauged the temper of the country and the Chamber for the Siccardi Laws were overwhelmingly approved on March 9, 1850—a turning point in his political career. It was also a milestone in the country's history, representing a radical break in its tradition of submission to Rome. The new policy was staunchly defended by Cavour's *Risorgimento* which deplored the higher clergy's violent attacks upon the laws.

In this fashion Cavour inaugurated his campaign to bring the democratic, anticlerical forces of the left-center to support the Piedmontese monarchy. Unquestionably the Ministry's intention of limiting the prerogatives of the Church convinced many democrats to abandon their far-reaching social policies and support the bourgeois monarchy. On the other hand, many deputies of the moderate right, Cavour's former friends and allies, could not second the approach that sought social stability at the expense of the Church. These men rallied about Balbo who fought the Siccardi Laws while the more pragmatic members of the *Destra,* or right, increasingly looked to Cavour for leadership. The editors of *L'Opinione* recognized the significance of the split in the *Destra* and called for an alliance of the "loyal" right and their friends on the left to combat the "clerical reaction." The Count was already moving in that direction, and the position assumed by the Church helped to consolidate the alliance of center-right and center-left.

Rome itself set the tone for the clerical response to the recently enacted measures. Cardinal Antonelli, on Pio Nono's behalf, protested against the legislation. Claiming that the Holy See had always assumed a deferential attitude towards Sardinia, the Secretary of State observed that the Pope—who still prayed for the Piedmontese people—did not deserve such shabby treatment in return. Was it legitimate, Antonelli asked, for a state, especially a Catholic one, to reorder its institutions to the detriment of the Church, without the consent of the Holy See? His response was an emphatic no!

The upper clergy in Piedmont supported the Pontiff's position. In mid-March Archbishop Fransoni of Turin returned to the capital after an absence of two years. Almost immediately he revealed his antipathy to the recent developments in constitutional Piedmont and expressed particular disdain for the recently passed Siccardi legislation. Resuming the opposition which had earlier forced him into exile, in April he directed a circular to the clergy ordering ecclesiastics, called in judgment, to procure the permission of their superiors before appearing in front of state judges. This, in effect, was a declaration that the law was null and void. The government responded energetically, sequestered the circular, and on May 4 arrested the Archbishop in his palace. Following his own directive, Fransoni refused to talk before a lay tribunal and was subsequently sentenced to a month in jail and a fine of 500 lire. His imprisonment won him the sympathy of the Catholic party and the conservative press as well as the support of Rome. Despite the punishment meted out to him, Fransoni's determination to combat the Siccardi Laws and its sponsors did not abate.

This became apparent later that year when Pietro di Santarosa, Minister of Agriculture, and a staunch supporter of the Siccardi Laws, fell dangerously ill and requested the last rites. The embittered and inexorable Archbishop, knowing of the impending death of the Minister, had issued specific instructions to his clergy to refuse the Minister's request for the last rites unless it was accompanied by a full and formal retraction of the part he had played in formulating and passing the controversial bill. Santarosa, a religious man, responded that he had acted in good conscience and attested that as regards any doubts that might have arisen between his conscience and God, he had already confessed to Don Ghirinbello. This did not satisfy Brother Pittavino, who following the orders of Fransoni refused to give the dying man religious consolation unless he gave an explicit retraction of all his hostile acts against the Church during his tenure in office. Persisting in both his religious faith and political beliefs, Santarosa died without religious absolution.

Cavour, a close friend and associate of Santarosa, witnessed his mental anguish due to the Church's refusal to grant the last rite, and was furious with the Servite brother who had refused his request." One must have seen what I have seen, and heard what I have heard," he later wrote, "to believe that such things are possible in the nineteenth century." Shocked by the intransigent and irresponsible behavior of the Archbishop and the servile obedience of the brothers, Cavour approved both the arrest of Fransoni and the decree expelling the Servite order from Turin. This unfortunate incident, which aroused part of the country against the clerical party, and the Minister's funeral, attended by thousands from all classes, rallied support for the Ministry's program. The public further reacted by erecting an obelisk to commemorate their "liberation from the clerical yoke."

The shrewd Count quickly appreciated the implications of the new militancy on the part of the Piedmontese. He took advantage of it by quietly putting forth his solution to the complex question of Church-state relations, calling for their absolute separation, as was the case in America.[15] Publicly his newspaper posited the need to separate civilian from ecclesiastical affairs. The principle of the separation of powers is eminently Catholic, ran one editorial in his journal, which reminded its readers that Christ himself had related that his realm was not of this world, and that one should render to Caesar that which belonged to Caesar. Rome reacted to the tone of his publication by prohibiting the circulation of *Il Risorgimento* throughout the Pontifical State.

Although many did not accept the Count's separatism, all concurred that his influence was increasing. Consequently, the position assumed by him and his newspaper were of interest to the government. To D'Azeglio's relief, Cavour in an address of early July, 1850, did not condone the attacks of the left upon the Ministry and showed an understanding of the need for its cautious approach. Nevertheless, he added that in the future he expected more of the Ministry and warned that unless it assumed a more energetic stance, he would not continue to uphold it. General Alfonso La Marmora, to assure the government of his support, suggested that the Count assume Santarosa's seat in the cabinet.

D'Azeglio was less than receptive to the suggestion that Cavour become his new Minister of Agriculture. "He would turn the Ministry topsy-turvy in a month," he asserted and the King, who "sought a more sympathetic nomination," concurred.[16] Still La Marmora persisted in calling for Cavour, promising that under their influence he would keep on a moderate course. Trusted by the King and D'Azeglio, La Marmora finally overcame the doubts of both men. When the position was offered, it was Cavour's turn to hesitate. Fully realizing that the portfolio offered was a secondary one, he was torn between entering the government immediately or waiting for a more prestigious post—possibly that of Prime Minister. Finally the prospect of immediate power overcame his ambition and on October 10, 1850, his appointment as Minister of Agriculture, Industry, and Commerce was confirmed. After years of waiting, at the age of forty, Cavour entered the government.

CHAPTER VI

Member of the Cabinet

ONCE INSTALLED AS MINISTER OF AGRICULTURE, CAVOUR DETER-
mined to provide Piedmont with a liberal image. His adherence
to liberal principles and his call for the reform of society and
governmental policy, aimed in part to improve his own life and
to satisfy his consuming ambition. He rebelled against the state
of affairs in which those like himself, who were second sons of
aristocratic families, had to accept primogeniture and a secondary
role in family affairs. Cavour would not submit to a subordinate
status. The fact that he was a second son, one of his aunts suggested, explained his combativeness, his overwhelming will to
succeed, and the fervor of his liberalism. Liberalism was to be the
mechanism to overturn the conservative establishment which
limited his horizon and earmarked those of his station for the
clergy or the military. It was also seen to be the best means of
combating the Austrians and the other absolutist regimes in the
peninsula.

In order to win domestic and international support, he called
for a series of reforms. To this end he proposed the adoption of
free trade to acquire the goodwill of liberal England and Napoleonic France. When various pressure groups in the country
fought his laissez-faire principles, Cavour attacked the problem
from another direction. Rather than tampering with the tariff
directly, the astute Minister concluded separate commercial
treaties with France, England, Switzerland, and the German
Zollverein, their combined effect substantially mitigating Piedmontese protectionism. Relying upon his background in agriculture, banking, industry, journalism as well as his fund of experience in economics, he explained the technical significance of the
commercial policy. In defending these treaties before the Subalpine Parliament, he argued that they were politically expedient
as well as economically sound. Even more than stimulating the
economic resurgence of the country, these treaties, he hoped,
would create a favorable climate for his country in Europe.

Similar motives served to shape his policy toward the Church in Piedmont and the Papacy. Although Cavour wrote Count Adolphe de Circourt that his most ardent desire was to conclude if not a peace, at least a truce, with the Holy See, his actions were better geared to provoke rather than placate the Pope. Recalling that his first great political success resulted from the position he had taken on the Siccardi Laws, he concluded that the conflict with Rome was the least dangerous means of promoting reform, impressing Protestant English opinion, and continuing the national campaign against Austria. This decision was to determine the course of the Count's political career.

The news from Rome encouraged him to follow a hard line vis-à-vis the Church. In early Autumn, D'Azeglio sent General Pinelli to Rome to win the Holy See's approval of the recently enacted Siccardi legislation. Accorded a number of private audiences with the Pope and the Cardinal Secretary of State, he was not permitted to present his credentials. By mid-October the Piedmontese representative returned from the Eternal City not only certain that it was impossible to come to an agreement with the Papacy, but that even the opening of preliminary talks was then out of the question. The Curia, it was learned, demanded revocation of the Siccardi Laws as a prerequisite for such negotiations—a call which aroused tempers in Turin. Cavour's *Risorgimento,* while proclaiming its respect for the traditional religion, insisted that the Ministry complete the civil reforms needed to implement the principles outlined in the Constitution—with or without the consent of Rome.[1]

The year 1851 brought no reconciliation between Turin and Rome. Whereas the pontifical government sought good relations with the other states of the peninsula, it shunned Sardinia as an outcast. The Piedmontese were disturbed that the Pope's brilliant Secretary of State, Antonelli, in planning for an Italian confederation, purposely excluded Sardinia. They were therefore delighted when the project failed. The Court of Rome as well as the Bourbons of Naples, in turn, recognized that the much vaunted reformism of Cavour aimed not only to please his own people but to discredit the other native regimes. "The measures of political progress and reform in operation and preparation under the government of Sardinia keeps the neighboring Italian states in a state of continual agitation," E. J. Morris, the Chargé d'affaires of the United States in Naples, informed Daniel Webster, in January, 1851. "The rapid advance of Sardinia in social and political amelioration forms such a striking contrast with the stationary policy of Naples, and the other Italian Kingdoms, that similar measures must be undertaken here, or violent insurrectionary movements will certainly take place." [2] This was precisely the Count's intention.

While keeping a close watch upon events in Rome and the mood of his own country, Cavour was kept busy by his work as Minister of Agriculture and his responsibility for the Navy. He was soon to be burdened with yet another responsibility. Despite the sacrifices made by Count Nigra in his capacity as Finance Minister, including his drawing upon his own personal account to come to the rescue of the treasury, he was forced out of the government, and in April Cavour became Minister of Finance as well as Minister of Agriculture. Aware of the pressing need for fiscal reform, the Count still insisted that the greatest problem facing the government centered about relations with the Church. On this issue, he insisted, there would be no temporizing, no compromise. "Thank heaven," he wrote Count de Circout, "the violence and bad faith of our adversaries make our game a pretty good one." [3] The game could not be discontinued for it brought the Count popularity and power as well as the support of part of the left, without undermining the social order.

The problem, as Cavour saw it, was to strike a balance between his policy of limited action against the Church and those who sought a more complete and violent confrontation. He knew that there was in the Chamber an element that was dissatisfied with his separatism and sought control of the Church by the state. The ecclesiastical left wanted the state to intervene even in internal Church matters, hoping to direct it along proper channels. From his exile Vincenzo Gioberti provided inspiration for this group. Disillusioned by the conduct of Pius in 1849, this earlier champion of the neo-Guelph program had radically altered his position. In his *Del Rinnovamento civile d'Italia* (The Civil Regeneration of Italy), Gioberti advanced a more revolutionary and far-reaching plan than the one gradually evolved by Cavour.

Claiming that Catholicism was not dead but burdened by defects and unnecessary responsibilities, Gioberti urged that it be shorn of its temporal dominion, which he labeled the cancer of the peninsula. In his chapter entitled "About the New Rome," Gioberti explicitly stated that the Pope must not be allowed to exercise sovereignty over a state or a territory. The dignity and security of the papal court, he explained, could be better guaranteed by the Italian nation. While Gioberti contemplated depriving the Papacy of every vestige of temporal sovereignty, he was unwilling to concede to the Church the liberty which Cavour's separatism promised. It was the ex-priest's contention that in a small state such as Piedmont, an institution as powerful as the Church could cause great havoc if given free rein. Thus the prophet explained that if the Jesuits had flourished in Piedmont as they did in France, the *Statuto* would have been destroyed long ago.

Angelo Brofferio emerged as the most eloquent and energetic spokesman for this view. He was willing to support the government only so long as it continued its campaign against clerical abuses, threatening that the moment it took one step backwards he would return to the opposition. Brofferio remained true to his promise and vehemently denounced Cavour's plan to exempt seminarians from the draft. "Does military service harmonize with the worship of a God of Peace?" Cavour asked, but he did not convince Brofferio. Brushing aside Cavour's argument of expediency as well, Brofferio showed that exemption from service was a violation of the constitution which declared the equality of all citizens—including religious—before the law. Some ten deputies from the ecclesiastical left joined him in denouncing the immunity enjoyed by seminarians and sanctioned by the Count. Agostino Depretis, the chief architect of the plan to curb clerical abuses, kept a close watch on the discussion and on the position assumed by the Ministry on this issue.[4]

Despite Cavour's conservative position on the draft, Depretis was pleased that he had parted with the right on questions of religious policy. The ecclesiastical left hoped the rift would broaden and sought to support and encourage the Count. However, in 1851 when he championed a bill to grant all the freedom to educate, he evoked an outburst of indignation from them. Valerio claimed that granting the Church the right to teach was a virtual invitation to that tyrannical organization to spread her poisoned shafts. He admonished the Chamber that the liberty Cavour praised so highly would result in a renaissance of Jesuitical influence, which would endanger the constitutional order. The law, he argued, granted supremacy not to the liberal and constitutional state, but to the autocratic and hierarchical Church.

Cavour, who insisted that liberty was inherently good, persisted in favoring freedom of education and rejected Brofferio's suggestion that the state supervise education in the seminaries. Even more so, he opposed those who wished to prohibit the teaching of theology in the seminaries, forcing the clergy to study in the secular universities. At the same time he contested the argument of the left that liberty of teaching was responsible for the powerful position of the clergy in France. Observing that freedom to teach was a relatively recent development, Cavour contended that it could not possibly be responsible for the prestige and power of the Jesuits there. Furthermore, the Belgian case amply illustrated that liberty of education worked for the benefit of the liberal party and its principles.[5]

The radicals of the ecclesiastical left remained unreconciled. They were further aroused in the fall of 1851 by the news that the Ministry intended to open negotiations with Rome for the purpose of settling their differences. Cavour, for his part, did not deny that he supported the discussions between Count Manfredo di Sambuy, the Piedmontese representative, and Vincenzo Santucci, Pius's plenipotentiary. This mission, which sought papal sanction for the current reordering of ecclesiastical affairs in Piedmont, the Count considered prudent. He hastened to add, however, that the opening of negotiations with Rome was not the reflection of a change of policy on the part of the government, whose conduct would remain constant. To further reassure the ecclesiastical left, he promised that the Ministry would implacably follow the path which the country favored.

The Count was not prepared to accept all the advice that came from the left, the element that clamored for state supervision of the Church. He found the policy of the extreme right, which he claimed sanctioned even violence to achieve its ends, equally repugnant. We do not intend to follow the examples of our adversaries, we do not intend to counterpoise vendetta with vendetta, persecution with persecution, he promised. We have too much faith in the principles that we advocate to adopt the arms of despotism in favor of the cause of liberty. In the face of the opposition of the two extremes, Cavour saw the need for constant vigilance. "The reactionary party, agitated for some time, seeks to employ the Senate as an instrument to overturn the Ministry, he wrote Castelli in April, 1851. To deal with this situation he called for firmness and prudence.[6]

His assessment was accurate for the far right was restive, while his political allies of the constitutional right were disturbed by the anticlerical turn taken by the Ministry. We do not want the Church to be separate from the state, declared one of Cavour's political supporters who could not second his ecclesiastical policy. We want one to be independent from the other, but united for a common interest: the prosperity of the nation. Clearly he was losing the confidence of the moderate right which was not prepared to sanction the anticlerical measures demanded by the left.

Deputies such as General Menabrea and Father Pernigotti even questioned the value of a free press if such would result in journalistic attacks upon the Church to the detriment of their faith.

Cavour did not share the fears expressed by his friends and seemed surprised by the intimations of Father Pernigotti. "I believe that when he manifests such fears, he is unjust to the religion itself," the Count responded. He was convinced that Catholicism could resist greater dangers than those presented by the attacks of the press. At any rate, he was determined to defend the freedom of the press, even at the cost of losing the support of some of his friends on the right. The danger from the right, in his opinion, had escalated as a result of Louis Napoleon's coup d'état at the end of 1851. This could be readily gleaned from the obvious satisfaction the coup produced in the King and the Court of the Two Sicilies, who regarded it as a guarantee for the maintenance of the existing order. The fall of the republic in France encouraged reaction elsewhere and certainly had an effect in adjacent Piedmont where constitutionalism was already under seige.

As a result Cavour and his friend Michelangelo Castelli saw the need to detach themselves from their colleagues on the right and find new friends elsewhere. The fact that the parliamentary right was becoming less compact and less able to defend the government also influenced their decision to turn to the left. In an attempt to increase faith in his liberalism, Cavour's speeches were more than ever filled with liberal sentiments while he spent long hours in the company of Urbano Rattazzi and other members of the center left. Castelli was no less active in turning towards a number of important figures of the constitutional opposition such as Urbano Rattazzi, Domenico Buffa, Giovanni Lanza, and Carlo Cadorna who had proved their loyalty to the monarchy. Numerous conferences were held in the Casa Castelli and at the beginning of 1852 Cavour and Rattazzi of the center left decided upon a program. "The principles that were to inspire the new party were basically two," Rattazzi later confirmed, "internally to resist any reactionary tendency that might arise as a result of the coup in France, while at the same time promoting, as far as circumstances would permit, a continuous and progressive development of liberty in accordance with our *Statuto*, in the political, economic and administrative spheres." [7] In international affairs they sought to prepare the way for Piedmont to liberate Italy from foreign rule.

Rattazzi and Cavour agreed that they would take advantage of the first opportune moment to affirm their new alignment. The opportunity arose sooner than either expected, for the Ministry, under the pressure of Louis Napoleon, who had been viciously attacked by the Piedmontese press, decided to present legislation facilitating action against journalists who abused foreign rulers. Cavour, who would not curb the press attacks upon the Church, recognized the need to satisfy a statesman as powerful as the ruler of France. Therefore on February 5, 1852, he rose to defend the law on behalf of the Ministry, explaining that the government intended to pursue a middle course avoiding both reaction and revolution.

He found it necessary to reassure Rattazzi who refused to sanction the bill which restricted the press, but who indicated he would support the Ministry so long as it operated constitutionally. Cavour welcomed Rattazzi's support, hoping that it would be forthcoming in the new session. At the same time he shocked the lower house and the rest of the cabinet by announcing that the cabinet had to expect to lose the support of Luigi Federico Menabrea and his followers. Without consulting his colleagues in the government or D'Azeglio, Cavour took it upon himself to assert that they had decided to renounce the assistance of Manabrea and the right. In the ensuing debate it was the astonished Count Ottavio di Revel, leader of the moderate right, who claimed that Cavour had done more than divorce the old right, he had married the center left. His description of the new alliance as a marriage of convenience caught the imagination of the deputies who clung to the term and from that moment the union was known as the *connubio* or marriage.

On the day that Cavour audaciously disavowed the support of the right and turned to the left, acting as if he already headed the cabinet, D'Azeglio was at home, bedridden by the wound he had received fighting the Austrians in 1848. When the explosion erupted, the perplexed Prime Minister did what he could do hide the division in his cabinet from the public, behaving like a general who conceals a mutiny by placing himself at the head of the mutineers. Cavour, however, did not apologize for his actions. "I am accused of having left my old friends," Cavour commented. "That accusation is not true," he continued. "I did not leave, rather I was abandoned by them, they did not wish to follow me. Should I, therefore, have remained alone and refused the support of those who were disposed to follow where I led?" [8]

Despite Cavour's protestations, his unilateral action on behalf of the Ministry, his disregard for the cabinet's decisions, and his frequent violations of the rule of secrecy concerning sensitive government business was less than honorable conduct. Interpreted in the worst light, this behavior reflected Cavour's "love of power," to use the words of the French Minister. It is true that the Count had tried to persuade his colleagues to pursue a more radical program in alliance with the "bourgeois party" of Urbano Rattazzi. When they refused, however, there followed an ugly scene in which the frustrated Count flung dishes about the room. Once he had consolidated his political power, Cavour was little disposed to acknowledge any error of discourtesy on his part, claiming that the *connubio* was not only opportune but necessary. Indeed, he was instrumental in having Rattazzi selected Vice-President of the Chamber and then against the Prime Minister's wishes had him elected President.

This last act of insubordination was too much, even for the tolerant D'Azeglio. On May 11, 1852, the day of Rattazzi's election, the Prime Minister wrote the King that his health prevented him from resisting these intrigues and submitted his resignation and that of the entire cabinet. The King understood his Minister's plight, and accepted the resignation. However, he commissioned D'Azeglio to form a new cabinet which excluded Cavour. Nonetheless, the position of the Prime Minister was not enviable. He could keep Cavour out of the cabinet, but he could not destroy his political influence. "At the appropriate moment D'Azeglio must leave," Cavour confided to a friend in June, 1852, "and then we can constitute a truly liberal cabinet." [9] D'Azeglio governed at the sufferance of the *connubio* bloc which wielded great influence and increasingly determined the tenor of government policy. Try as he might, D'Azeglio found himself unable to take decisive action without its support. Within five months this alliance and its insistence on effecting a broad program of ecclesiastical legislation brought about the downfall of the Ministry.

The chief tactic of the Rattazzi-Cavour bloc was to call for the full implementation of the Siccardi legislation, which made provision for the introduction of a law regulating marriage. This call for civil matrimony served to aggravate the political tension and religious conflict. The debate had raged for two years with clericals saying that it would legalize concubinage and liberals maintaining that matrimony in its relation to civil law was a contract and hence it was a function of the state to prescribe its form, determine its validity, and define its civil effects. On June 12, a law project providing for civil matrimony was presented to the Chamber. As proposed it made the civil as well as the religious ceremony necessary. Only in certain special cases was the civil service valid in itself; in all cases, however, registration was to be placed in the hands of lay authorities. Passed in the lower house by a large majority in early July, it could proceed no further. A series of petitions was presented to Parliament, protesting against the law and declaring it incompatible with Article I of the *Statuto*.

Pio Nono, having read the decree by which the Attorney General presented the civil matrimony bill, wrote to the King that the project was neither constitutional nor Catholic. "Your Majesty, we implore you in the name of Jesus Christ, whose vicar we are, no matter how unworthy, and on behalf of his Holy Name we ask you not to sanction this law which would produce a thousand problems." [10] In this letter the Pope also asked for some curb upon the country's journalistic excesses and immorality. Issuing a thinly veiled warning to the King, he expressed the hope that these sins would not fall upon the head of those who had the power to put an end to this deplorable state of affairs, but did not do so. Meanwhile the clergy frantically promoted the signing of petitions and otherwise protested against the proposed legislation. Actually they did naught but exercise a right permitted by law. Nonetheless, the liberal press and the government persisted in construing what the religious thought as work in defense of the Holy Faith, as demagogic intrigue and an attempt to overturn the country's institutions.

As soon as the debate on the law on matrimony had been completed, the Chamber adjourned on July 15 and Massimo D'Azeglio left for the Ligurian riviera for his vacation. Cavour took advantage of his freedom from office to travel to France, Belgium and England—a trip that was to prove important to him and Piedmont. The Count's vanity was somewhat deflated when he discovered that abroad D'Azeglio was the Piedmontese politician best known and respected. He and even more so Rattazzi were suspected of radicalism. Among other things, Cavour hoped to dispel this negative impression and acquire something of an international reputation. He was gratified by the fact that some of the Italian emigrés in the French capital recognized his prominence in Piedmontese politics. In fact, Gioberti expressed the hope that Cavour would be called to guide the country, for he considered him the sole figure capable of setting it straight.

When Cavour left the French capital rumors circulated in Piedmont that the ex-Minister had headed south to Civitavecchia, Naples, and possibly even Rome. The editors of the Catholic

L'Osservatore Ligure Subalpino derided the suggestion as prepos-
terous, as ridiculous as Kossuth going to Hungary to give his
salutations to the Emperor, or to Verona to pay a courtesy call
upon Field Marshal Radetzky. Actually, Cavour had headed
north to Protestant England where his ecclesiastical legislation
earned him a warm welcome. The English public was informed
of developments in the peninsula through the work of organiza-
tions such as the Society of Friends of Italy which published its
Monthly Record from 1851 to 1855. In London, Cavour spoke to
Lord Malmesbury, the Foreign Secretary in the Conservative
stopgap Ministry of Lord Derby, and Lord Palmerston, who had
occupied the Foreign Office in the Liberal Ministry of Lord John
Russell (1846–1852). The Count was delighted that the Conservative government was no less friendly to Piedmont than the previous Liberal Ministry. "Our antipapal policy," he wrote Castelli,
"has endeared us in their eyes." [11] This was yet another reason to
continue the campaign against the Church.

The news which reached Cavour in London about the King's
vacillating attitude in ecclesiastical matters in general and the
issue of civil matrimony in particular distressed him. More than
ever the Count considered it necessary to "manage" the King. At
the moment he did not feel qualified to do this. The King had
been cold to him lately, indeed had last received him at the
doorway, he complained to Castelli, as one would a common
peddler. For this and other reasons, D'Azeglio, who maintained
a good relationship with Vittorio Emanuele, was indispensable.
His visit to England reinforced this impression, for there almost
the entire political world knew no one else but D'Azeglio and
attributed to him all the progress that Piedmont had made.

Cavour was pleased to hear from Lord Malmesbury that both
England and France desired to see a reconciliation between him
and D'Azeglio and wished he would rejoin the Ministry. Somewhat more surprising, the English Foreign Minister informed
Cavour that he had been entrusted by the Piedmontese Prime
Minister to ask his visitor to return to the cabinet. Flattered, but
suspicious of D'Azeglio's intentions, Cavour was neither startled
by the invitation nor by the fact that it should be extended by
the minister of a foreign power. Unperturbed, he replied that he
had no personal antipathy for D'Azeglio and agreed that his own
principles were compatible with those of his former colleague. He
hastened to add, however, that he represented a party which had
been mistreated and could not return to power until such time
as that party had been granted full satisfaction. Aware of

D'Azeglio's difficulties, Cavour was not disposed to help him maintain his ministry; he looked forward to replacing him.

On his way home Cavour again stopped in Paris, this time asking for a special audience with Prince Louis Napoleon, President of the Republic. In order to improve the image of Rattazzi in certain quarters of the French government, Cavour arranged for his political ally to meet him in Paris. Both were invited to dinner by Napoleon and later accorded a private audience. On both occasions the French President was amiable and talked with great interest about the affairs of the peninsula. From that moment on Cavour understood the true sentiments of Napoleon on the Italian question. Despite the emergence of ultramontanism among the French clergy, Cavour judged that Napoleon was in complete control of the situation, and would do something for Italy.

In October, when Cavour left Paris, France was on the verge of being transformed into an empire. Cavour believed that the proclamation of empire would render more perceptible the direction of Napoleon's policy, which he prophesied would be favorable to the Italian cause. When the Count returned home later that month, he did not find any improvement in the crisis created by the civil matrimony bill. If anything, the situation had deteriorated. Clerical journals in Piedmont such as *L'Osservatore Ligure Subalpino* and *L'Armonia della religione colla civiltà*, taking their cues from the *Civiltà Cattolica*, which had moved from Naples to Rome, did not relent in their criticism of the proposed marriage law. In Savoy the episcopate published a warning to the faithful, threatening excommunication for those who should marry according to the new norm. Only the fact that the proposed law had not yet been approved by the Senate and promulgated, restrained the government from proceeding against the hierarchy. To make matters worse, Vittorio Emanuele now confirmed to his Ministers that, being ready for any sacrifice for his country, save at the expense of his conscience, he could not sanction "a law which might displease the Pope."

Knowing that the Rattazzi-Cavour alliance would not permit its withdrawal, D'Azeglio had no other recourse than to resign. Since control of the Chamber had fallen into the hands of the center, D'Azeglio's last suggestion to the King was to call upon Cavour, its leader. Never one to bear a grudge, D'Azeglio judged Cavour best able to cope with the present difficulties and to continue the work he had commenced. The Marquis was impressed not only with the Count's intellectual capacity, but also with his "devilish activity" and his willpower and stamina as well. Finally, he knew how much Cavour wanted the post.[12]

Vittorio Emanuele took D'Azeglio's advice, summoned Cavour, and offered him the presidency of the ministry on the condition that he enter negotiations with the Holy See to resolve all pending difficulties with the Church and, above all, the civil matrimony controversy. The Count responded that he would not be the instrument of a policy condescending to the pretensions of Pio Nono. Actually he could not pursue such a conciliatory course —his association with Rattazzi and the left would not permit it.

The most that Cavour was prepared to promise was to open new talks with the Holy See. With this aim in mind, he went through the procedure of asking several clergymen who were close to Pius if he inspired sufficient confidence to be able to conduct fruitful negotiations. Archbishop Andrea Charvaz of Genoa, Vittorio Emanuele's old teacher, frankly told the Count that the political activity displayed by him thus far did not create any trust in Rome, and that no government presided over by him would have the confidence of the Pontiff. Consequently Cavour informed the King that it was necessary either to openly break with Rome or to call upon Count Balbo. In this fashion he expressed the opinion that the government had two choices: it could follow a national, antipapal policy, or give up its national aspirations and pursue a policy in accord with the Church.

Vittorio Emanuele, to Cavour's chagrin, chose the latter course and in October, 1852, entrusted the propapal Cesare Balbo with the task of forming a ministry. More than ever the King was determined to have the Senate revise or reject the marriage law. In his correspondence Cavour commented that the priests of Piedmont were happy for the moment. He doubted, however, that their joy would be permanent for he knew that anticlerical agitation was at a high point and he believed that a constitutional monarch could not long remain immune to public opinion. There remained the possibility that the King would overturn the country's institutions to initiate a personal regime which would placate the Papacy, but the Count did not question the loyalty of the *Re Galantuomo*—the gentleman King. Rather, Camillo predicted that as soon as their monarch assayed the sentiments in the nation he would send the clerical party to the devil.

Cavour's confidence also stemmed from the realization that he and Rattazzi controlled sufficient votes in the Chamber to make the life of any pro-Catholic, antinational government impossible. He was right. When a Ministry of the moderate right (Balbo-

Revel) proved as illusive as one of the center right (D'Azeglio), the King reluctantly summoned Cavour. Vittorio Emanuele told him that he did not wish to be excommunicated, whereupon the Count coldly replied that even less should he want to give up his rights. He did promise not to make a cabinet issue of the civil matrimony law then pending before the Senate and on this condition was confirmed in office on November 4, 1852.

The new Prime Minister did not take into his hands the Ministry of Foreign Affairs which was assigned to General Giuseppe Dabormida, keeping for himself the Portfolio of Finance. Determined to create a central bank of emission in the country, which he envisioned as a necessary instrument for his policies, he took the portfolio which he felt would best enable him to strengthen the position of the *Banca Nazionale.* Another general, his friend Alfonso La Marmora was retained as Minister of War, then engaged in the task of reorganizing the army. Count Carlo Boncompagni remained as Attorney General while Count Pietro Paleocapa assumed the Portfolio of Public Works and Luigi Cibrario that of Public Instruction in the "great ministry." Shortly thereafter Rattazzi joined the cabinet as Minister of Justice, later occupying the more important position of Minister of the Interior.

The first major issue confronting the new cabinet was the civil matrimony bill. On December 20, the day before the Senate voted on the matter, the King wrote a note to Cavour reminding him that if the law which he did not approve should pass the Senate, he would find himself in a grave situation. Describing his predicament, he called upon Cavour to act in accordance with his conscience and his friendship for him. Cavour did not disappoint his monarch, and allowed the civil matrimony bill to be defeated by one vote. Despite this concession, really made at Rattazzi's expense, the new government initiated a policy in line with the *connubio* agreement by implementing a more radical ecclesiastical policy than had been pursued by the former government. There were those in Italy and abroad who questioned this policy, but Cavour concluded that it was the best for Italy at the moment. He frankly admitted that the conflict with the Pope was a political necessity and believed its termination would be interpreted as a capitulation to Austria and absolutism—something that public opinion would not tolerate.[13]

Count Manfredo di Sambuy, the Piedmontese negotiator sent to Rome, did not agree. He believed that the signing of a convention between the Holy See and Turin would be advantageous to both. If the King could come to terms with the Pope, he wrote Archbishop Charvaz, he would have the strength to separate himself from the enemies of religion. Not surprisingly, Cavour commenced his Ministry's ecclesiastical policy by recalling Count Sambuy, asserting that it was time to abandon the policy of appeasement that had been characteristic of previous governments. This was but the beginning, for between November, 1852, and January, 1853, the period when the civil matrimony laws were being withdrawn, the question of the religious orders and their property came before Parliament. Even among some moderates there was hostility towards the orders and a predisposition to suppress those congregations not involved in instruction or assistance of the infirm. This distressed Pio Nono who was also disturbed that Cavour retained Boncompagni, the Attorney General who had proposed the civil matrimony legislation.

Cavour was not surprised by the criticism of his religious policy or economic program. Criticism of the latter was prompted, in part, by the country's difficult condition. That autumn the high price of foodstuffs increased the opposition to the policies of the Minister of Finance, especially since word circulated that he had speculated upon the misery of the poor to enhance the family fortune. On the evening of October 18, 1853, an angry group met in the Piazza Castello and then poured out towards the Casa Cavour shouting, "Down with the Prime Minister! Death to Cavour!" Castelli who saw the angry crowd approach, alerted the servants of the house to bolt the gates and doors and scurried to summon the police. They arrived just as the mob had forced open the gate and had entered the hallway of the house. Together with the servants of the household they managed to keep back the surging crowd until other *carabinieri* arrived. When reinforced, they arrested the leaders of the demonstration and dispersed the rest.

Cavour, who happened to be presiding over a commission at the Ministry of Finance, missed the entire spectacle, but was given a vivid account by his friends and family. Always alert, he took advantage of the demonstration against him by claiming that it was a malicious maneuver of the two extremist parties which had joined forces against his Ministry of the middle. The Count thus used the outburst of public sympathy to strengthen his government and censure the clerical right and the extreme left. Undaunted, the following morning the Count walked to the Ministry to the applause of the citizenry, which was outraged by the conduct of his critics.

Cavour was also applauded for his first diplomatic conflict with Austria. Paradoxically, Mazzini and Young Italy were in part responsible for this confrontation. At the beginning of 1853 the indefatigable Mazzini had produced yet another pamphlet, this one entitled, *Il Partito D'Azione*. In it the patriot insisted that the national party transform itself into a Party of Action, asserting that the period of education had to be followed by one of action. The governing classes in all the Italian states viewed this work as a prelude to yet another insurrection, and they were not mistaken. In February, Mazzini arrived in Lugano and from his Swiss base attempted to direct a revolutionary outburst in Milan; it erupted on the sixth. The Mazzinians had counted upon some 500 Milanese joining their cause, as well as the assistance of the Hungarian troops garrisoned in the city. Neither materalized. As usual his rebellion found few adherents, but the smaller the number the more intense seemed the Austrian reaction.

The Piedmontese, perhaps even more distrustful of Mazzini than the Austrians, had learned of his plans and acted in good faith towards neighboring Lombardy. The Cavour government shared the information they had available with the Austrians and prohibited volunteers from crossing the Ticino. Following the abortive revolution in Milan, Cavour escalated his harassment of the republicans. Emigrés suspected of complicity in the plot were summarily sent to the island of Sardinia or exiled, radical and democratic journals were mercilessly pursued, and though the courts sided with the papers, the Count achieved his objective of ruining most of them. The Mazzinian *L'Italia del Popolo,* though sequestered fifty times in a period of months, was one of the fortunate few to survive.

Unfortunately the Austrians showed little gratitude in return. In part this was due to the fact that Vienna, like the Vatican, was convinced that the revolutionary wave that threatened to inundate Italy was reinforced by supplies from Turin. In February, 1853, the Austrian government passed a decree sequestering all the property of exiled Lombards. Piedmont was affected, for some 20,000 Lombard families had found a home there, and at least 1,000 of these still had personal and real property in Lombardy. Although the Austrian action clearly violated international law, the Austrian Ministers refused to rescind the decree. Realizing that the Austrians wanted to humiliate Piedmont, Cavour also saw that his small state could not wage war upon an empire of forty million. Instead he was content to present his country's case to England, France, and Russia while recalling the Piedmontese ambassador to Vienna in the spring of 1853.[14]

Cavour's moderation had achieved a triumph of sorts, for Piedmontese patience was contrasted with Austrian aggression. He gloated over the fact that Austria had provoked against herself all the governments of Europe and had thus rendered Piedmont a great service. Cavour promised to profit from this by crossing into Lombardy all the sooner. Undeniably, it would now be more difficult for Austria to seek refuge behind the sanctity of treaties and law—now that she had so blatantly violated both. "While the star of Mazzini began to pale, the first rays of new light broke upon our horizon," observed Visconti Venosta. "The dignified attitude of the Sardinian monarchy and its King in the face of the threats from Austria; the seriousness with which Piedmont had reorganized its finances, its army, and public services; and the order with which liberty progressed, attracted anew the sympathetic regard of the people of Lombardo-Venetia towards the Ticino." [15]

Within Piedmont, itself, however, there were those who feared for its future. In 1853 a fear gripped certain groups, especially on the left, who suspected that the Austrians abroad and the clericals at home were conspiring to overturn their parliamentary regime. In view of this danger they called for renewed legislation against the Church. Cavour did not comply, and to their disgust, in May, 1853, he proposed that seminarians be exempted from the draft, arousing suspicion and provoking the accusation that he violated his own principle of separation. The Prime Minister denied that clerical exemption from the levy constituted a violation of the separation of Church and state, claiming it was not a privilege but a necessity for the clergy. The left was not convinced.

There was even greater opposition to his attempt to entrust the functions of the treasury to the National Bank and to create a separate bank of issue on the island of Sardinia. Once Cavour had pushed the bill through the Chamber, the fight against the measure shifted to the upper house. In fact, Carlo Giulio, who reported upon the law before the Senate, announced that his committee found itself unable to approve the Prime Minister's bill. Citing the awesome power of a large, privileged bank, Senator Giulio opposed the concession of a monopoly, warning that such a union of bank and state would produce only difficulties to the detriment of both. Cavour tried to convince the opposition that their union would be advantageous to both, asserting that bankers exercised greater influence upon the government in those states that lacked great banking institutes. This paradoxical theory did not convince the upper house which rejected the measure by a vote of thirty-two to twenty-eight.

Certain that the present legislature would not enact his bank bill, Cavour decided to dissolve it, using the divergence of the two houses on the bank issue as his excuse. Anxious to secure a new mandate for his government, he campaigned vigorously for a victory. Warning that no less than the high regard held for Piedmont abroad was at stake, Cavour called upon liberals to rally to his support. The struggle was not between Cavour and Brofferio or between Cavour and Fransoni, he warned, but between those who wanted to preserve and those who would overturn the constitution. The alternatives being posed in these terms, the country responded by returning the friends of the Ministry to power while failing to reelect some of the most vociferous extremists of the right and left—with Angelo Brofferio the most notorious victim. The Cavour-Rattazzi government, thus reinforced, was determined to implement the program of the *connubio* agreement. Their resolution was for many the sign of a new direction in Piedmontese politics and the occasion for patriots throughout the peninsula to change their opinion of Cavour.

CHAPTER VII

Crimea and the Church-State Conflict

IN CONVOKING THE FIFTH LEGISLATURE ON DECEMBER 19, 1853, Vittorio Emanuele expressed the sentiments of his Prime Minister in enumerating the vital tasks ahead. Instructed by Cavour, the King stressed the importance of financial questions and the relations between Church and state, urging the legislators to devote their maximum attention to these two pressing issues. Of the two, the religious one engendered greater interest—enough perhaps to overshadow Cavour's less than popular activities in the financial sphere.

For this reason, among others, Cavour did not intend to come to terms with the Holy See, even though Archbishop Charvaz of Genoa and the Bishops of Maurienne and Annecy were apparently sent to Rome to secure such an accord. The Pontiff suspected as much. Both he and Cardinal Antonelli questioned the goodwill of a government which allowed free reign to the anticlerical press and did little to curb its most flagrant excesses. Most troublesome to the Holy See was one of Rattazzi's journals, La Maga, which led the campaign for the suppression of the religious houses. "What do we ask of the government?" it repeated at the head of each of its numbers, and the answer was always the same—"the occupation of all the monasteries." Meanwhile Giuseppe Farini's radical pamphlet, "The Nation is Unitary and the Real Owner of all Ecclesiastical Property," 1854, was permitted wide circulation in the subalpine state much to the consternation of Pio Nono.

The Catholic element in Piedmont was equally distressed. Count Solaro della Margarita expressed its concern when he interrogated the Ministry to know at what point negotiations with Rome were, and why there was no termination of a disagreement in which the religious and civil interests of the country were so deeply involved. Unwilling to say so publicly, privately Cavour admitted that reconciliation with Rome was then out of the question for the Turin government. "The Pope is not unpopular because he is the head of the Church, but rather because he is the principal cause of Italy's misfortune," he wrote Baron Hambro, the head of the well-known banking house of London, in March, 1854. "If we had yielded to Rome, the entire liberal party would have abandoned us, and we would have been forced into the arms of Austria." [1]

As before, Cavour did not wish to intensify the conflict with the Church to the point where it would arouse conscientious Catholics to defend the traditional faith. Hence he had serious reservations when in March, 1854, his political ally, Rattazzi, presented a project which envisioned the suppression of a good number of Piedmont's ecclesiastical orders, prevented new ones from emerging without the consent of Parliament, and turned over to the state the revenue from the suppressed congregations. In part, this bill represented a reaction to the recent study of the situation of the Church in the country. Among other things, the investigating commission found that in proportion to population the ecclesiastical income of Piedmont was triple that of France.

Another disturbing disclosure was that, while the Church as a whole was rich, many parishes were poor, forcing the government, whose finances were already in difficulty, to provide a subsidy of almost one million lire to the lower clergy. Rectification of this impossible situation was sought by the Rattazzi bill which provided for the elimination of over 300 religious houses: only orders engaged in public instruction, preaching, or care of the infirm were not to be disbanded. At the same time the projected law provided that subsequent to the sequestration of these convents, the government would provide the impoverished lower clergy with one million lire a year.

As expected, the Pope and the Catholic party raised objections. One deputy, suspecting that the government had not negotiated with Rome in good faith, asked that the record of these talks be made accessible to the Chamber. Confronted with this request, Cavour had to admit that the question of the convents had not formed a special topic of discussion. This admission served to further arouse opponents of the move to strike at the country's religious houses. "The law which is proposed is more than an insult," declared Solaro della Margarita, "it is an injury to the Church; it is more than an insult to justice; it is a betrayal of the public which applauded the first article of the constitution." [2] Della Margarita, ultrasensitive to every pronouncement from the Holy See, could not understand how Catholic deputies could vote for a measure that had been censured by the Pope. In his opinion, one who upheld a provision condemned by the Church *ipso facto* ceased being a Catholic.

Pius responded with the publication of an allocution which deplored the grave damage done to the Church by the Piedmontese government in general and specifically attacked the pending legislation. Not only did he declare that law to be impolitic, he repeated the canonical censure of those who were responsible for the measure. This admonition provoked a new deluge of protests and petitions and another campaign in the clerical press. The Bishops of Savoy and Terrafirma compiled two petitions, which at Di Revel's request were read to the Chamber and inserted into the parliamentary records. For public peace, as well as to safeguard the principle of private property which they knew the Prime Minister valued, conservatives urged that the bill be defeated.

The Count found himself in a most difficult position. He still did not agree with Brofferio, who returned to the Chamber early in 1854, just in time to take part in the debate on the law of convents. Having long opposed these "antiquated" institutions, Brofferio had since 1848 sought their indiscriminate abolition. Cavour could not sanction such an attack upon all the religious communities. In fact, while the debate was raging, the Prime Minister wrote to assure Sister Marie-Angelique of the Sisters of the Visitation that no government, and certainly not his, would think of suppressing their holy and eminently useful order. His brother Gustavo was even more favorable to the orders, calling upon the character Father Cristoforo in Manzoni's *Promessi Sposi* to plead for his fellow friars.

Noting Cavour's hesitation, the Mazzinians screamed that he was a satellite of Cardinal Antonelli; at the same time the Jesuits claimed that his government wanted to destroy Rome, religion, and morality. All of this upset the Prime Minister who was not anxious to effect this legislation, fearing that it would provoke further unrest. His hands were tied, however, for his association with the left restricted his freedom of action. Consequently Vittorio Emanuele was made to understand that an accord with Rome was then out of the question and if the government delayed presenting the law of convents, it ran the risk of having the extreme left seize the initiative, with all the danger this entailed.[3] The entire issue was also intertwined with the question of Piedmont's participation in the Crimean War and the divergent views of Cavour and Rattazzi on the matter.

The tensions which had been mounting in the Near East at the end of 1853, led to a Russian declaration of war against the Ottoman Empire, countered by an Anglo-French intervention the following spring to save the Turk and Constantinople. As soon as the conflict erupted, the Piedmontese Prime Minister saw the advantage of having his state allied to the liberal powers against conservative Russia and Austria. Understandably Cavour was upset when Austria, following a tortuous course, chose to remain neutral. Still, he was inclined to join the western powers in return for a promise of territory or support for the withdrawal of Austria's sequestration decree against the Lombard exiles. Vittorio Emanuele was even more strongly inclined to support the allies than his Minister and it was who had instructed Cavour to offer them 15,000 troops.

Mazzini opposed Piedmont's participation in the conflict, warning that it would be no less than a misfortune. In his opinion the country should retain its freedom of action and be ready to attack Austria if it joined in the fray and thus had its hands full. Even if Vienna remained neutral, Mazzini explained, England and France occupied elsewhere would perforce have to neglect Austria's interests, providing Piedmont with an opportunity to strike. Perhaps more important, Cavour's colleagues also opposed unconditional entry. As a result, the Prime Minister reconsidered his position, deferring to his cabinet's wishes not to enter the alliance unless something tangible was promised in return. Since the allies were not prepared to make any commitment, the prospect of Piedmontese participation in the war seemed remote.

Vittorio Emanuele, however, refused to stand by and watch the opportunity to use his army pass. He even dreamed of taking personal command of the French and British forces in the Crimea. Privately he assured the French that he would bring his country into the war. "It was on my orders that Cavour spoke of it, and if the ministers have to be changed, I shall change them," the King confided to the Duke de Guiche in early June, 1854. "But don't say anything about it; leave me to act. You know what is at the back of my mind." [4] When the new year opened, and Piedmont had not as yet entered the war, the French insisted that Vittorio Emanuele keep the promise he had made to their ambassador. Once again the King indicated he would enter the Crimean conflict and was prepared to overturn the Ministry if it did not follow his directive.

This time the Duke was indiscreet and revealed Vittorio Emanuele's confidence to the Count de Salmour, a close friend of Cavour. Salmour's warning served to make up Cavour's mind to force his colleagues to join in the war. The alternative was dismissal. Aware of Rattazzi's opposition, Cavour first considered the possibility of forming a new Ministry with the support of Massimo D'Azeglio, sacrificing his friends on the left. When this failed, he again turned to Rattazzi, promising complete support for the law of convents in return for the left's unconditional support of the alliance with France and England.

On this basis the *connubio* was resumed and reconciliation consummated in February, 1855, when the alliance for war was approved. The prospect of Piedmont fighting alongside England and France was discussed not only in Parliament but throughout the peninsula. Cavour considered this participation eminently useful for, like the Ministry's ecclesiastical policy, it improved the country's image abroad. "If Piedmont performs well, as I believe it will," he explained, "it will see its authority and credit grow, and its allies will be obliged to support and second its aims. If instead—and this I do not believe—Piedmont should not do its share, all the conditions, all the promises, will remain a dead letter." [5]

Although the King was delighted to have his way on the Crimean issue, he was perturbed by the thought of having to sanction the law of convents. His reluctance was reinforced by the publication of Pio Nono's allocution of January 22, 1855. Attached to it was an *Exposition Supported by Documents* which traced the history of the relations between Piedmont and the Papacy, outlining a series of wrongs to which Sardinia had subjected the Holy See. The thrust of the work was to expose the provocations Rome had to endure and to reveal simultaneously how the Papacy had shown the greatest willingness to come to terms with the desires of the Turin government, as far as it could without violating its fundamental principles.

"If the Court of Rome with the canon law in one hand and the Concordat in the other screams that we have violated the faith," wrote Massimo D'Azeglio, "we can retort that it has shown an appalling lack of discretion and charity." The present Prime Minister was more pragmatic if less anticlerical than his predecessor. He urged the ambassador in Paris to let it be known that the clerical party's opposition to the treaty revealed its profound antipathy for England and France. The wily Cavour considered even the papal publication of its *Exposition* advantageous, and called upon Villamarina to use it to demonstrate the impossibility of reaching an understanding with Rome.[6]

The King, on the other hand, did not look so dispassionately on the papal reaction. Distraught by the loss of three members of his family, he believed that this might be divine retribution. Within one month, his wife Marie-Adelaide, his brother, the Duke of Genoa, and the Queen Mother, Maria Teresa, had all passed away. The latter, a devoted daughter of the Church, had on her deathbed allegedly reproached her son for his government's attack upon the Church. Suffering from pangs of conscience, the King sought consolation from the Pope. Calling for moderation and understanding from the Pontiff, the grief-stricken monarch stressed that he had no malice for the Church or its head, pointing out that the recent ecclesiastical legislation had been demanded by the exigencies of the times. In a postscript to his letter, the King reassured Pius that he would do all in his power to prevent passage of the law regarding religious orders.

Unaware of this promise, the Prime Minister proceeded to implement his bargain with Rattazzi by favoring the law on the congregations. Unlike Brofferio who sought revenge against the clergy for keeping Italy disunited, Cavour justified his support on economic grounds. On February 17 and then again on the 23, the Prime Minister stated the need for passage. In his speech of February 17, Cavour defended the law upon two grounds. In the first place he asserted that the economic situation and the country's finances rendered the bill necessary. Secondly, he maintained that the religious corporations were no longer fulfilling the functions for which they had been established. Lamenting that the religious orders no longer attended to agriculture and the mendicant orders had abandoned their attempt to aid the lower classes, Cavour affirmed that immediate action was necessary.

Although Brofferio and the ecclesiastical left condemned Cavour's defense of the measure on economic rather than ideological grounds, it was overwhelmingly approved by the lower house at the beginning of March, 1855. In the Senate it found a more hostile climate, which was encouraged by the King, who announced that he would not sign the measure. In fact, he told the Foreign Minister that if Cavour's cabinet did not intend to respect his wish on the matter, it had better be prepared to resign —an indication of the fact that he and Revel already had another cabinet selected.[7] At the same time the King, in association with some of the leading members of the Piedmontese episcopacy, conspired to defeat the bill in the Senate.

Since the head of the government had justified the legislation as an economic expedient to provide funds for the underpaid curates, the King and the Bishops sought to eliminate that argument by having the upper clergy voluntarily give the money to the lower clergy. On April 26, 1855, Nazari di Calabiani, Bishop

of Casale, proclaimed before the Senate that the Church of Piedmont, with the permission of Pius IX, was willing to provide the
million lire which the state had promised the lower clergy, thus
removing the economic need for the suppression of the convents.
Confronted with this offer, Cavour called an emergency meeting
of the cabinet to vote upon the compromise. Unanimously rejecting the offer, the Ministers followed Cavour and tendered
their resignations.

Out of office, Cavour argued that though deprived of its financial motives, the law represented the sentiment of the liberal,
progressive elements in the state opposed to the stagnant, conservative forces. A victory of the latter, he intimated, would
jeapardize the constitutional order and undermine the liberal
image he had worked so hard to project. For this reason he called
upon men of influence, such as Massimo D'Azeglio, to persuade
the King to reconsider his actions.[8]

D'Azeglio, ousted by the Count from the Presidency three years
earlier, had from the first considered the Rattazzi bill, inopportune. Nevertheless, he thought it his duty to safeguard the constitutional order. Having been denied an interview with the
perplexed monarch, D'Azeglio wrote him a letter repeating
Cavour's contention that the Bishops' offer constituted a dangerous attempt to compromise the constitution.

Most likely it was not so much D'Azeglio's plea but political
considerations that induced the King to reexamine the road he
was traveling. A Di Revel Ministry, of which he had boasted,
failed to materialize because the leader of the moderate right
opposed Piedmontese participation in the Crimean war without
any commitment on the part of England and France. Vittorio
Emanuele was thus forced to turn to Giacomo Durando, a member
of Cavour's old cabinet, to preside over the Ministry. With the
Cavour-Rattazzi bloc intact and intransigent, General Durando
had no more success than Balbo had had in 1852. There were
those who counseled the King to overturn the existing parliamentary structure, but he hesitated going that far. Having no viable
alterative on May 2, the King had to recall the *bestia nera*—
Cavour.

Within the same month that Cavour returned to office, the law
of convents, sparing one order that had been the favorite of the
Queen Mother, was pushed through the Senate. Cavour was more
than ever convinced that the country would more readily support
Austrian rather than clerical oppression. To prove his point he
referred to the adverse effect produced upon public opinion when

it was believed he had been sacrificed to satisfy that party. This thought sufficed to make his fellow citizens forget the burdensome taxes he had imposed upon them and it also served to make him extremely popular.

Vittorio Emanuele did not share his Minister's satisfaction. Before placing his signature upon the convent bill, he asked Rattazzi, its chief sponsor, if he could sign it in good conscience. Rattazzi, naturally, reassured his vacillating monarch. Cavour was relieved. "The law of convents has received royal sanction," he wrote the Marquis of Villamarina at the end of May, *"consumatum est! the crisis is over, and for the moment the various internal factions are reduced to impotence."* 9 The King, visibly perturbed, told Durando that he was lucky to be able to fight the Russians while he had to combat monks and nuns. Pius reacted as the King feared, and in his address of July 26, 1855, *Cum Saepe,* excommunicated all those who had approved, sanctioned, or executed the controversial law.

The furor caused by the suppression of the monasteries had not yet subsided when Cavour led the country to believe that he sought to reach a reconciliation with Rome. Apparently to facilitate this, Luigi Cibrario, a man of extremely moderate sentiments, was entrusted with the Portfolio of Foreign Affairs. Reports circulated that the French government had offered to mediate between Turin and Rome, but the pretensions of the papal court were such as to discourage the French ambassador. Actually Piedmont posed as many problems as the Papacy, thus barring a solution to their bitter conflict. Although the Prime Minister had every intention of continuing his struggle with the Church, he wished to convince the public that this struggle was the result of Roman intransigence rather than Piedmontese provocation. The need to attract anticlerical radicals at home combined with the need to impress liberal opinion abroad to render the struggle with Rome too essential to be abandoned.

Pio Nono questioned Piedmont's policies. When at the end of November, 1855, Cavour had a long cordial talk with Carlo Sacconi, the papal Nuncio at Paris, he justified his ecclesiastical policy by separating his private from his public conscience. Within his private conscience, Cavour admitted that he could see things in the same light as the Nuncio; as President of the Council he had to see things differently. In 1855 it was Cavour, the man not the Minister, who sought to assure himself of religious consolation should he be stricken by the cholera which was then raging. Not even the anticlerical Rattazzi, who happened to walk into the Casa

Cavour as the Count was making this arrangement, found cause to criticize his political ally for taking this precaution.

As a politician, Cavour appreciated the popularity of Piedmont's action against the Church and was loath to lose the goodwill it brought. For this reason he bitterly criticized the harassment of English Protestants and their Bible societies in San Remo, labeling this contrary to the country's political interests in that it alienated the party that was most favorable to Piedmont.[10] When he, at the end of the year, accompanied Vittorio Emanuele on a tour of Paris and London to consolidate the Crimean coalition, the importance of the conflict with the Church was made manifest to the latter. In Paris the man who had earlier taken part in a rebellion against the Pope had neither forgotten nor forgiven the misrule in the papal states. Now that he was Emperor, he asked Cavour and D'Azeglio what he could do for Italy. In London Bible societies and other Protestant groups, pleased by Cavour's quarrel with the Pope, hailed him as the hero of a new reformation.

Cavour, who had persuaded the King to make the trip, achieved a diplomatic success of sorts when he convinced Vittorio Emanuele to shorten his ferocious-looking moustache. Knowing the King's appetites and his lack of finesse, he worried about his conduct and was embarrassed by Vittorio Emanuele's barrack-room language at the Tuileries and his open advances to the ladies of the court. Cavour was not prudish, merely prudent. Since his tragic romance with the Marchesa, he too had sought the favor of a series of ladies, but his approach was always more subtle and less boisterous than that of the man he served. Furthermore, he was not prone to boast of the escapades which provided some relief from his increasing preoccupation with political matters. Indeed, following his affair with Melanie Waldour it was she, not Cavour, who publicized it in the romantic novel *Alphonse et Juliette.*

With the passage of time Cavour's private life was not only subordinated to but absorbed by his political career. Following his entry into the diplomatic arena, Cavour the statesman completely dominated Cavour the man. Thus every setback had more than political consequences and was perceived as a potential obstacle to his ambitions and a challenge to his very reason for existence. Since his success in politics was never complete, seldom certain, he had to endure many sleepless nights and countless disappointments.

Even the applause that his policies had received in the allied capitals was soon countered by the premature talk of peace. True enough, the Piedmontese forces under La Marmora had seen fire in the valley of the Tchernaja on August 17, 1855, and had fought well, but this action did not justify Cavour's boast that the shame of Novara had been removed. The Prime Minister hoped that the Piedmontese would truly distinguish themselves so the allies would be indebted to him. Austria's diplomatic maneuvers, which aimed to end the war, seemed to deny Piedmont the opportunity to justify her participation in the quarrel.

Fearing the public reaction to the Austrian-inspired peace, Cavour instructed his Minister in London to urge Her Majesty's government to consider the detrimental effect this would have upon the constitutional party and its leaders. At the same time Cavour instructed Emanuele D'Azeglio to pander to Protestant antipapal sentiments by suggesting that the Jesuits would profit most from Piedmont's misfortune. He sought to jolt the leading evangelical Protestants, such as Lord Shaftesbury, by raising the specter of popery, hoping that the extreme Protestants would in turn push the Ministry to prolong the war.

In light of the benefits that the Count derived from his conflict with the Church, he was not about to terminate it. Hence his Ministry's attempts to reach agreement with Rome were more apparent than real. Cavour admitted to friends that while he never refused to negotiate with the Holy See to keep the King satisfied, one had always to arrange things in such a way that an accord could never be concluded. Whatever the Count's thought about an eventual accord, he was convinced that the moment was not propitious for a reconciliation with Rome. In fact, in his private correspondence he indicated that despite the best of intentions, it was impossible for the moment to come to terms with the Church. When in 1856 it appeared as if the King would provide a rapprochement with Pius by means of personal diplomacy, Cavour was alarmed. In his view the King was endangering the entire political edifice, the fruit of eight long years of laborious work. "It is not possible to conserve our influence in Italy if we come to an agreement with the Pontiff," he confirmed to his ally, Rattazzi, and for this reason he would not retreat one step.[11]

Following the conclusion of the concordat between Vienna and Rome, Turin could not follow the Austrian example and still retain her identity and independence. Clearly Cavour found it far easier to condemn that concordat, claiming that it reduced relations between Church and state to the point they had been in the Middle Ages. Still he did not wish to completely exasperate the Pope or his resourceful Secretary of State, lest they take some step which might prove injurious to Piedmont's plans. Hence he contrived to send his parish priest, Father Giacomo of the Madonna degli Angeli, to Rome to soothe Pius if not settle the conflict.

In 1856 Cavour confessed to the Marquis Migliorati, provisional representative to the Holy See, that he never doubted the good disposition of the Papacy towards Piedmont. He also understood why Antonelli, for political reasons, desired an end to the conflict. It was Piedmont that could not make a short-term settlement; she could not reach an accord with the Papacy until the question of civil matrimony had been settled—something which was not likely to occur in the near future. Were this obstacle removed, Cavour continued, he could not guarantee a settlement. Due to the universal detestation he claimed the papal government inspired, the Count warned that his cabinet might find it difficult to sign even a favorable agreement. In reality, his antiecclesiastical policy was politically rather than ideologically motivated. It was a necessary tactic to maintain the *connubio* agreement, thus preserving a dialogue with the left without threatening classes, institutions, and values which the socially conservative Count cherished and did not wish to disturb.

Although there were profound political reasons and obvious international advantages that accrued from the struggle with the Church, from time to time Cavour confessed that he was disturbed by the difficulties involved in the ceaseless conflict. Exhausted, following passage of the law abolishing the convents, he swore to Minghetti that he would never again involve himself in such a matter—he would prefer to leave the government, indeed the country, rather than repeat that ordeal. Undoubtedly the Count's problems were magnified by his family situation, for his older brother, the Marquis Gustavo di Cavour, a faithful son of the Church and loyal to the Papacy, had been much distressed by Camillo's actions.

Gustavo Cavour could not accept his brother's religious policies. Constantly immersed in philosophical studies and in correspondence with Catholic scholars such as Father Antonio Rosmini, Gustavo showed a reverence for the traditional faith not shared by his younger brother. In fact, when the dowager Marchesa di Cavour pleaded with Rosmini to convert Camillo, Rosmini suggested prayer and the excellent example set by his brother. While Camillo had worked to establish *Il Risorgimento* his brother and a group of Catholic moderates founded *L'Ar-*

monia della religione colla civiltà. Established as a biweekly
when launched in July, 1848, the paper seemed sincere in its
desire to create an atmosphere that would approximate its name
and goal, *The Harmony of Religion with Society.* Even in this
initial period, however, the newspaper rejected Camillo's separatism and sought to show that society and religion were inextricably interrelated.

Father Audisio, its first editor, was succeeded by Carlo
Emanuele di Vische and Father Giacomo Margotti within the
initial few weeks. Gustavo di Cavour, in fact if not in name, was
for more than two years the director of *L'Armonia,* assisted by
collaborators who were moved by a common religious outlook
but who did not always share the Marquis's political ideas. In
the first issue the editors expressed their aims. They indicated
the desire to raise a Catholic and Italian battle standard, defending it with that moderation they considered consistent with
courage.

In the political arena the Marquis shared his brother's conviction that the future belonged to the liberals who were animated
by an idea which could not be suppressed. Consequently, he
approved of the peaceful installation of constitutionalism in
Piedmont and elsewhere. However, he was as vocal as conservative Catholics in defending the unchanging religious dogmas of
the Church. Asserting that this immutability of tenets could be
conciliated with the natural desire for progress, he termed as
empty prejudice every claim that religion and progress were
irreconcilable.

Despite this belief, the Marquis opposed the organization of a
Catholic party. Fearing that such a party would arouse suspicion
of the Church, he concluded that it would do more harm than
good. Gustavo did not mean to imply that Catholics should
estrange themselves from political life. Rather he felt that individual Catholics, following the dictates of their conscience,
should defend their religion with moderate ideas and means
against the extremists. This was precisely what he attempted to
do. At times his conscience led him to assume a position that
coincided with that of the hierarchy; at other times his posture
was contrary to theirs and approximated the position enunciated
by his brother.

Gustavo agreed with Camillo that as a Catholic he could support the law which recognized marriages contracted before the
civil authorities, without the intervention of the Church. He was
not prepared, however, to sanction the spoliation of the privileges

of the Church or the attacks upon its head. Thus when his younger brother deplored the "betrayal" of Pio Nono, Gustavo defended the Pontiff's refusal to attack Austria, observing that even the most resolute atheist had to recognize that as Prince of Peace his conscience forbade him from taking part in an offensive war. Small wonder that Gustavo's newspaper considered French intervention against the Roman Republic legitimate and approved the Pope's decision to withdraw the constitution he had earlier been forced to grant his subjects. While most liberals applauded the state's actions against the Jesuits, *L'Armonia* defended the Society. Although the editors of the paper approved of liberty of conscience, they did not intend for all the cults to be treated equally—Catholicism was still the religion of state.

Despite the protestations of the editors of *L'Armonia* that they profoundly respected and carefully observed the terms of the constitution, almost from the beginning within the pages of the periodical were found the basic premises of conservative Catholics. Defending the Church and the Pope against all their religious and political adversaries, the paper was Catholic first and Italian second. Opposed to freedom of religion and education, *L'Armonia* questioned the value of Italian unity, which it feared would be detrimental to the temporal power. Gustavo's position varied, but on religious issues and on political matters which touched on the Church's mission, he was severe and relentless in his opposition to his brother and was not far removed from the reactionary tone of his journal.

Gustavo was as much a critic of the divine right of kings as Camillo, though his reasons were not the same. The Marquis considered this principle untenable because it made the monarchical power into an idol which usurped the place of religion. At the same time he displayed a vivid aversion to the reactionary party, holding it responsible for the rise of the revolutionary party which had risen in reaction to it. Thus as *L'Armonia* moved politically closer to the extreme right, Gustavo Cavour became increasingly alienated and his articles more and more rare. In May, 1851, he withdrew from the journal which had become politically reactionary and blatantly violent in its tone, producing discord rather than harmony between religion and society. He confessed that during the years he had been involved as an editor he had always hoped he could bring into harmony the doctrines of true constitutional liberty and the immutable principles of the Catholic faith. He no longer nourished the hope that *L'Armonia* could serve this pacific function. Since the paper had come under the influence of doctrinaire conservatives and implacable clericals, the Marquis decided that it could not serve as a vehicle of conciliation between Church and state.

Gustavo Cavour found that his program of achieving harmony between Church and state was as difficult to promote as his brother's principle of separatism. "For wanting to uphold these principles in Piedmont in the midst of the excitement of the parties in these stormy times, I have earned the reputation of being a reactionary and antiliberal from the one side," he complained. "The other side accuses me of possessing illusions about certain impractical utopias, and of being the exponent of dangerous novelties." [12] Like his younger brother, Gustavo condemned both reaction and revolution. Unlike Camillo, he was so concerned about the well-being of the Church that he considered reaction the lesser of the two evils and was prepared to accept it, were there no other viable choice. Gustavo's willingness to go this far to preserve the prerogatives of the Church alarmed his younger brother, who had before his eyes a personal example of the devotion that Rome could inspire.

Nonetheless, in the middle fifties the religious question was to be temporarily overshadowed in the Count's mind by the impending congress to settle the terms of the peace following the Crimean War. Cavour intended to send the elder statesman and former Prime Minister, D'Azeglio, to Paris. The latter was disturbed that Cavour had shunted aside his magnificent missive to Walewski, in which in more than forty pages he had answered Napoleon III's query as to what he could do for Italy. Even more humiliating was the fact that Cavour had in the place of the opus, upon which he had worked for a month, substituted a letter he had drawn up in one morning. Adding insult to injury, D'Azeglio was shocked to learn prior to his departure for Paris that Cavour had deliberately kept from him the decision of the powers to have the Piedmontese representative take part only in those sessions directly affecting Piedmont's interests. Declaring that he would not humiliate himself or his country by accepting these conditions, D'Azeglio refused to go to Paris.

Learning of this decision on February 8, only a few days before the opening of the Congress, the Prime Minister had no alternative but to put his own prestige on the line and left for the French capital on February 13. He was soon to reveal a flair for diplomacy that surprised contemporaries. Cavour did not intend to complete his mission alone, enlisting the services of colleagues and allies, including his ravishing patrician cousin.

The vivacious Countess di Castiglione was barely nineteen when she arrived in Paris early in 1856 to ensnare the Emperor and incite him to wage war against Austria. Presented at court by Walewski, who described her as "the loveliest woman in Europe," she possessed a physical beauty that more than compensated for her lack of mental maturity. Almost immediately, Cavour's ward became the sensation of the social season. Upon meeting her even men of letters overlooked the fact that she had no wit, being enthralled by the proportions of her form and her exquisite face. It was at fancy dress balls that she created the greatest astonishment. Dressed in the latest fashion, she caused a commotion as she moved sultrily through the throngs that venerated her like some pagan princess. What made her enchanting to bystanders was the fact that she seemed oblivious to the sea of admirers surrounding her, reacting only to the Emperor and those who moved within his circle.

Having already seduced Vittorio Emanuele on the eve of her departure, the Countess easily overcame the weak resistance of the French Emperor. Cavour had thus conspired to make the Sardinian King and the French Emperor share the same mistress; he hoped to make the two companions in arms for a more worthy venture. The Countess, meanwhile, with the help of Cavour had deceived herself into believing that upon her actions hinged the fate of Italy if not Europe and assiduously reported her conversations with the Emperor to the Count. Cavour soon concluded that although Napoleon may have had the carnal appetite of Louis XV, he was jealous of his power and at any rate his young cousin was not another Madame Pompadour. Still the cynical adventure continued, as Cavour sought all means, no matter how coarse, to win the goodwill of Napoleon.[13]

Once in Paris the Count sought to convince the English and French to admit him as an equal to the deliberations. He utilized every means at his disposal to the point of paying court to Lady Holland's dog and patronizing the Marchioness of Ely, an intimate correspondent of Queen Victoria. With Napoleon's active support and Lord Clarendon's tacit approval, the Piedmontese were accorded an equal status, with the understanding that Cavour had too much tact to meddle in discussions that did not concern his country.

When the Congress finally opened at the end of February, the Count realized that the more pressing issues had to take precedence over the Italian question and remained modestly quiet and purposely inconspicuous. Behind the scenes he weaved plans for the acquisition of some territory, preferably the union of Parma and Modena to Piedmont, but all his schemes proved abortive. Unable to obtain satisfaction, he settled for some moral victory, but his initial efforts in this direction also met with scant success. While he found England and France well disposed toward Italy, he discovered that the first, preoccupied with the Russians, did not wish to upset Austria unduly while the latter seemed determined not to offend the Pope. He and his chief lieutenant, the Marquis di Villamarina, the resident ambassador at Paris, realized that Count Alexander Walewski who presided over the Congress did not share Napoleon's pro-Italian sympathies. Consequently, only the Emperor's pressure could bring the Italian question to the negotiating table.

By mid-March the most that Cavour had managed to obtain was a promise that the Italian problem would be aired after the signing of the peace and prior to the departure of the representatives. At the end of the month Cavour wrote Castelli that Piedmont had gained some advantages. For one thing, both allies now realized that the present state of the peninsula was intolerable and were reaching the conclusion that only Piedmont could regenerate Italy. Not able, for the moment, to wage war against Austria, the Piedmontese could not expect to receive any territory. They had to prepare for the future.

Meanwhile the work of the Congress continued and on March 30, the peace was signed. On April 8, the President of the Congress, Walewski, proposed an exchange of ideas on matters that might threaten the peace in the future. He brought forward the Greek question, expressing the hope that the occupying forces would be able to leave soon, and displayed concern about the question of the press in Belgium. In this incidental fashion he brought up the Italian question, pointing to the French and Austrian occupation of the Papal States, which he hoped would soon end, and the mismanagement of the Bourbon government of the Kingdom of the Two Sicilies.

Lord Clarendon, who spoke next, was clearer and more concise in his criticism of the Papal and Neapolitan governments and pressed for reforms. Critical of the Papal regime, he condemned that of Naples as the worst that had ever existed. The Count was delighted by the strong, almost extra-diplomatic language of Clarendon and hoped it would lead to some positive action.

At last it was Cavour's turn to talk and present the Italian view before the Congress of European powers. Satisfied that his main points had been made by the English, Cavour was moderate in his speech to the point of recognizing the position of those representatives who did not wish to discuss the matter because they lacked precise instructions. Since others had introduced the issue, however, he felt compelled to talk about the fate of the peninsula. Distressed by the occupation of the Roman States by Austrian troops, Cavour declared that this intervention was provoked by the irregular state of affairs there, which disrupted the political equilibrium of the peninsula. He called the attention of the powers to the abnormal and dangerous situation resulting from the indefinite occupation of large parts of Italy by the Austrians. His moderate approach had a twofold purpose—to discredit Austria abroad and the radicals at home, thus proclaiming to the entire world that only he and the moderate liberals could avert a revolution in Italy.[14]

The session of April 8 was of historic importance because for the first time official Europe heard from the mouth of an Italian representative the difficult situation of the peninsula. Still, Cavour was aware of the limitations of diplomacy and did not conceal his sentiments from Clarendon. From his conversations with the latter, and as a result of their private conference of April 11, Cavour came away convinced that the English looked favorably upon a third war of liberation in Italy and would lend active support. In part he reached this conclusion because of his exaggerated notion of the impact he had made on Clarendon; he estimated this impact to be "electric," a description not supported by Clarendon's correspondence from Paris.

Possibly Cavour's keen perception was blurred by his disappointment at not securing Parma and his fear of returning home empty-handed, which he felt would inevitably weaken his parliamentary position. He had also to cope with the threats of his sovereign, Vittorio Emanuele, who had recently humiliated him by threatening to visit Paris incognito to provide him with lessons in diplomacy. Wishful thinking may have led him to overestimate the commitment of Clarendon, and this was facilitated by the fact that the two spoke French and did not clearly understand one another. The discrepancy between Cavour's and Clarendon's account might have resulted from the fact that Cavour had "a rush of blood to the head" an experience, which from time to time made him all the more daring, and according to Vittorio Emanuele, left him with no recollection of what had been said while in that condition. Finally, Cavour may have overestimated the influence of his anti-papal policy in arousing a Protestant England to champion Piedmont's cause against Catholic Austria.

Whatever fired Cavour's imagination, he had the good sense to pay a short visit to England to see if Lord Palmerston and the other members of the cabinet shared what he construed to be Clarendon's views. Although he was shown many civilities and courtesies, it did not take long for the perspicacious Count to conclude that the English had no intention of turning against their Austrian ally. "Madame, you are the best friend of Piedmont in England," he told the Queen in the hope of winning her support, but his words were wasted. Following his dinner with the Queen all she noted in her diary was that Cavour was agreeable and had some amusing anecdotes about the Congress. More than ever, Cavour recognized Napoleon III as the sole force capable of implementing his designs.

Napoleon's words and actions were such to reassure Cavour. It had been reported to him that during the tense days in mid-March, when the Emperor was anxious for the safety of his wife and expected child, he had cried out, "Certainly, something should be done for Italy." [15] All of Cavour's conversations with the Emperor convinced him that one day he would throw his support behind Piedmont in her struggle against Austria. Consequently, in April Cavour wrote Castelli from Paris asking him to caution the directors of the journal *Il Fischietto* to cease their counterproductive attacks upon the French ruler. None other than Vincent Benedetti, Corsican by birth but Italian in heart, had urged him to take this step. "Let that journal attack my Ministry, let it attack me personally," Cavour wrote, asking Castelli to use his influence to see that it leave alone the one individual who held the keys of Italy's political future in his hands. Without entering into particulars, Cavour let Castelli know that he had nothing to lament about Napoleon's conduct and took special delight in reporting his premonition that the present peace would not last very long.[16] Within three years we shall have war, Cavour prophesied.

CHAPTER VIII

Cavour's Second Connubio

ALTHOUGH CAVOUR RETURNED FROM PARIS WITH PROMISES RATHER than provinces, he was given a hero's welcome. Vittorio Emanuele embraced him warmly and personally placed around his neck the collar of the Annunziata. The Tuscans sent him a bust of himself with the inscription, "He who defended her in the open." Invited by the two houses of Parliament to explain his conduct at the recent Congress, the moral victory he had achieved won their unanimous approval. Garibaldi acknowledged that Cavour's success had awakened the pride of the Italian people. It was said that the Count had left Turin as the plenipotentiary of the King of Sardinia and had returned as the Prime Minister of the King of Italy.

In his speech before the Chamber on May 6, 1856, Cavour aroused new expectations when he indicated that the conflict between Austria and Piedmont could not be settled peacefully. Cavour's confidence in no small measure stemmed from his belief that the French Emperor nourished a secret rancor against Austria and still bright in his memory were the events of 1831 in which he had taken part. Cavour insisted that it was possible to come to an accord that would conciliate the interests of France with the independence of Italy—at the expense of the Habsburg monarchy. "In marching with him [Louis Napoleon], we shall arrive at our end," he wrote the Count de Salmour.[1] For the moment he felt the need to convince others of his convictions and to keep the radicals from taking precipitous steps.

In this campaign Cavour received assistance from an unexpected quarter. From his exile in Paris Daniele Manin, the heroic defender of the Venetians in 1848–49, cautioned against sporadic violence which would hurt rather than help the Italian cause. Although Manin recognized Mazzini's patriotic contribution, he insisted that this prophet cease his conspiracies and that the republicans repudiate the "theory of the dagger" which sanctioned the doctrine of political assassination. In September, 1855, an open letter to the House of Savoy by Manin appeared in

Valerio's paper, *Il Diritto.* Convinced that Italy had to be made, this being the first and most important question, he said to the monarchy of Savoy: "Make Italy and we are with you—if not, not," while he urged the constitutionalists to think about making Italy and not of enlarging Piedmont. In this fashion he censured the doctrinaires of the Piedmontese as well as of the Mazzinian party and called upon them to place unification above partisan interests.

Manin was thus one of the first of the revolutionary party openly to break with Mazzini and champion unification under the constitutional monarchy of Piedmont. He sacrificed his republican and federalist sympathies to the need to create the unitary state and asked the House of Savoy to risk losing the throne of Piedmont for the chance of gaining that of Italy. A Lombard nobleman, the Marquis Giorgio Pallavicino, who had spent a number of years in that infamous Austrian prison, the Spielberg, and was later forced into exile, shared Manin's belief that Italian independence might be achieved under the aegis of Piedmont. Although much of his wealth had been seized by the Austrian authorities, he contributed generously to the work of forming a national organization which had independence as its first aim. Even Garibaldi could not contest the logic of collaborating with the Piedmontese. If anything, his chief complaint was the slow pace of cooperation.[2]

Actually, the delay in consummating an alliance between the National Party and the government resulted more from Cavour's hesitations and doubts than from the suspicions of Manin and Pallavicino. The Count feared that an official connection with any element of the revolutionary party would alarm England and France and alienate the goodwill of Louis Napoleon. Hence, prior to the Congress of Paris, Cavour had virtually ignored Manin's overtures for collaboration. At Paris Cavour awoke to the reality of the limitations of diplomacy and the need to convince the Emperor that his cause had popular support. Belatedly Cavour reconsidered Manin's offer of cooperation, though he refused to compromise Sardinia or its dynasty.

Cavour met with Manin early in April, 1856, and though he found some of Manin's ideas utopian—his preoccupation with unification of the peninsula—Cavour concluded that he could render great assistance at the appropriate moment. He informed Minghetti that he should remain in continuous contact with the members of the National Society, without entering or becoming a member, conserving in any event his full freedom of action.

"The National Society causes the Mazzinians to lose ground," Cavour responded to those who asked him about that organization, "therefore, I cannot, I must not oppose it." [3] The adherence of Garibaldi was an acquisition of vital importance. From that moment the general resolved to abandon Mazzinian conspiracies and to coordinate his activities with those of the Piedmontese.

In late August Garibaldi took a trip to Turin and was privately received by Cavour who hinted that when the time for action arrived, the general could count upon considerable official support. Delighted by the Prime Minister's promises, Garibaldi was encouraged by the thought that Cavour was seriously contemplating the political redemption of the peninsula. Writing to La Farina soon afterwards, he referred to Cavour as *il nostro grande amico*. Since Cavour knew that the Party of Action would inevitably follow Garibaldi's lead, his summons to the general was a stroke of genius and provides yet another proof of his statesmanship. Until then the underlying assumption in the peninsula had been that Piedmont had to be pushed, she could or would not take the initiative though she might be drawn into a conflict against the Habsburgs. The Count's call to Garibaldi showed not only that Piedmont would most likely commence the campaign, but that the Piedmontese Minister recognized the importance of having the people of Italy on his side.[4]

Part of the left remained unreconciled. Crispi, in fact, wrote Valerio that Cavour cared as much for Italian unity as they did for Austrian rule in the peninsula. Mazzini, too, remained aloof and skeptical, attacking monarchical Piedmont as readily as royalist Naples, while accusing Manin of political naiveté for placing his trust in Piedmont rather than the Italian people. He predicted that as soon as Garibaldi realized that Cavour could do nothing for Italy, he would resume his role as revolutionary leader and restore unity to the Party of Action. Pallavicino, who distrusted Cavour, responded that they would entice or if needs be force the Piedmontese to act alongside them by the threat of a republican revolution.

The threat posed by the son of Joachim Murat, Luciano, and the Muratist party in Southern Italy provided another stimulus for cooperation between Cavour and the National Party. Inspired by the support of Louis Napoleon, who had bestowed both a princely title and a pension upon Luciano, and the obvious dissatisfaction with the Bourbon regime in the south, the Muratists hoped to deprive Bomba of Naples and perhaps even Sicily. Unwilling to antagonize the Emperor of the French, who had tacitly supported the Muratists since the start of the Crimean War, Cavour indirectly opposed the enterprise. On the one hand, he alerted the English to the French scheme, arousing their suspicion. On the other, he met with Giuseppe La Farina who in his pamphlet *Murat and Italian Unity* had condemned the Muratist movement. Persuaded that a majority of Italians looked to Vittorio Emanuele for leadership, La Farina was willing to let the revolution come in his name—so long as it came. He placed his trust neither in the King nor Cavour but in the inexorable logic of events.

According to La Farina, his meeting with the Prime Minister on September 12, 1856, in the Casa Cavour on the Via dell' Archivescovado, was the first of a series of secret conferences. Given access to a private staircase which led to the Count's chamber, La Farina clandestinely visited the Prime Minister at the break of dawn to map out future strategy. "Go ahead and prosper," advised Cavour, the man who posed before Europe as the enemy of the revolutionary party, "but if you fail, or if I am molested by the Chamber or diplomacy, I shall be forced to deny you like Peter." [5] Whatever words passed between them, following the initial meeting the men of the National Party expressed a new confidence in the Piedmontese Minister.

In fact if not in form, Cavour had consummated a second *connubio* which brought to his camp the great mass of Italian patriots. The avowed aim of the National Party was to undermine the existing order in the peninsula and to overturn the governments of the other princes. Encouraged by Cavour, who was a master at adapting to new and unpredictable situations, the National Society was formally organized in 1857 under the direction of the Sicilian La Farina. Having Manin as its prophet and Pallavicino as its paymaster, the organization renounced counterproductive conspiracies and stressed the need to await the signal of Cavour and Piedmont. Although the Society's newspapers barely reached ten thousand and its membership never made that number, the organization aided Cavour in channeling the dynamic though disruptive elements of the far left and served to confirm Piedmont's leadership in the national movement. When asked what part his government had played in its formation, Cavour replied that he could only say that he preferred that association to that of Mazzini.

Cavour's understanding with the National Society was important because the situation in Italy remained tense and relations between Austria and Piedmont did not improve. At the end of

1856, one of Ferdinand's soldiers rushed at him with a bayonet and the King of Naples barely escaped death. In the north, despite the new leniency of the imperial regime, disturbances broke out in Milan. Questioned about these developments in the Chamber of Deputies early in 1857, Cavour responded that his Ministry's politics and policies neither supported nor encouraged such disturbances or revolutionary attempts. Publicly he still clung to the posture of the man of order; privately he spoke a different language.

The Count feared Austria's conciliation more than he did her provocation, a position strikingly similar to the one he maintained toward the Church. When Vienna, having failed to crush the passive resistance in her Italian provinces, sought to cajole and persuade the Milanese, the Count found himself in difficulty. Had the Austrians lifted the sequestration decree earlier, he observed, it would have caused even greater embarrassment for his government. Taking a page out of the radical program, he called for political agitation and relentless opposition. In fact, he made the Princess Christina Belgiojosa his agent provocateur to lead the campaign to turn a deaf ear to the blandishments of the Viceroy in Milan, the popular archduke Maximilian, and his fascinating wife, the Princess Charlotte.

Determined to prevent a reconciliation between governed and government in Lombardy, Cavour, the apostle of order, showed little concern for legal niceties. "It is urgent that you force the Austrians to renew the state of siege in Milan," he confided to Count Cesare Giulini, without placing any restrictions on the methods to be employed. "Throw stones at the sentinels, scribble *Viva l'Italia!* on every wall," he urged Emilio Dandolo, anything to prevent the emasculation of Italian patriotism.

To dispel the notion that Lombardy and Venetia were on the verge of revolution, Franz Josef visited Italy at the end of 1856. Aware of the significance of the visit, Cavour issued a call to the Lombards to undermine this goodwill tour by veiled opposition if not open resistance, exposing its failure to the entire diplomatic world. Following his instructions, the best society was conspicuous in its unwillingness to pay homage to the Emperor, and those who attended his court did so at the risk of social ostracism. This, in part, accounted for the poor reception Franz Josef received in Milan. When he made his solemn entry into that city the blinds were drawn and few houses were festively arrayed. Ordered to open her blinds and decorate her house, the Countess Dandolo flung a tiger skin from her window to the chagrin of the authorities. When questioned, she claimed that was all she had in the way of decoration.

To complete the Emperor's humiliation, Cavour chose the very day the Emperor entered Milan to reconfirm his country's liberal and nationalist policy in Parliament and to have the Piedmontese press announce the decision of the city of Milan to offer the city of Turin a monument to the Sardinian army. At the same time news spread of the determination of the cities of Lombardy to offer one hundred cannons to the fortress of Alessandria. These steps encouraged the people of the provinces to continue their passive resistance, but infuriated the Austrians to the point where some feared they might sanction some rash action against the Piedmontese. They continued to complain about the tone of Piedmont's newspapers, to which Cavour responded that free discussion formed an essential base of his political regime and refused to silence it.

Turin was tense with excitement on the evening of February 26, when King Vittorio Emanuele attended the Royal Theater in the company of the Grand Duke Constantine of Russia, who was his guest. Shortly after the entrance of the two, Cavour appeared in the royal box with a broad smile on his face and handed a letter to the King. After reading it, the monarch turned to his Minister and vigorously shook his hand. The audience, having witnessed the entire event, suspected that the news was good and broke into spontaneous applause. The next morning the entire capital sighed with relief when it was learned that the Austrians had decided not to wage war, but merely to break official relations with the Piedmontese government.[6]

In point of fact, there had not been an Austrian Minister at Turin nor a Sardinian one at Vienna since the time of the Austrian sequestration decree. From that time the two legations had remained open under the direction of their respective secretaries. Now even this secondary representation was to come to an end as diplomatic relations were completely severed. Cavour told Count Paar, who was recalled to Vienna, that he hoped to see him again when relations had improved. However, he was determined that relations be normalized upon his conditions, and this necessitated the withdrawal of Austria from Italy. In June, 1857, he wrote Madame de Circourt that Austria's open enmity had served one positive function—it had rallied honest men of all parties round the government. Though he reassured her that war was not imminent, he left no doubt that he would not shy from it at the appropriate moment.

No less bold in conceiving public work projects than in political matters, Cavour pressed for the construction of the Mount Cenis tunnel. In 1857 he proposed legislation to finance the enterprise, and Parliament, fascinated by his vision, voted the monies. In England, Lord Palmerston was so impressed with the gigantic task undertaken by tiny Piedmont that he instructed the Sardinian representative in London to tell Cavour that one would no longer have to look to the Roman past for impressive public works projects.

The economic reforms and public projects which made Piedmont the showcase of Europe cost a good deal of money. In addition there was the need to be prepared for an armed conflict with Austria, and this meant greater expenses for the military. Together they imposed a heavy financial burden and an increase in taxes which part of the population resented. Such dissatisfaction was ominous because the Chamber elected in 1853 was almost in its fifth year of existence and, according to the constitution, had to be dissolved. This proved to be a potent weapon in the hands of the conservative-clerical opposition. Understandably, the situation caused the Count great anxiety. "Abandoned by England, faced by a malevolent and hostile Austria, obliged to struggle against Rome and the other Italian princes—you will understand how difficult our position is," he wrote to William de La Rive in October, 1857. "For all that I am not discouraged, for I believe the country is with us. The general election will prove it." [7] Confident of success, neither Cavour nor his followers actively campaigned. The following month Cavour was caught completely by surprise when the elections showed a strong shift of sentiment to the right. In the minds of many this was the result of the concerted efforts of the conservatives, who in the last days before the elections made a number of dramatic appeals to the electorate. *L'Armonia* published a letter by Monsignor Fransoni in which he affirmed the obligation of Catholics to vote, and to vote well—that is, to support candidates of secure Catholic principles and therefore antiliberal and antiministerial. Thus encouraged, the clerical party of Piedmont continued its determined campaign against Cavour's government. This was the first time in Piedmont that there was an organized intervention by the clergy in favor of its own candidates, and the results were impressive.

Cavour had indicated that if the elections did not solidly support his Ministry, he would resign. To his chagrin, not one of his Ministers was returned by an outright majority, while his conservative rival Solaro della Margarita was elected in four districts.

All told, more than sixty conservatives won election. However, both for political and personal reasons, the Prime Minister was not prepared to resign. Outside the exciting political arena Cavour's life was not a rich or varied one and by his own admission had little meaning. His energies had been channeled into the government to the detriment of his other interests, talents, and relationships. It is true that his genius and pragmatism won him the admiration of colleagues and even rivals, while his charm and daring enabled him to fascinate women as varied as Madame de Circourt and the Princess Belgiojoso. But these associations left much to be desired, many of them were maintained through an occasional letter rather than frequent contact.

The Count did have a number of friends, but these were men who shared his economic aims and political aspirations and were part of the world that Cavour did not wish to abandon. Cavour could never forget that while he was the most important figure in the King's government, and a personality of Europe-wide importance, at mealtimes in the Casa Cavour it was his elder brother, the Marquis Gustavo di Cavour who sat at the head of the table, and was the effective head of the household. Unable to acquire primacy in his own family, Cavour was unwilling to relinquish the political primacy he exercised in the state.

Cavour immediately perceived that the clerical-conservative victory endangered his political future and might return the country to a more conservative course, overturning the work of eight years. "But this must not happen," Cavour repeated to himself. "Our policy must triumph, the work of eight years must not be lost." Rejecting the suggestion that he resign, he again pointed out that it was not a question of one liberal ministery being replaced by another, but of a virtual coup which compromised the entire liberal system. "In 1849 we had to confront the red crisis, and we overcame it," he told friends, "in 1857 we have the black crisis, and we shall overcome this too."

Soon after the disastrous election Cavour expressed his concern to Emanuele D'Azeglio, a nephew of Massimo and then Sardinian Minister to London. Suspecting that the clerical party would obtain a good number of seats in Savoy and Liguria, he had not believed it would obtain more than thirty deputies. As it turned out, it won more than sixty. Convinced that the liberal cause had received a grave wound, he insisted that only a strong counter-offensive and a series of fierce battles would enable the liberals to regain the initiative. In concrete terms, the strategy to be employed against the clericals and conservatives was to call into question their right to retain the seats they had won by charging that extralegal means had been employed.

Personally and politically threatened, Cavour argued that the use of the pulpit had been unconstitutional in a number of elections and that the victors should be deprived of their seats. Conveniently forgetting that in previous elections episcopal intervention had been at times actively encouraged, and that his government had actually supported one of the canons in the elections, the Count decided *ex post facto* that canons fell into the category of ecclesiastics who were entrusted with the cure of souls, and therefore not eligible to sit in the Chamber. Perhaps even more arbitrary was Cavour's refusal to refer the matter to the courts, claiming that the Piedmontese judges would only consider the legal aspects of the problem, to the exclusion of the more important political considerations.[8]

Accusing the clergy of employing spiritual arms to obtain political ends, the liberal majority reacted vindictively when the Chamber met and invalidated a good many clerical victories. As a result some ten percent of the seats in the Chamber were declared vacant in the drive to secure the government a majority. Don Margotti, the fiery editor of the opposition paper *L'Armonia,* was denied his seat on the pretense that his election had been vitiated by errors of procedure, and the conservative Birago de Vische's victory was overturned because it had been allegedly attained by clerical pressure. As a result of these reversals, Farini and Domenico Buffa, close friends and supporters of Cavour, won back their seats. Such illiberal tactics scandalized even a part of the liberal camp which benefited most from Cavour's investigations and invalidations. Impartial observers acknowledged that electoral corruption and irregularities had not been the monopoly of any one group in the elections, though Cavour conveniently made the clerical-conservative forces bear the brunt of the cost.

At the end of 1857 the energetic leader defended his actions before the Chamber. Denying the charges that he sought to keep Catholics and conservatives from the polls, he affirmed that what he vehemently opposed was the use of spiritual threats to cow the electorate. This he considered not only a violation of his principle of separatism but a dangerous abuse of the Church's authority. "When the clergy could with impunity denounce its political adversaries in electoral meetings, beginning with those who govern the state to the last in favor of liberal views, as bitter enemies of the Church, as men stricken by divine bolts," Cavour warned, "it could also easily cause a people to oppose the government . . . not only with legal means, but with material means as well, so that we would be threatened with virtual civil war." [9] It was such tactics, he continued, that he opposed. To maintain his liberal image, he reasserted that clerical participation in an election was not, in itself, an evil and therefore was not to be condemned or discouraged. On the contrary, he maintained that it was good that the clergy take part in public life and not estrange itself from the state.

While Cavour publicly called for civic responsibility and moderation from the clerics, in his correspondence he admitted that if they became truly moderate, they would become all the more dangerous. The shrewd Count frankly admitted that the violence of the clerical party and the exaggeration of that violence worked for the benefit of the liberal party. He and his followers, as much as Don Margotti and the clerical conservatives, were responsible for the Catholic party's practice of antagonistic absenteeism. The arguments advanced by Don Margotti in his article "Nè eletti nè elettori" in which he advised Catholics neither to run as candidates nor vote in the elections of 1861 were in large measure based upon the actions of Cavour following the elections of 1857.

Catholics in Piedmont were not reassured by Cavour's policies toward Rome, and the Pope continued to share their suspicions. Pius was disturbed by the treatment accorded Catholicism, the state religion, and by the reports he received of the outrages upon the Church, which Cavour permitted. Events in Piedmont seemed to confirm his belief that liberalism and anticlericalism were synonymous and he wanted neither one nor the other. Cavour's Piedmont was not as honest as states of the past which had openly attacked the Church, the Pope told Minghetti in the summer of 1857. Its persecution was more pernicious for it daily despoiled the convents and attacked the clergy. If Turin desired changes, the Pope exclaimed, it could have turned to Rome and requested permission before acting precipitously. Pius confided that in regard to the abolition of ecclesiastical immunities, he would have been inclined to approve this, if properly asked.

During that same summer Pius stopped at Imola and spoke to Giuseppe Pasolini. Discussing liberalism, the Pope admitted that he wanted nothing to do with it if it should resemble the anti-Austrian development in Piedmont. The liberal journals that emanated from that state removed any pleasure he might have derived from granting reforms. Eventually the talk turned to

Cavour, and the Pontiff asked Pasolini his opinion of the Piedmontese Minister. Unable to give Pius a first-hand impression of
the Count, Pasolini assured him that despite his attempts to
curb the Bishops, the faith had in no way been injured. "Perhaps
so," answered the Pontiff, who had questioned the country's motives and policies since 1848. The Pope was also suspicious of
Napoleon who had confided to Gioacchino Pepoli, sent to Paris
by Cavour, that the difficulties in Rome had to be resolved by
taking the government from the priests without making them
cry.[10]

Cavour did attempt to allay the fears of Pius, for he and the
King decided to send Carlo Boncompagni to Bologna to placate
him. The Prime Minister admitted that the purpose of the visit
was not to enter into negotiations with the Court of Rome, but
merely a gesture to show deference for the head of the Church.
In Machiavellian fashion he argued that Napoleon III would
approve of such an attempt to humor the Pope, and the Count
wished to maintain the goodwill of the Emperor. Cavour realized
that it would be difficult if not impossible for the Pope to accept
a partial solution of the existing problems between Rome and
Turin. However, he felt that Piedmont had all to gain from
advancing proposals to the Papacy, for in rejecting them it would
weaken its position before the whole of Europe. He was therefore delighted by the reports that Boncompagni had been coldly
received by the Pope.

While pretending to conciliate the Pope, Cavour had to be
careful not to lose the confidence of the radicals lest they return
to the Mazzinian camp. Although the prestige of the Party of
Action had fallen to a new low following its fiasco in Milan in
1853, Cavour did not underestimate the energy and dedication
of Mazzini. He knew that this prophet still had fanatical supporters and claimed there was no absurdity of which they were
incapable.[11]

In 1857 Mazzini, who coordinated the plans for a joint rebellion in Northern Italy and Naples, proved he was a formidable
competitor. Still, Cavour could not believe he would be so audacious as to venture to Genoa to direct the revolution personally
in that port city, as the French reported. The Prime Minister
sought to convince Napoleon that Piedmont was impervious to
the revolutionary agitation that rocked the Austrian-controlled
provinces and the regimes of the Pope and Bomba. This was
difficult to see in light of the fact that neither his police nor the
special agents sent by the French were able to apprehend Mazzini

who remained in Genoa from April to August, 1857. Thus, even though Mazzini's coup in Genoa was as abortive as the Neapolitan venture in which Carlo Pisacane sacrificed his life, Cavour's confident claims of the immunity of Piedmont to revolution were shattered.

Cavour admitted that the situation was critical. Every day the radicals became more unrestrained, he wrote Castelli in January, while their excesses served to strengthen the forces of reaction. Even more frightening was the possibility that the Mazzinian outburst would make an unfortunate impression upon Napoleon, causing him to cast aside those plans he was disposed to realize on Italy's behalf. Cavour hoped that the recent disturbance would have a contrary effect, pushing the Emperor to act with greater vigor against the Pope and Austria.

Nonetheless, the Count recognized that Napoleon disliked disorder, especially when it occurred so close to his frontier and person. For this reason, Cavour was tormented by the events of January 14, 1858. That Thursday Napoleon and the Empress attended a performance at the Paris Opera House. As their party arrived at the main gate at Rue La Pelletier at eight-thirty, three successive explosions rocked the air. The first bomb exploded in front of the imperial carriage, the second to the left, and the third directly under Their Majesties' carriage. Although the royal couple only left the carriage following the last explosion, they miraculously escaped unscathed. Many of the men, women, and children surrounding the carriage were not as fortunate, for over one hundred fifty innocent bystanders were wounded of whom eight subsequently lost their lives. This incident led to a public outcry in Paris and all of France, and to make matters worse for Cavour's ambitions, it was soon learned that the anarchists and would-be royal assassins were Italians: Antonio Gomez, Carlo di Rudio, Giuseppe Pieri, and their leader, Felice Orsini.

While Orsini's accomplices told one story and then another, they consistently refused to assume responsibility for their act, asserting that they were at most agents. Orsini, alone, during the trial admitted his guilt, saying that he was motivated by the desire to give Italy independence by bringing about a change of government and policy in France. Earlier, he explained, he had offered his daring and energy to Cavour to use on behalf of the nation, but the Piedmontese Minister had spurned his offer. Orsini therefore decided to act alone. "I came to the conclusion that there was only one man in a position to bring an end to the occupation of my country by foreigners, and that man was Napoleon III, who is all powerful in Europe," Orsini told the startled but sympathetic throng in the Palais de Justice. "But all his past led me to the conviction that he would be unwilling to do what he alone could do. I admit frankly that I considered him an obstacle. Then I said to myself: he must disappear. I acted as Brutus did." [12]

Orsini's courage and composure, as well as his open contempt for his cowardly co-conspirators, soon won him a grudging respect. Even the Empress, whose life he had attempted to take, complained Count von Hubner, the Austrian ambassador in Paris, was charmed by the "murderer" in white gloves. Less sentimental than his wife, the Emperor was less concerned about the fate of Orsini than about the agitation which had prompted his actions. Even before the assassination attempt he had instructed his ambassador at Turin, Prince La Tour d'Auvergne, to call to Cavour's attention the need to modify his country's press law so as to end the incessant and insulting attacks upon the person and policy of the French Emperor and to encourage the removal of Rattazzi from the cabinet. Having attained the latter aim early in 1858, the ambassador noted the Count's reluctance to discuss the second matter. He received the distinct impression that the journalist turned minister did not wish to curtail freedom of the press.

Despite, or perhaps because of his position, the French Foreign Minister sent another note on January 22 to the resident ambassador in Turin, instructing him to urge the Sardinian government to put a quick end to demagogic demonstrations in its territory. At the same time the French Minister was to relate that his government would consider it regrettable if Sardinia, and Genoa in particular, continued to offer refuge to the greatest enemies of European society and their revolutionary prophet, Mazzini. The latter's paper, *L'Italia del Popolo,* especially outraged the French. Both the King and Cavour were told to turn their attention to the criminal abuses committed in the name of liberty of the press. Cavour found himself in a most difficult position for, as much as he desired to retain the friendship of France, he could not easily disown the liberal principles which permitted the press to attack the French Emperor, nor could he maintain his national position if it were known that he had bowed to the dictates of France.

At first the Minister attempted to avoid the problem, but found the French ambassador persistent in his demands. Then the harassed Cavour assumed the offensive, observing that it was the imprudent policy of the Roman government, which Napoleon still protected, that provided Mazzini with the material for his revolutionary army. Consequently he contended that, if the French wanted to dry up the sources of conspiracies and infamies, it should address itself to Rome rather than Turin. This maneuver failed to deter the French ambassador who asked that Cavour's government suppress *L'Italia del Popolo,* prohibit foreigners from contributing articles to Piedmontese papers, and initiate official persecution of offenses committed against sovereigns.

Little inclined to follow these guidelines, the Count realized that expediency necessitated some step to placate the French. He therefore proposed legislation that would provide a more precise definition of activity which could incite political assassination or similar outrages, all punishable by law, radical modification of the law on the composition of juries, and official persecution of slander directed against foreign sovereigns. Cavour hoped this would satisfy Napoleon for he would go no further, threatening to resign rather than violate his principles. Should the French government prove unrelenting and induce him to take such a step, he warned, it would make a twofold mistake. It would place power in the hands of the legitimists—who distrusted Napoleon —while wrecking the prestige of the moderate party to the advantage of Mazzini and the Party of Action—whom the Emperor feared.

The misunderstanding with France not only threatened the Ministry, it also cast a shadow upon Cavour's national program and Italy's future. To his dismay, reports from Paris seemed to go from bad to worse. At a reception early in February, General Enrico della Rocca, chief aide-de-camp to Vittorio Emanuele, was signaled into the Emperor's study. Napoleon then proceeded to criticize the deplorable conditions in Genoa and Savoy where the press was permitted to continue unrestrained, showing no respect for morality, order, or persons; he warned the general:

I love your country. I love your King. I am sympathetic toward your colors, toward the cause it represents in Italy; but if nothing is done, if no way is found to restrain the press, protect morality and religion, if there is no law and order, my friendship will cool and I shall be forced to align myself closely with Austria. Then what will happen to Piedmont? So let this be well considered.

Make sure you realize that I am your only ally; do not imagine that

England will help you! What can she give you? Some money perhaps, but not a single man. There must be a choice between France and England: and that choice cannot be in doubt. I insist that everything necessary be done, everything I have the right to demand.[13]

On February 8, Louis Napoleon decided to present his demands directly to Vittorio Emanuele in a frank and forceful letter. He advised his brother monarch that if his country pursued a liberal but firm policy, then she could count upon the support of France. If, instead, demagoguery was tolerated if not encouraged, incendiary journals were allowed openly to preach revolution, assassination, and contempt for religion, then the Emperor claimed, he would suppress his natural inclinations vis-à-vis Piedmont and would look upon it as a source of agitation and a menace to the entire world.[14] There was, according to Napoleon, but one honorable road for the Piedmontese to pursue, and that was to cut themselves off from the ultraradical party and promote the principles of order, justice, and morality as well as the national cause.

The Emperor's letter excited Vittorio Emanuele's profound indignation and produced a lively irritation in his Prime Minister. Together they collaborated to produce a response which, though amicable towards the Emperor's person, revealed their country's determination to risk all rather than compromise the national honor by making humiliating concessions to France. Although addressed to General della Rocca, its contents were made known to Napoleon. Indeed, Cavour hinted that it would not be improper for the general to reveal the missive to him. Combining tact with tenacity, the King resented the reproaches directed against his government, observing this was not the way to treat a friend and ally. Noting that for eight hundred and fifty years his dynasty had carried its head high and had never been forced to bow it, Vittorio Emanuele insisted that he was responsible only to God and his people for his position. Still he desired the friendship of the French and would do all within his means to please the Emperor. To this end, he let it be known that his Minister was in the process of proposing a law which would legally curb the excesses of the press.

This proud, but not provocative, Piedmontese response won the respect of the Emperor. He charged Della Rocca to let the King know that he did not intend to contradict the procedures or policies of the Piedmontese government, did not call for a change of cabinet, and had full confidence in Cavour. Napoleon was pleased by the steps the Piedmontese had taken to meet his demands, and it appeared that the Emperor's thoughts on the Italian question, which had wavered, became more resolute. One indication of this new position was his decision to permit the publication of the patriotic plea that Orsini had directed to him from prison. Orsini's audacity and patriotism awakened thoughts and memories of Napoleon's own revolutionary past in the peninsula, while his analysis of the Emperor's prominent position in Europe flattered his ego. Calling upon him to return to Italy that liberty the French had helped her lose in 1849, Orsini warned that neither France nor Europe would enjoy tranquility until Italy were free.

The Count was delighted with Orsini's letter because it presented arguments which he intended to advance and he had it published in the *Official Gazzette*. To retain the goodwill of Napoleon, Cavour introduced the legislation which more clearly defined the crime of supporting political assassination, while providing penalties for those who conspired against the lives of foreign sovereigns and heads of governments. It was practically impossible to draft a press law which would at one and the same time offer the French certain immunity from attack and provide no protection for Vienna or Rome. Consequently the Count let his friends know that the De Foresta law had been drafted to placate the French, not to prohibit criticism of the Pope. However, certain elements of the extreme right allied with part of the liberal left to oppose his attempt to stiffen Sardinia's press law, rejecting the bill in committee.

Cavour realized that good Franco-Sardinian relations depended upon its passage and made the De Foresta law a cabinet issue. During the session of April 16, 1858, he rose to defend the proposal. Intimating that the Mazzinians might possibly make their next move against Vittorio Emanuele, he called upon the Chamber to condemn the villainous doctrine of political assassination by punishing those who supported it by word and deed. Denying that the bill was motivated by foreign pressure, Cavour claimed that the only pressure was that of conscience before which all honest men must bow. Mazzini's outburst against this obvious political device only made Cavour's ruse all the more effective, and the measure was overwhelmingly approved. The fact that it was submissive surrender, as Mazzini claimed, was immaterial. For Cavour it was important because it paved the way for French assistance.

Cavour knew that Napoleonic France was a revisionist power

anxious to overthrow the settlement of 1815 and looked upon Piedmont as a useful sword against Austria—the self-assigned guardian of the status quo. He therefore waited for the Emperor to take the initiative, and was not disappointed. As early as March, Cavour received word from his friends in Paris that Louis Napoleon was disposed to act on Piedmont's behalf, but negotiations could not be conducted along ordinary diplomatic lines. Cavour was not averse to secret diplomacy. His policy of provoking Austria and the Church while courting the French and secretly working with the National Society was not universally accepted, even in Piedmont. Moderates as well as conservatives feared the consequences of his brinkmanship. "Cavour seems to me to be a terrible man," wrote the Marchesa D'Azeglio. "He has arranged affairs in such a way that only he can manage them, and to remain at his post he exacts that our fate should be wholly placed in his hands." [15] The fate of Italy as well as Piedmont did rest in the Count's hands.

CHAPTER IX

From Plombières to Villafranca

THE POLICY PURSUED BY CAVOUR AFTER THE ASSASSINATION AT-
tempt of Orsini was bound to bear fruit. The Count had shown
himself sensitive to the French requests to curb the press and had
passed legislation to punish those who preached as well as practiced regicide and political assassination. Turin had shown its
goodwill; the time had come for Napoleon to translate his declarations of sympathy for Piedmont into positive action on its
behalf. Its Prime Minister waited anxiously, knowing that he
could not permanently restrain his revolutionary allies who had
ceased their agitation in the expectation that Piedmont would
henceforth take the initiative. Piedmont, however, could not act
without the consent and cooperation of Paris.

Early in May, 1858, a series of communications were transmitted to Cavour in the name of Prince Jerome Napoleon. These
messages contained notice of propositions which could not be
discussed either by mail or diplomatic agents, no matter how
trustworthy. In response Cavour communicated with Doctor
Conneau, the Italophile personal physician of Napoleon III and
an acquaintance of the Count's since 1856. "If things were more
advanced and basic principles had been agreed [sic], perhaps it
would have been best for me to go to Paris and talk personally
with the Emperor," Cavour wrote, "But, in the present European
situation, a step of that kind would make everyone suspicious
and would provide a pretext for tendentious comment; it might
even harm the very object of our negotiations; so I feel it should
only be tried if a definite agreement seemed probable, if not
certain." [1]

The Count preferred that the Emperor secretly visit Turin,
promising that matters could be discussed in his capital under
maximum security. In the interim Cavour took the precaution
of sending Costantino Nigra to Paris and developed a code of
conventional phrases so that they could communicate freely by
telegram. On Sunday, May 9, Nigra telegraphed that Napoleon
had confirmed three points: a marriage uniting his family with

that of the Savoy dynasty, a joint war to be waged against Austria, and the formation of a Kingdom of Northern Italy. From the beginning the Emperor insisted that the war had to be justified in the eyes of public opinion, so a plausible motive for the war was imperative. Concomitantly, he indicated that the cooperation of Russia was essential and therefore urged the Piedmontese not to offend the known predilections of the Tsar for the Court of Naples.

Citing the need for absolute secrecy, Napoleon promised to send Conneau to Turin at the end of May. As a result of his visit, Cavour learned that the Emperor desired to talk to him. The emissary made repeated references to the fact that his sovereign planned to spend a month at Plombières and would be close to the Piedmontese frontier. Disregarding the geographical error, Cavour recognized the political import of the hint and responded that he planned to spend his own vacation in Switzerland, but would be happy to visit the Emperor. Aware that the doctor had to report back to Paris, the Count awaited confirmation.

On July 11, 1858, Cavour received the Emperor's invitation to visit him at Plombières before the 24th of the month, when he was scheduled to return to the capital. Realizing that news of a meeting with Napoleon would cause a commotion, Cavour contended he was going to Switzerland to breathe the fresh mountain air, free of the pollution of politics. Going to visit the De La Rives, he felt that no one would suppose he was conspiring against the peace of the world. Despite his protestations to the contrary, this was precisely his intention. "The drama is approaching its climax," he wrote to La Marmora from Geneva, hoping fervently that he would not blunder in the supreme moment. He left accompanied only by a young undersecretary of foreign affairs, so that no one would surmise the importance of his mission.

In his notes he had outlined the most pressing problems. Specifically, he wanted to thrash out the aims of the war, the pretext for its declaration, the mode of cooperation with France, and the ticklish financial questions. He also wished to know what their position would be toward the other Italian states, if there would be a treaty and a military convention, and finally if the marriage of Prince Napoleon to Princess Clothilde was a *sine qua non* condition of cooperation.[2]

No sooner was Cavour ushered into Napoleon's presence on Wednesday, July 21, than his host raised the very questions that weighed upon his mind. Without hesitation Napoleon informed the Count that he had decided to champion Piedmont's cause against Austria in Italy, provided the struggle were undertaken for a non-revolutionary end and could be justified before the courts of Europe. Since the search for a plausible pretext was of paramount importance, Cavour presented two proposals: one dealing with commercial questions, the other protesting the illegitimate extension of Austrian power in the peninsula. Neither satisfied his co-conspirator. Embarrassed because he had no other precise plan, Cavour and Napoleon pored over the whole peninsula, finally settling upon Massa Carrara as the area where they could best entangle Austria and arouse her to declare war.

In response to Napoleon's insistence that the Pope and the King of Naples be treated with circumspection, Cavour indicated that the Bourbon King could be left unmolested so long as he did not champion the Austrian cause while the Pope would be assured of his possession of Rome by the French garrison when the Romagna rose in revolt. Cavour then questioned the Emperor about the subsequent political organization of the peninsula. After a lengthy discussion the two agreed that the lands of the Po, the Legations, and the Romagna would be united to form a kingdom ruled by the Savoy dynasty. Rome and its environs would be kept by the Pope. The remaining lands of the Pope would be joined with Tuscany to constitute a kingdom of Central Italy while the Neapolitan kingdom would be left unchanged. Cavour was skeptical about the possibility of an Italian confederation under the presidency of the Pope, but accepted Napoleon's condition that this dubious distinction be conferred upon Pio Nono in compensation for the loss of most of his lands.

Having discussed these general goals, Napoleon wanted to know specifically what he could expect in return for his services. Not surprised when the Emperor mentioned Savoy and Nice, Cavour was prepared to cede Savoy which was French-speaking and to discuss the cession of Nice which was thoroughly Italian. This answer did not disturb Napoleon, who moved on to military matters, promising to provide 200,000 men while the Italians would provide another 100,000. All these details were settled in less than four hours. At three in the afternoon they separated, but not before the Emperor granted Cavour another appointment for the next day.

The following afternoon he took the Prime Minister for a three-hour drive in his carriage through the countryside surrounding Plombières. On this occasion the Emperor brought up the subject of a family alliance with the House of Savoy and the means of attaining it: the marriage of his cousin Prince Napoleon to the King's fifteen-year-old daughter, Princess Clothilde. Knowing Vittorio Emanuele's reluctance to give his young daughter away in marriage, especially to one with as tarnished a reputation as the rotund and far older Prince, known derisively as Plon-Plon because of his huge bulk and less than military bearing, Cavour took pains to make no commitment. He did, however, promise to inform Vittorio Emanuele about the proposal and warned his sovereign of the consequences of a refusal. He cautioned the King not to put the entire enterprise in jeopardy out of sour aristocratic scruples and he wrote General La Marmora begging him to support his position.

Cavour was pleased by the promises made by Napoleon. "I can assure you that throughout our talks I was persuaded that as regards Austria, the Roman Question, our institutions, our past and on the probable future of Italy," he wrote Castelli, "the Emperor thinks as we do. Considering the frankness, indeed the abandon with which he expressed himself on all these points, I felt I was not speaking with the Emperor of the French but with a real Italian liberal." [3] Napoleon, for his part, concluded that Cavour was the only true friend he had in Europe. From Plombières Cavour ventured to Baden-Baden, where he gathered from his talks with the various diplomats that Russia would be friendly should a Franco-Austrian war erupt, while Prussia and the small German states would remain neutral.

Among others, he met William, soon to be the Prince Regent of Prussia, who was pleasantly surprised that Cavour was not the turbulent revolutionary he expected. Indeed Manteuffel let it be known that Cavour had captivated the future King. Cavour came away from the encounter convinced of the possibility of a future Piedmontese-Prussian alliance, which would not only be compatible with but would complement the French connection. For the moment he was content, certain that, if Vittorio Emanule consented to the marriage of his daughter, northern Italy would be liberated.

Convinced of the necessity for the marriage, the mettlesome Minister determined to have his way. Upon arriving in the capital, he again brought the matter to the attention of his sovereign, who instructed him to let Napoleon know that he approved the project. "Yet the King cannot pledge his word in a definitive manner without the free consent of the Princess his daughter to the union," Cavour wrote to Napoleon in early August. "For that reason and also because the King wishes that the Prince, before engaging himself irrevocably, should have seen his daughter from close at hand and should have judged whether she conforms to the idea he has of her, he proposed to Y.M. to urge the Prince to come to Piedmont upon his return from Algeria, on the pretext of fulfilling the promise made a year ago to visit our country." [4]

Despite Cavour's anxiety that Napoleon might be alienated, the Princess Clothilde could not be pushed into any marriage, especially one which was contrary to her hopes. Although the architect of the French alliance pretended to understand, he was furious with the Princess, who in his eyes did not understand her duty to her country, and with the King, who allowed his young daughter to take such an independent position. The Prime Minister realized that Vittorio Emanuele wanted the marriage. "Only as he has an extraordinarily weak character, he does not dare to be really firm with her, he wants to appear in her eyes as one obliged to yield to a political necessity," he wrote to Count Villamarina of the royal household. "In a word, he wants me to play the part of the tyrant, while he keeps for himself the part of a noble and affectionate father. Perhaps such conduct may be called neither noble nor affectionate. But no matter if the King is weak, I am as strong as a rock. To attain the sacred goal we have set ourselves, I would be prepared to face far worse dangers than the hatred of a girl and the wrath of courtiers." [5] He proved to be true to his words.

All the secrecy surrounding Cavour's meeting with Napoleon did not prevent official Europe from learning of it from the Belgian press. Thought of it haunted the Austrian ambassador to France, who discovered that no one in the French Foreign Ministry seemed to know what the two had agreed to do. Even Walewski knew little about the matter, though he feared that Cavour had some international intrigue in mind. Rome was no less disturbed and the reports sent by the Nuncio from Paris were not reassuring. Sacconi directed Antonelli's attention to an article in the *Constitutionnel* which he believed to be inspired by the government. Among other things the article affirmed that the Emperor's government was concerned about Italy and sympathetic to its interests and "glorious nationality."

The fears of Vienna and Rome were not groundless for no sooner had Cavour set foot in Turin than he commenced his campaign to promote war. "We are moving toward war with Austria," he told the Neapolitan Giuseppe Massari at the beginning of August. Predicting that hostilities would erupt before the next legislative session in France, he called for a concentration of forces.[6] To this end he was willing to cooperate with the revolutionary National Society of La Farina, noting that to make music many instruments were needed. At dawn one day at the end of 1858, Garibaldi, wearing a frock coat and top hat, was brought into Cavour's study and informed of the agreement made at Plombières. Apparently the wily Count conveniently failed to mention Napoleon's design on Nice, for the general readily accepted the suggestion that he enroll and command a volunteer force. Anxious for action, Garibaldi agreed to await the signal of La Farina, the National Society, and above all Cavour. The guerrilla chieftain thus renounced his association with the Mazzinians and placed himself at the disposition of the Count who promised to address himself to the Italian question.

Napoleon opened the new year dramatically when at his reception for the diplomatic corps he turned toward Baron Hubner, the Austrian representative, and expressed regret that relations between their governments had become so strained. His words fell like a bolt from the blue and produced a panic in Paris and consternation throughout the continent. The Papal Nuncio, who left the reception "pale as death," wrote Antonelli that rumors had mushroomed as a result of the words directed by the Emperor to the Austrian ambassador. Perhaps to calm opinion, Napoleon and Eugenie sought to soothe Hubner at the reception at the Tuileries the next evening. Meanwhile Count Walewski tried to convince diplomatic Europe that there was no belligerent intent behind Napoleon's remark and the official journal Le Moniteur also discounted the notion of an impending conflict. Apparently there was to be no war—at least for the moment.

The Austrians were not assured, especially when they learned that Garibaldi had held a long conference with Cavour a week before the Emperor's ominous words. The Vatican was even more concerned than Vienna. Since the start of the year the Nuncio at Florence had warned of the underhanded dealings of Piedmont with the revolutionists of Tuscany. According to his reports, Cavour was the instigator and La Farina his revolutionary instrument.[7] Even in friendly capitals it was acknowledged that the war clouds resulted from the machinations of the Count and the Emperor.

On January 10, when Vittorio Emanuele opened Parliament, his words echoed Cavour's sentiments. The response to the King's remark that his country was not insensitive to the cries

of anguish arising from all parts of Italy was electric. Senators
and Deputies were joined by spectators in shouting *Viva il Re!*
applauding him as much for what he had meant, as for what
he had said. Hudson, the Italophile British Minister at Turin,
compared it to a rocket falling on the treaties, while Cavour
promised there would be no turning back. Diplomatic Europe
was frantic. Among those perturbed was Count Malmesbury, the
English Foreign Minister. This Tory, who was determined to
preserve the peace, became increasingly hostile to Cavour when
he discovered that he was intent upon provoking a war. Unlike
Cavour, Malmesbury looked for, and believed possible, an Italian
regeneration unstained by violence and bloodshed. He therefore
wrote Hudson reproving the belligerent speech of Vittorio Emanuele and criticizing Cavour for the awesome responsibility he
had assumed. From Rome Pio Nono launched the charge that
the King's speech was calculated to arouse revolutionaries the
length and breadth of Italy.

Cavour knew that both Rome and London supported the
status quo, but counted upon the French to break the Gordian
knot. His confidence was confirmed by the arrival of Prince
Jerome Napoleon in Genoa on January 16, and a short while
later the marriage contract between him and the King's daughter
was signed at the royal palace, with Cavour acting as notary of
the crown in the matter. Cavour, who believed that brilliant men
should have no children, left the wedding with a magnificent
ring presented to him by the King. To the protestations of the
Count that he had no wife nor would take one, Vittorio Emanuele responded, "Your bride is the *Patria*."

"I hope this alliance will prove more profitable to you than
our own numerous ones with the House of Savoy have been for
us," Count Buol, the Austrian Foreign Minister, commented to
the French chargé d'affaires at Vienna. It was to prove fruitful
to Piedmont, for at the same time a formal treaty between
France and Piedmont was concluded but antedated to December,
1858, to remove suspicion. Although the treaty was secret, Napoleon had perforce to discuss the terms with his Foreign Office
and perhaps this is why its terms were less generous than those
outlined at Plombières. One article, for example, stipulated
that the entire cost of the war was to be borne by the Kingdom
of Upper Italy, while another provided that both Nice and Savoy
were to be turned over to France. Nothing was said about the
territories to be included in the new Northern Kingdom, al-

though it was noted that its population would be about eleven million. About the rest of Italy, the treaty remained silent.

Determined to have his war, Cavour sought to broaden the coalition against Austria and to do so he thought in terms of having his sovereign marry the Russian princess Marie de Leuchtenberg. Having subordinated romantic connections to political ambition, the Count expected others to do likewise. Vittorio Emanuele, who had showered his attentions on Rosina Vercellana in the four years since his wife's death, thought otherwise, and word leaked out that the monarch planned to marry his mistress. Scandalized that the King should even consider a marriage with the daughter of a corporal of low birth, the aristocratic Cavour determined to use any means at his disposal to put an end to this liaison. Against the wishes of his cabinet, the Count attempted to convince the two lovers that the other had not been faithful. Unfortunately, the actress Laura Bon refused Cavour's bribe to substantiate his story to Rosina, while the latter countered the reports of Cavour's detectives by claiming that the King's demands upon her time were so frequent and forceful that she had neither the opportunity nor the inclination to see other men. Thus all of Cavour's deception and diplomacy did not separate the two lovers. Indeed, they were drawn more closely together and never forgave the Count for meddling in their private lives. The entire affair had political consequences, for badgered by Cavour, the King turned to Rattazzi for advice and support, creating a potential rival for the powerful Count.

The King could not immediately dispense with his troublesome Minister because he more than anyone else had been responsible for the French alliance, and he alone, it was believed, had the force and cunning to force Napoleon to fulfill his promises. Early in February, Napoleon announced to his Ministers that soon a brochure would appear which reflected his views on the Italian question. Inspired if not prepared by the Emperor in consultation with the Viscount de La Guerronière, the pamphlet, entitled *Napoléon III et l'Italie,* foreshadowed the war in Italy. This alone was sufficient to disturb Rome but specific reference to the "abnormal" situation in the States of the Church and the criticism of the clerical character of the government aroused Pio Nono. The fact that its author recommended a federal union in the peninsula with the Pope as President did little to console Rome. In London the reaction was almost as bitter.

February 3, the day the polemical pamphlet appeared on the bookshelves of Paris, Queen Victoria in her speech opening Parliament expressed her determination to maintain the peace and public treaties. The following day she wrote a letter to Napoleon urging him to calm the apprehensions of Europe by declaring his adherence to international treaties and by revealing his pacific intentions. This posture distressed Cavour, who considered it certain that England would be against him, but found it impossible to turn back to please Victoria. "The cause of Italy is no less sacred, no less worthy to stir the hearts of generous souls, than that of the Irish or that of the black race," which had already moved the English, Cavour observed in his parliamentary speech of February 9, 1859. "It too will triumph before the tribunal of English public opinion," he predicted. Meanwhile he hoped to prevent the English government from preserving the Austrian-imposed peace, which he deemed unsatisfactory for Piedmont and Italy. "I am persuaded that England sincerely desires the preservation of the constitutional system in Piedmont," he confided to General Fox, who was passing through Turin, "but does it not realize that it is absurd to think of conciliating the existence of that constitution with the continuation of Austrian domination in Italy?"[8]

Toward the end of February the English Foreign Secretary, still determined to preserve the peace, asked Cavour to catalog his country's grievances. In his March Memorandum, Cavour recapitulated the complaints of the people of the peninsula and suggested the most important remedies: autonomous governments for Lombardy, Venetia, and the pontifical provinces east of the Appenines, and the canceling of Austrian military conventions with the Grand Duke of Tuscany as well as the Duchies of Parma and Modena. These suggestions could be implemented only if the Habsburgs resolved to abandon their Italian provinces—a most unlikely eventuality. Rather, the Austrians called upon the English to maintain the sanctity of treaties and thus preserve their position in Italy.

Resigned to the meddling of the English, Cavour more than ever counted upon the resolve of Napoleon to wage war. Unfortunately, his policy continued to vacillate. On February 7, when he spoke at the opening session of the Corps Législatif and the Senate, he recalled his promise that the Empire meant peace, but added that his government would remain immovable in its defense of right, justice, and national honor. Subsequently, the Count was distressed by the public disavowal of the Emperor's intention to wage war which appeared in *Le Moniteur* in early March. "The Emperor has agreed to help the King of Sardinia defend himself against any aggressive move on the part of Austria," it was reported. "He has promised nothing else, and we are certain that he will keep his word."[9] Understandably, Cavour was in a bitter mood the next day, complaining that the article was another of Napoleon's customary tricks. Undaunted, he told friends that he was ready to set fire to the four corners of the world rather than back down.

The Prime Minister's optimism and daring were not shared by all his colleagues. Even La Marmora expressed grave concern about the mounting sentiment throughout Europe against a European war, and the great opposition to an Italian war in France itself. Matters grew worse in March, when the Russians proposed calling a conference to settle the Italian problem. Meanwhile, the British sent Count Cowley, their resident Minister in France, to Vienna on a special mission.

Cowley, who left Vienna on March 10, was convinced that it was necessary for Piedmont to disarm before Austria would negotiate. The Piedmontese, who had already mobilized their troops at the frontier to forestall any Austrian aggression, responded by calling to active service all soldiers dismissed from the class of 1828 to 1832. Shortly afterwards Cavour's government published a decree authorizing the formation of free companies and resisted diplomatic pressure to stop the enrollment of the flood of volunteers. "They could throw me into the Po," he argued defiantly, "but I shall not stop this movement." Having been excited and pushed forward, he and his colleagues insisted that the bomb they had packed must shortly explode. It was clear that Cavour's frantic armament was designed not only to protect Piedmont but to force Napoleon's hand. The wily Minister held out the specter that if abandoned, Vittorio Emanuele might abdicate, and a pro-Austrian ministry might be formed to the detriment of France's influence in Italy.[10]

Unwilling to have his plans for war and political readjustment shattered, Cavour wrote to his fellow conspirator, Napoleon, relating the difficulty of his position should the Italian question be discussed at a congress from which Piedmont was excluded. He suggested that Napoleon support his admission to such a congress, knowing that Austria would refuse, sparing him further difficulty. Appealing to the Emperor's Corsican pride, he indicated that Austria had miscalculated in assuming a menacing tone toward him. Avoiding threats and declarations, Cavour flattered Napoleon by asserting that he trusted he knew how to frustrate the attempts of those who would frustrated his noble Italian design.

On March 25, the Count left for Paris at the invitation of the Emperor. Arriving in the capital the next day, Cavour was immediately closeted with him. The news of the meeting precipitated a new round of rumors. Supposedly the Emperor had called the Count to induce him to disarm at the same time Austria did—before the congress. Others reported that Napoleon had refused to support Cavour's position of having Piedmont play an integral part at the coming congress. Baron Rothschild, who visited and questioned Cavour, was little satisfied with his response that the chances for peace were as good as war. Jokingly Cavour suggested that the two buy securities; he would then leave his post and they would profit from the increase of three francs his resignation would encourage. "You are too modest, monsieur Count," retorted the famous banker, smiling, "you are well worth six francs."[11]

It is not known what words passed between Cavour and Napoleon; whether the Count catered to the Emperor's ego or played upon his fear of exposure of their plot or explosion of revolution. Whatever was said, the troubled visitor was reassured. War was inevitable. Small wonder that the Nuncio's reports from Paris proved disappointing to the papal Secretary of State. Rome responded less than enthusiastically to Napoleon's plan to present his proposal for an Italian confederation to the proposed congress. The other Italian states, Sacconi explained to Walewski, would find it difficult to join such a confederation and would not consent to sit by the side of Piedmont which had intimidated them. Antonelli, therefore, informed the British at the beginning of April, 1859, that the Pontiff considered the calling of a congress to solve the Italian question, unwarranted. In fact, if invited to participate the Pope would certainly decline.

Nonetheless, England remained a problem to Cavour as well as the Pope, for her government persisted in proposing peace overtures. In mid-April the British called for Piedmontese disarmament as a preliminary to peace. Cavour remained deaf to their pleas, prepared to turn the world upside down rather than comply. He could afford to be rebellious because Napoleon III had secretly told him to refuse to submit. The Nuncio at Paris, in his reports to Rome, corroborated Cavour's judgment that Napoleon would fulfill the promises made at Plombières. "Taken together, it is more and more obvious that the Emperor is dominated by liberal ideas," Sacconi wrote Antonelli, "and wants to arrange things by obtaining great sacrifices from Austria and realize his well-known ideas."

The evening of April 18, Prince Latour d'Auvergne was officially informed by his government that France had accepted the English plan for disarmament. Since Count Walewski had specified that the Prime Minister should be immediately informed of this decision, the Prince ordered the Secretary of the Legation, Baron Aymé d'Aguin, to the Palazzo Cavour to bring him the telegram. Awakened to receive this disastrous news, Cavour went into a state of convulsive agitation. Beating his forehead with his hands while a wild gleam flashed from his eyes, revealing at once fury and frustration, he cried out that the only alternative he had open was to shoot himself, blow off his head. "The Italian question is not lost," he told Massari whom he called at five that fateful morning, "but Piedmont and I have been beaten."

Later that morning Prince Latour personally went to see the Count, who unburdened himself, indicating that he had been seriously wounded by the recent communication. Mincing no words, he added that he would not counsel his sovereign to pursue any course other than the one they had jointly embarked upon—and which they thought Napoleon sanctioned. He preferred to resign, even leave the country, rather than accept defeat. This declaration frightened the French Minister who considered such a step no less than a catastrophe and most likely encouraged the telegrams of Napoleon and Prince Jerome which sought to calm Cavour.

The Prime Minister recognized that if Napoleon accepted disarmament, he had to submit. Nonetheless, he considered this a tragic mistake. From Paris came word that the matter was now in Austrian hands; if she accepted Piedmont in the congress, Cavour would have to disarm the country. Because the Count was so despondent, his friends determined to keep a close watch upon him. When Minghetti heard that Cavour had closed himself in his study, giving his servants specific orders to admit no one, they urged his closest friend, Castelli, to go immediately to see him lest he do something desperate.

Upon hearing the news Castelli rushed to the Palazzo Cavour and was welcomed by the head servant, Martini Tosco, who was relieved to see him. "The Count is in his room alone," he blurted out, "he has already burned many of his papers and left instructions not to permit anyone to enter, but for mercy's sake, you go, no matter what the cost." Thus encouraged Castelli entered

Cavour's room and found him encircled with papers he had torn
to shreds, while some were already burning in the fireplace.
Fearing that his distraught friend would take more drastic steps,
he asked, "Does this mean that the Count of Cavour wants to
desert the field before the battle, wants to abandon us all?" and
then overcome by a burst of emotion, burst into tears. Embracing
Castelli, Cavour quickly said, "Calm yourself, we will confront
everything and always together."[12]

Just when everything seemed lost, the Count's plans were res-
cued by the Austrians who did not specify their acceptance of
Piedmontese participation in the conference. From Berlin came
the news that the Austrians, bent upon humiliating Piedmont,
would not accept the English proposal and that the Vienna
government would demand Sardinian disarmament under the
threat of war. Similar reports were received from the Russian
legation in Turin while Walewski instructed Prince Latour to
inform Cavour of Austria's intransigence and to count upon
their most energetic support. On April 21, this was confirmed
by a telegram from Lord Malmesbury which specified that the
Austrians had sent a three-day ultimatum to Turin. Delighted
by the news, Cavour rubbed his hands energetically, but without
losing control of his emotions before the English representative
he claimed that he had done all he could to avoid the confla-
gration.

The afternoon of April 23, Castelli ran into a friend who had
just received a telegram reporting that the Austrian representatives, Baron Kellesperg and Count Ceschi, were on a train
heading for Turin, carrying the fateful ultimatum. Cavour appeared and, seeing his friend jubilant, tore the telegram from
his hands, read the first few words, and then galloped down the
stairs to the Chamber of Deputies to announce the news to
others. During the course of the session, he asked for and obtained a vote conferring full powers upon the King for the
length of the inevitable conflict. As the excited Deputies shouted
"Long live the King" and "Long live Italy!" Cavour received
word that the Austrian emissaries had reached the capital. Rushing out of the Chamber, Cavour was heard to remark that he
was leaving the last sitting of the Piedmontese Parliament, the
next would be that of the Kingdom of Italy.

When the Austrians arrived, the Prime Minister received them
politely in the Ministry of Foreign Affairs. Given three days to
meet their demands, Cavour decided to take the full time, promising he would reply on April 26. When Castelli and his friends

entered Cavour's office, the Count reacted like a small boy given a new toy. "It's here," he shouted, "it's here, go read it." While completing a letter, he told his friends who were devouring the ultimatum with their eyes, *"Alea jacta est."* Having finished the letter, he invited them all to dinner to celebrate the momentous occasion. Friend and foe alike recognized Cavour's achievement. Even Mazzini termed the Count's provocation and rejection of the ultimatum "a master stroke."

Cavour's success was made possible in no small measure by the incompetence of Austria. As early as April 20 she had revealed her intention of sending an ultimatum to Piedmont, but waited a full three days to do so, waited another three days for the expected rejection, and another three days before crossing the border on April 29. Once across, the Austrians moved foolishly here and there instead of throwing themselves on Turin. As a result the Habsburg hope of defeating the Piedmontese before the arrival of the French proved completely vain. Even friends marveled at the madness of the Austrian course of action.

The day the Austrians crossed the frontier, Vittorio Emanuele issued a proclamation, written in fact by Cavour, which served the dual purpose of rallying Italian support as well as justifying Piedmont's actions abroad. "Unable to accept the example set by our institutions and not wishing to subject herself to the judgment of a European congress on the evils and dangers of which she is solely responsible," the Count wrote, "Austria has violated her promises to England and makes her code of honor a cause for war."[13] But Cavour went beyond this and had the King assert that he was defending not only his throne and the liberties of his people, but the honor of the Italian name. In this fashion the resourceful Minister served to advise the people of the peninsula that this was a national rather than a dynastic struggle.

The Count's joy was not shared by the Pope. Rome was upset by the national tone Cavour had given the war and feared its repercussions. As soon as Antonelli believed war between France and Austria to be inevitable, he had tried to free himself of the French and Austrian occupying forces in order to prevent the embarrassing presence of warring armies on papal soil. He did not succeed. Neither he nor Pio Nono was reassured by the Emperor's pledge that no matter what happened, His Holiness could count upon Napoleon's complete support. For one thing, the Holy Father doubted Napoleon's will and ability to control Cavour. He could point to the fact that despite the promise the

Count had given to employ regular troops only in the war, he proceeded to unleash Garibaldi, having the general appointed commander of the *Cacciatori delle Alpi.* This audacious act, which absorbed the revolutionary element and aroused popular enthusiasm in England, caused consternation in Rome. The fears of the Pope and the other Italian princes were to be justified by events.

The announcement of the war, the King's proclamation, and the enlistment of Garibaldi served as a signal to overturn the established order throughout the peninsula. Despite Napoleon's admonition to use caution as regards the Pope, the Turin cabinet informed Rome that it would seek the Austrians wherever they were to be found. In the two Duchies, the Legations, and Tuscany, there were similar national manifestations. The Duchess of Parma, the Duke of Modena, and the Grand Duke of Tuscany outdid one another in fleeing the wrath of their own subjects and were followed by provisional governments that proclaimed their allegiance to Vittorio Emanuele and favored union with constitutional Piedmont. Such an amalgamation could not be easily accomplished.

In the first place, no provision for Piedmont's incorporation of the duchies had been provided by the treaty with France. Secondly, diplomatic opinion was already suspicious of the activities of France and Piedmont, and such a step would only create new hostilities. Sacconi, the Nuncio at Paris, reported to Rome that Cavour and the Piedmontese were directing the revolution in Central Italy, and the Marquis Pepoli, the leader of the revolution in Bologna, took frequent trips to Turin and Paris. Queen Victoria, too, was prone to protest against Sardinian activity in Tuscany and Massa Carrara.

The Sardinian Minister, having foreseen the diplomatic difficulties, took no official action to incorporate these territories. He did wish to send the Prince of Savoy-Carignano to Tuscany in the King's name, but Napoleon objected and despatched the Fifth French Army Corps under Prince Napoleon to Leghorn, in the face of Cavour's protests. Having lost the battle, the Count did not concede the struggle for Tuscany, suggesting to Vittorio Emanuele that he appoint the Prince by his order. Napoleon resented both Cavour's tactics and the King's order which addressed the Tuscans as if they were already incorporated into Piedmont. To minimize the misunderstanding, Cavour sent out unofficial commissioners with instructions to assume power and contribute to the winning of the war. Later they would tackle the ticklish question of amalgamation—but from a position of strength. The same instructions were given to Count Diodate Pallieri who was sent to Parma, to Luigi Carlo Farini who was sent to Modena, to Massimo D'Azeglio who was sent to Bologna, and to Carlo Boncompagni who was sent to Florence. To quiet the Pope, the King wrote him a personal letter assuring him that he had nothing to fear from Piedmont's movements, and that he would always be defended by the King and his troops.

The presence of a strong autonomist movement in Tuscany worried Cavour, so that he pressed for a fusion with Piedmont before the autonomists or the French could forestall this. Already suspicion divided the two allies. The French were no more sincere than were the Piedmontese. Their ambassador in London, the Count de Persigny, attempted to place the entire responsibility for the war upon Cavour's shoulders, claiming that Napoleon had had no intention of waging war in Italy, but had been blackmailed to do so by the unscrupulous Prime Minister of Piedmont who threatened to publish his most confidential correspondence.

Intially this suspicion did not hinder the effectiveness of the allied campaign. Since General Gyulai had failed to take decisive action and continued to vacillate, the allied forces were permitted to join and won the battle of Magenta on June 4. The road to Milan was now open. The following day Cavour had a proclamation issued to the citizenry of that city, informing them of the victory, the Austrian withdrawal, and the achievements of Vittorio Emanuele who had for ten years planned and sacrificed for the reannexation of Lombardy to Piedmont.[14] From Milan Napoleon issued a proclamation to the people of Italy, calling them to arms under the banner of Vittorio Emanuele. This served as an affront to the Court of Rome as well as that of Naples. Antonelli protested to Turin and Paris, but his words seemed wasted.

Cavour, it appeared, was master of the situation. Diplomatically, too, he seemed to have things his way. Russian friendliness assured the allies of Prussian neutrality, and on June 10, Palmerston's liberal government replaced the conservative Derby cabinet. Cavour learned from Emanuele D'Azeglio that the new government favored the formation of a Kingdom of Upper Italy which would include not only Lombardy-Venetia but Parma, Modena, Tuscany, and the Legations as well. Even the Queen could not ignore the fact that though English public opinion favored neither Austria nor France, the sympathy for Italy was general. To crown their success the French and the Piedmontese won the double battle of Solferino and San Martino on June 24.

At the moment when complete success seemed to be within Cavour's grasp, Napoleon thought of bringing the war to a halt by negotiations. Historians have long sought to understand why Napoleon reversed his position. Undoubtedly Cavour's activities in Central Italy played a part. On July 4 Pio Nono appealed to Napoleon to restrain the rapacious activities of Piedmont which threatened to destroy the temporal power of the Church. Two days later the French leader attempted to negotiate with Austria through the British government. This proved abortive. Meanwhile Cavour learned that the Russians wished to mediate the conflict. "At this moment mediation cannot have but unfortunate results," he responded, "it is necessary for Austrian influence in Italy to disappear completely before the peace can be solid and durable." The Emperor apparently thought otherwise and resorted to direct negotiations.

On July 8 an armistice was agreed upon and a few days later the Emperors met at Villafranca to outline the terms. The two, upon meeting, greeted each other in the most cordial manner, as if no issue separated them. When they were alone, it was Franz Josef who took the initiative. In a friendly manner, as one brother monarch to another, he cautioned Napoleon of the company he kept, observing that revolutions overturn, but do not construct. Then turning to particulars, he announced that he was prepared to cede the territory the French now occupied, and they were free to turn it over to the Piedmontese. He would concede no more.

Napoleon accepted these terms and also agreed to support the demand that the Grand Duke of Tuscany and the Duke of Modena be returned to their states. In this fashion he at once countered Cavour's interference in the Romagna as well as the prospect of working in alliance with the Italian revolution. At the same time the French and Austrians agreed to the creation of an Italian Confederation under the honorary presidency of the Pope, permitted Venetia, though under the crown of Austria, to form an integral part of the union, and promised to press the Pope to introduce a number of reforms in his states. Neither Vittorio Emanuele nor his Foreign Minister had been consulted by their French ally in the elaboration of these terms. Hudson's words of warning flashed through Cavour's mind, "Take care, Napoleon will start you dancing, then leave you alone."[15] The Count was not ready to leave the floor; for him the music had just begun.

CHAPTER X

Creation of the Unitary State

CAVOUR, WHEN INFORMED OF THE ARMISTICE NAPOLEON HAD CON-cluded with the Austrians, was furious, for it left the peninsula vulnerable to Habsburg depredations. Initially his anger took the form of a quiet irony. "What a marvel!" he blurted out. "The Emperor wants to give a limited wedding gift, only Lombardy." When Pasolini observed that the arrangement left the quadrilateral in Austrian hands, the Count sighed and said, "The fortresses, besides these he would have given Milan—even Turin for he was tired and hot." Since the armistice terms called for return of the old rulers in Central Italy, Cavour was perplexed as to the instructions he should send to his representatives there.

As one problem after another confronted the bewildered Minister, he fell into a state of feverish agitation and made an abortive attempt to postpone the time the armistice was to go into effect. He then hoped that his King would not submit to this humiliation. This desire was not unreasonable; in fact, when the King read the terms he too was upset, insisting that they were different from what he had been led to believe they would be on July 8, when the truce had been concluded. Unable to control his temper, Vittorio Emanuele threatened to continue the war without the French. "Do as you please," the Emperor cynically replied, warning him that instead of one enemy he might find two. After considering the matter and recollecting his father's fiasco when he tried to fight alone, he resigned himself to Napoleon's decision. Having no viable alternative, he had to sign the armistice, but took care to give his approval only to those aspects of the document that concerned him—a reservation that was later to prove eminently useful.

Cavour could not as easily swallow Napoleon's treachery. His opposition, in part, was based on the fact that so long as Austria remained entrenched in the northern fortresses and occupied Venetia, Piedmont and Lombardy could not be secure. Napoleon had earlier admitted as much. In his proclamation to the French people at the start of the war he had indicated that there were only two alternatives: either Austria would dominate northern Italy up to the Alps or Italy would be free to the Adriatic, because the Habsburgs considered any independence in the peninsula detrimental to their own position. There were signs that the Austrians intended to reopen the Italian question at a more convenient time. Franz Josef, as he left the war area, was heard to say that he would reacquire Lombardy in a year or two. Small wonder that the Count found the terms of Villafranca unacceptable.

When the King returned to his camp at Monzambano, Cavour descended on him like a thunderbolt, openly denouncing the faithless Emperor. He stormed into his sovereign's quarters, his face scarlet, his motions violent and erratic, his voice vitriolic. For two hours he was locked with the King in a violent confrontation. Insisting that his and Italy's interests had been betrayed, he hounded his depressed monarch to continue the war alone, and in the final analysis to abdicate rather than accept Napoleon's conditions. Apparently the outraged Count, who was used to having his way, was so disrespectful to his sovereign that Vittorio Emanuele felt constrained to turn his back on him, all his verbal attempts to calm Cavour having been to no avail. Calling to his attention that he after all was the King, Vittorio Emanuele was enraged by his Minister's response that since he knew the Italians better he was their true king.

Unable to impose his will, Cavour left in a rage. Even after this tempestuous scene of July 10, 1859, Cavour continued to oppose a negotiated peace until such time as northern Italy had been liberated from the Alps to the Adriatic as Napoleon had pledged. To the various explanations or excuses to justify the French action, Cavour replied that promises were promises and had to be kept. Seeing the labor of so many years stultified, his dreams shattered, the Count preferred to promote a revolution rather than quietly submit to the betrayal. When Napoleon visited Turin on July 15, Cavour went with his colleagues to the station to receive him, but the former allies did not exchange one word.

Still enraged, Cavour expressed his sentiments by not attending the dinner in the Emperor's honor. Napoleon, however, called for Cavour that evening to explain his controversial decision. He justified his steps solely on military considerations, claiming that it would have required 300,000 men to occupy Verona and he did not have them. Cavour did not contest this observation since the Emperor's decision appeared irrevocable, but he expressed concern for the fate of these states abandoned to their former sovereigns: Tuscany, Modena, and the Romagna. Happily the Emperor promised to plead their case before the projected European congress, asking only that pending a decision the Piedmontese prevent the old dynasties from being reestablished. This was a suggestion the Count was most eager to carry out, and to this end he wrote General La Marmora requesting that he immediately release the Tuscans, Modenese, and Romagnols in the army so they could play a prominent role in preventing the princes from returning.

During these dark days Cavour could also find some consolation in the fact that Lord John Russell, the new English Foreign Secretary, was more favorably disposed to the Italian cause than had been his predecessor. Indeed, the English position toward Italy was in the process of change. "The Emperor Napoleon is left in a position of great power," Lord John informed Queen Victoria after Villafranca, implying that he enjoyed that position because he was the sole champion of the Italian cause. The purport of these words was that in the future England might vie with France in order to win the goodwill of the Italians—a situation which Cavour could use to good advantage. For the moment, however, the situation remained deplorable and the Count was exhausted from functioning not only as Prime Minister but as Foreign Minister, Minister of the Interior, and Minister of War as well. He took advantage of his differences with the King and Napoleon to resign in mid-July, 1859. "I have been criticized for not wanting to sign the peace, but I could not do otherwise," he told Massari, "that peace I could not, I cannot sign."

Cavour's outburst of indignation against the Emperor and his own King was not totally spontaneous or devoid of purpose. It sought to convince and succeeded in convincing Italians that he was an Italian patriot as well as a son of Piedmont and provided a ray of hope when the terms of Villafranca were made public. Very likely it also helped to shame Napoleon into giving up any claims to the territories he had earlier been promised. "Your government will pay me for the expenses incurred during the war," Napoleon whispered to Vittorio Emanuele as he left Turin and promised to say no more about Nice and Savoy.

Even this concession, won in part by Cavour, did not pacify Vittorio Emanuele who vividly recalled his Minister's blistering attack upon him. He remained convinced that he had gone too far, too fast in attempting to subvert the Papal States against Napoleon's interdiction, thus provoking the Emperor's withdrawal from the war. Neither could the King condone his Minister's resignation at a moment of crisis. "He is a muddle-head who is always pushing me into some wasp's nest or other," he told the British military attaché. "Cavour is mad. I have often told him he was off his head. He goes off playing with follies like this rising in the Romagna, and heaven knows what else. But he is finished now. He did a good job, but he is finished."[1]

Despite his diatribe against Cavour, the King consulted him in choosing a successor. The Count pointed to Count Francesco Arese, and when he refused, to his old friend General La Marmora, who agreed to head a new Ministry. Assisting him in the important post of Minister of the Interior was Cavour's former ally Rattazzi. It fell upon the shoulders of this government not only to annex Lombardy but to execute the terms of the armistice of Villafranca. Apparently to implement the latter, the Piedmontese commissioners in Central Italy were formally recalled. Cavour, however, encouraged them to remain in an unofficial capacity, to direct public opinion against a restoration and to wait for the appropriate moment for annexation to Piedmont. Luigi Carlo Farini thus remained in Modena and from there influenced events in the Romagna as well, until Minghetti arrived. On the withdrawal of Boncompagni from Tuscany, the Baron Ricasoli advanced Turin's interests there.

Even from behind the scenes Cavour had to move cautiously and not create any undue embarrassment for Napoleon who could not sanction those steps which violated his formal pledges to Austria as well as his voluntary obligations to the Pope. "If annexation should cross the Appenines, unity would be accomplished, and I will not have unity; I only want independence," Napoleon confessed when asked to permit the central states to join Piedmont. "Unity would make trouble for me in France, on account of the Roman Question, and France would not be pleased to see on her flank a great nation that might diminish her preponderance."[2] The business in Central Italy was a labyrinth which required the conspiratorial ability of Cavour to find the way out. He, however, continued to remain out of the government.

Napoleon publicly opposed the development in Central Italy whereby the Piedmontese, counseled by Cavour, unofficially though relentlessly consolidated their position. Yet the enigmatic Emperor let the Austrians know that he would not tolerate their intervention either in Tuscany or the Romagna—thus providing the provisional governments with the protection they needed to defy the terms of Villafranca. He still clung, it seems, to the idea of an Italian confederation which would encompass Austria and the Papal States. Fortunately, Lord John Russell let the French know that his government would not be a party to the creation of a confederation which included Austria and would deliver Italy, bound hand and foot, to Vienna. He and Palmerston favored the annexation of Central Italy by the Piedmontese and reminded them that God helps those who help themselves.

Cavour, who had unraveled the riddle of the Emperor and penetrated his reserve, was convinced that under the appropriate conditions Napoleon would be willing to see Piedmont annex Central Italy including the Romagna, but had to be able to justify his actions before European diplomatic circles and French public opinion. Thus Cavour confided to Count Arese that even as regards the policy to be pursued toward the Papal States, he and the Emperor were again in accord. Audacity and resolution, he believed, would bring success. He therefore criticized the vacillation and indecision of the La Marmora-Rattazzi cabinet.

While Cavour brooded over missed opportunities, Bettino Ricasoli in Florence and Luigi Carlo Farini in Modena fearlessly clung to a vision of unification far transcending Cavour's plan for a North Italian kingdom. The Count recognized their contribution, confiding to Castelli that if there were anything that mitigated the pain of the unfortunate peace, it was the admirable, indeed heroic conduct of Central Italy. If these areas could succeed in remaining free by preventing the return of their petty rulers, the results of the war would be better than if Napoleon had continued his Italian campaign, since they would owe their independence to their own actions rather than foreign arms. Actually, the Count not only sanctioned the illegal activities in Central Italy, he encouraged and acted as an accomplice and guide of the revolutionary movement he had promised he would prevent.

Following his suggestions, the assembly in Florence in its session of August 20, 1859, unanimously declared the deposition of the House of Lorraine and the annexation of Tuscany to Piedmont. Meanwhile in Modena, Farini, almost under the guns of the Austrians, convoked a popular assembly in mid-August which promulgated the Piedmontese *Statuto* as well as the codes and laws of the Sardinian state. He was made dictator pending annexation to Piedmont. A few days later Parma did likewise. A

short while after a similar assembly in the Romagna elected
Marco Minghetti President, while it voted the abolition of the
temporal power and asked for annexation to Vittorio Emanuele's
kingdom.

It was known in Turin that Cavour aided and abetted these
actions and thus continued to possess the esteem and sympathy
of a good portion of the population. "I have no family," he told
Massari, "I will always do all I can for the Italian cause." He had
not renounced politics, he wrote Castelli, and would only do so
when Italy was free; then his work would be finished. So long
as the Germans remained south of the Alps, he continued, he
deemed it a sacred duty to consecrate what life and power he had
left to the national goal. He promised that he would not be discouraged either by the ingratitude of some or the villainous
activity of others. Above all, he would not waste his strength in
sterile agitation and party conflict.[3]

Nonetheless Cavour was dissatisfied with the conduct of the La
Marmora-Rattazzi cabinet which he felt was too timid vis-à-vis
Napoleon and too sensitive to the vacillations of Vittorio Emanuele. The latter wavered between an audacious and a conservative course of action. He looked longingly at Central Italy but
hesitated alienating Napoleon or further antagonizing the Pope
to the point where he might hurl an anathema. On Cavour's
suggestion, on September 15 the King entrusted Vittorio Stellardi
with the mission of secretly informing the Pope that the Piedmontese government had been constrained by necessity to place
the Romagna under its authority in order to rescue it from
greater evil. Above all, the King's envoy was to persuade the
Pontiff to content himself with only a nominal sovereignty over
this area, which would be recognized by the payment of an annual tribute.

Later in September when Stellardi visited Pio Nono, he found
him moderate in his references to Vittorio Emanuele. Toward
Cavour he was bitter, and even more so toward Napoleon. Actually, the Pontiff could not help but admire the political crafts-
manship of Cavour—even though his actions proved detrimental
to the Pope's temporal power. When he had granted the Marquis
Gustavo di Cavour an interview earlier in the year, he had
jokingly alluded to the agitation in the Romagna and Emilia
saying, "If I had your brother for my minister, I would not find
myself in this awkward position." Nonetheless, when threatened
with the loss of the Romagna he responded by his consistorial
allocution of September 26, 1859, *Maximo animi,* in which he

reaffirmed the censure he had earlier issued in *Ad gravissimum*. He also observed that all those who by their aid or advice took part in, or approved of the spoliation were included in the ecclesiastical censure.

Unperturbed, Cavour continued to stress that the key to Central Italy was to be found in Paris and only the consent of the sphinx-like Napoleon was essential for its absorption. The sympathy emanating from the new English government he found encouraging; the approval of the French he deemed absolutely essential. For this reason he was discouraged with the Treaty of Zurich signed in November, for the French once again adhered to the terms of Villafranca, though no plans were made for the implementation of the provision calling for restoration in Central Italy. Consequently, Cavour could not decide what course of action to follow. What is certain is that he did not believe Villafranca or Zurich to be adequate and would not accept one or the other. Increasingly he realized that he would have to formally resume direction of affairs to set things straight.

The Count waited for the proper moment to return, and in December, 1859, the French provided assistance. On the night of December 22, another anonymous pamphlet appeared in Paris —this one called *Le Pape et Le Congrès*. Once again word soon spread that it was written by La Guerronière, but it contained the thoughts of the Emperor. It dealt with the problem of Central Italy in general and the Pope's temporal authority in particular. Rome, it was argued, could give up the Romagna without any real harm to the position of the Pontiff or the Church. Without wishing to make the Pope subject to anyone, in fact stressing his sovereignty, La Guerronière argued that he could retain his temporal power if he reduced the size of his holding. The Pontiff, he explained, could keep Rome and its immediate vicinity. The Catholic states would then collectively assure the Pope of the rest of his possessions. It thus advanced the extraordinary principle that the powers which in 1815 had restored the Pope to his states now had the power to deprive him of them.

The appearance of the pamphlet caused an enormous sensation and a violent reaction. Italian liberals of Cavour's stamp were enthusiastic not so much because of its content—for they had already set their heart on the possession of Rome—but for the recognition that the Pope could not possibly retain the Romagna. On the other hand, it threw French Catholics into alarm, aroused Cardinal Antonelli, and made it impossible for Rome or Vienna to sanction a European congress to settle the

Italian question. Not only did the pamphlet put an end to the projected congress, its publication brought about the resignation of Count Walewski and the selection of the anticlerical Thouvenel as the new French Foreign Minister. One more obstacle was thus removed for the return of Cavour.

Adding insult to injury, Napoleon had written to Pio Nono at the end of December, 1859, claiming that one of his greatest preoccupations during the last war had been the condition of the Papal States. According to Napoleon, the inexorable logic of an awakening nationalism in the peninsula, as well as the Pontiff's failure to follow his advice to provide a separate, lay administration for the Romagna, had led to the agitated situation there. Napoleon suggested the Pope show himself magnanimous and resign himself to the loss of the Romagna, thus rendering a great service to the people of the peninsula as well as the peace of Europe.[4]

The Pope refused to follow this advice. On January 1, 1860, when General Goyon, commander of the French forces in the Papal states, went to bring his salutations to the Pope for the new year, Pius welcomed his assurances that they were there to defend the rights of the Church. He offered his prayers that God would shed his light on the head of the French army and nation so that they could see and comprehend the falsity of certain principles that appeared in the pamphlet the Pontiff termed a monument of hypocrisy.

Antonelli, meanwhile, protested that the Piedmontese not only had provoked the rebellion in the Romagna, but favored and furthered it with arms and men.[5] His protests, however, fell upon deaf ears. Rome found itself almost totally isolated as even Austria advanced the notion of turning the administration of the Romagna to the Grand Duke of Tuscany, as if that province were irrevocably lost—thus adhering to the French position. Cavour assumed the offensive by claiming that Antonelli's attempt to defend the area by hiring a "detestable group of scamps" would not succeed. To calm conscientious Catholics, however, he predicted that religion would not suffer as a result of the overthrow of the papal regime. To prove his point, he contended that since the end of that government in the Legations, priests were more respected, churches better filled, and the precepts of the Church more faithfully observed.

The supple papal Secretary of State was prepared to take advantage of any diplomatic overture that was not offensive to the moral scruples of his sovereign, but found there were precious few. Antonelli could derive little satisfaction from the English position, whereby Lord John Russell admitted the possibility that his government would support Napoleon against an Austrian attempt to impose an unpopular government in Italy. The way that even wise and moderate men spoke of the affairs of Rome was indicative of the great change which had occurred in public opinion; actions toward Rome that would have been impossible a year earlier were now held probable.

Cavour took advantage of this favorable diplomatic climate to return to the post of Prime Minister. "I want to become Premier again," he told friends, "in order to complete Italian unity." The King, who recalled Cavour's unfortunate words and actions after Villafranca, accepted his apologies, observing that it was not the time for recrimination. He had to accept the services of the rambunctious aristocrat because he deemed them necessary to fulfill the destiny of his dynasty and country. Lord John Russell was delighted to have Cavour's good sense and ability to conduct the affairs of Turin. In Bologna the municipality ordered public establishments illuminated on January 20, 1860, to celebrate Cavour's return to the helm.

Within the last few months Cavour had reviewed the political situation and assessed the best means of overcoming the obstacles imposed by Villafranca. His first objective was to annex the Romagna and the central duchies and he understood that such a solution required French approval. Thus he found the recent changes in the French government encouraging. Furthermore, he appreciated the Emperor's frank statement to the Cardinal Archbishop of Bordeaux, in which he had left no hope or illusion for those who dreamed that his arms might restore pontifical control in the Romagna. The intransigent position of Rome simplified matters, for on January 19 Pius issued his encyclical *Nullis certe* in which the policies of Napoleon's government were openly attacked and his proposal to bring about cession of the Romagna absolutely rejected.

The attempts of the Cavour government to persuade Pio Nono to abandon the Romagna proved as abortive. In early February, 1860, Vittorio Emanuele sent Father Stellardi to Rome with a letter explaining why he had to maintain control of that region. "The government wishes to be able to say that all means of conciliation were exhausted," commented Sclopis, "and that the Pope persists in not yielding." As expected, Pius responded that his conscience forced him to restrain from any action that would even indirectly sanction such an unjust and violent spoliation of the Church's lands. Cavour remained confident despite the Pope's rejection. "In Italy matters will for the moment arrange themselves without a Congress. Sooner or later, the supreme tribunal of Europe will give a definite sanction to what is going to happen; but from that moment we are still very far," the Count wrote in February, 1860. "The blindness of Austria and the obstinacy of the Holy Father make me dread many a crisis before diplomatists round a green table cloth will be able to regulate the destinies of Italy in a stable fashion."[6]

So long as the Piedmontese Minister could count upon the support of France, he was not unduly disturbed by the refusal of Rome to yield the Romagna. What he feared most was that Napoleon would once again falter in his resolve. For this reason he panicked when he heard of an Anglo-French agreement to grant Piedmont only Parma, Modena, and the Legations and turn Tuscany into a separate state. Terming this proposal an ultimatum sprinkled over with rose water, he was prepared to run the risk of antagonizing France rather than force the Tuscans to renounce their union with Piedmont. At any rate, he urged General Fanti to push forward his armament of the local population and to be prepared for any eventuality. He also exhorted Farini to increase the pressure for annexation in Central Italy, observing that he could not rely upon diplomacy alone to accomplish his aims.

Actually, Cavour considered acting without French sanction, a dangerous expedient to be employed only as a last resort. In turn, Napoleon did not wish to alienate the Piedmontese, but merely wanted them to understand that they could only absorb Central Italy by paying his price—the cession of Nice and Savoy to France. Benedetti of the Foreign Office, who was sent to Turin, told the Prime Minister that the Emperor wanted this territory, even at the cost of turning the whole of Europe against him. Reluctantly but realistically, on March 12, 1860, before the new Parliament had been elected, Cavour signed a secret agreement promising to turn the two provinces, with a population of some 800,000 to France, in return for Napoleon's support of his annexation of Central Italy with a population of eight million. When the treaty was stipulated and signed Cavour turned to one of the French plenipotentiaries and said, "Now you are definitely tied to us, you have become our accomplices, our cohorts even in folly." Little did his Gallic allies suspect how far the bespectacled and innocent-looking Minister intended to carry this advantage.

The treaty did provide that the transfer of territory would occur only after the popular will had been consulted, so there was provision for plebiscites not only in Central Italy but in Nice and Savoy as well. However, Cavour and Napoleon decided beforehand how these elections were to turn out, and made arrangements to assure that the popular will conformed to their plans. Thus, before the Piedmontese could properly evaluate the treaty, the French moved into Nice and Savoy and arranged for the plebiscite which would sanction the *fait accompli*. Afterwards the Count had to justify his actions before the Chamber and the country, and tried to argue that Nice like Savoy was more French than Italian. His sophistry convinced few, but the prospect of obtaining the whole of Central Italy won over all but the most idealistic. During the same month plebiscites were held in the Central Italian states on the question of consolidation with constitutional Piedmont. No one who knew Cavour was surprised that the results were almost unanimous in favor of union.

Capitalizing upon his success in absorbing Central Italy, on March 25 Cavour called for new parliamentary elections for the enlarged Kingdom of Northern and Central Italy. The results proved gratifying as the Prime Minister saw his supporters elected to the Chamber. He was also assured that the Assembly would now approve the treaty by which he had ceded Nice and Savoy to France. Nonetheless, the victory was at best bittersweet. General Fanti, the Minister of War, warned that the cessions made Turin vulnerable to attack. The King, too, was less than pleased at having to resign himself to the loss of the cradle of his dynasty and favorite hunting ground. Having already sacrificed his daughter to procure the French alliance, he commented stoically, "Since the child has gone, why not the cradle as well?" Garibaldi did not accept the loss of Nice as magnanimously, complaining that Cavour's intrigues had made him a foreigner in the land of his birth. Henceforth he regarded the Minister as a dangerous enemy. Diplomatic complications also arose as the British cabinet expressed alarm at the French acquisition and feared that the emerging state would become a French satellite.

From Rome Cavour expected the pronouncement of the decree of excommunication as soon as the popular vote in the Romagna was made public and formal notification presented of the annexation of the province. While claiming to be faithful to the principle of liberty Cavour wrote to Depretis, then Governor of Brescia, urging him to prevent any person or group from using the excommunication to excite public opinion or to turn people against the government by attacking its King, Ministers, or institutions. In addition, he cautioned Depretis to prevent anyone from giving the expected bull any publicity, calling for immediate action and the arrest of anyone who should attempt to make themselves the champions of disorder.[7]

To awaken the Pope to the fact that the King was personally implicated in the absorption of his territory, the Prime Minister arranged for Vittorio Emanuele to visit Bologna. State visits were also made to Milan and Florence and in both cities Cavour, whose entire existence had become enmeshed in his political career, derived obvious satisfaction from the fact that he was cheered louder than the King. In part, this reception rendered all his activity, all his scheming, all his sacrifices, worthwhile. Unhappily, he was not able to savor this success for long; his satisfaction was punctured by the King who criticized his cession of Nice and Savoy. This verbal attack so outraged the Count that he left the King in Florence and returned to Turin alone. Following this experience, Cavour was visibly dejected, and for days afterward was easily moved to tears.

Despite Vittorio Emanuele's ingratitude, Cavour decided not to resign. For one thing he suspected that this was what the King wanted, so he could appoint his rival, Rattazzi, Prime Minister. Then, too, he concluded that his work was not yet complete, particularly as regards Rome. In the hope of pacifying the Pope and placating public opinion in Catholic Europe, Cavour conceived of sending Federigo Sclopis di Salerano on a mission to Rome. Prior to accepting the task, Sclopis met with Cavour and expressed his misgivings about the annexation of the Romagna and listed all the difficulties which, in his opinion, rendered a rapprochement with Rome impossible. Cavour, for his part, did not conceal his conviction that the proposed talks would do little to reconcile the Pope to the loss of his province. Still he wanted the discussions, to secure further proof of the lack of conciliation to be found at the Court of Rome. Publication of Pio Nono's bull of excommunication on March 29, 1860, while a liability with the Catholic population of his state, could be used to advantage by Cavour to bolster his case against Rome among the anticlerical and Protestant powers.

Napoleon, having made himself Cavour's accomplice in the annexation of the Romagna, seemed determined to preserve the rest of the Papal State. In fact, the Duke de Gramont urged de Martino, the Neapolitan envoy in Rome, to have Neapolitan troops occupy part of the States of the Church, up to Ancona, assuring him that the French would guarantee these troops against any Piedmontese aggression.[8] Fortunately, the Neapolitans did not accept the offer, both because they distrusted the French Emperor and because early in April, 1860, an insurrection erupted in Sicily, which turned their attention to that troubled island.

When news was heard of the Sicilian disturbances, Francesco Crispi called upon Garibaldi in Turin to lead an expedition to liberate Sicily, begging Vittorio Emanuele to entrust the general with a brigade of the Piedmontese army for the venture. The King, following consultations with Cavour, felt constrained to refuse publicly not only material support but also to withhold any moral approval. Their position reflected the Prime Minister's fear of Mazzini's involvement and his concern that Garibaldi antagonize Napoleonic France or Catholic Austria and thus disrupt his own plans in Central Italy. For these reasons Cavour sought to discourage the expedition, but not to the point of preventing the enlistment of volunteers and the collection of guns and ammunition.

On May 6, Cavour's government permitted Garibaldi and his "thousand" volunteers to embark from Quarto near Genoa, carrying 1,000 muskets from the government depot, and did little to hinder his arrival in Sicily five days later. The Count ordered Admiral Persano to cruise in the water surrounding Sardinia and to stop Garibaldi's two vessels only if they entered some port. He was not to interfere with them if he happened to encounter the Garibaldini on the high seas. Fearing that this campaign might destroy the tenuous understanding he had with the French, Cavour hastened to explain his position to Napoleon. Knowing the latter's desire that the territories promised him be legally transferred, Cavour shrewdly suggested that he could ill afford to alienate public opinion if he were to get the treaty ceding Nice and Savoy passed in Parliament. He let it be known that if he had allowed the Garibaldi expedition to leave for Sicily, he did so because the alternative of keeping him back was dangerous and might well mean the loss of public and parliamentary support.[9]

Whatever his motivation, reports reached Rome and Naples which tended to implicate the Sardinian government in the project, providing ample proof that Garibaldi had received arms and other aid from the Piedmontese. When Cavour heard the news that Garibaldi had landed safely in Sicily, he cried out,

"There is no point in hesitating, it is necessary to help him."[10] Having made that decision, he allowed some four thousand men to be collected for the guerrilla chieftain, and these were armed and supported by Cavour's government working in conjunction with the National Society. The Count had chosen wisely, for by mid-May the General had proclaimed himself dictator of the island while his victory at Calatafimi paved the way to Palermo. The next day, May 16, Cavour revealed his attitude toward these developments:

> Garibaldi has landed in Sicily. It is very lucky that he did not execute his intention of attacking the Pope. We cannot stop him from making war on the King of Naples. It may be a good or a bad thing, but it was inevitable. Had we tried to restrain Garibaldi by force he would have been most dangerous within the country. What will happen now? It is impossible to predict. Will England help him? It is possible. Will France hinder him? I do not think so. And we? We cannot support him openly, neither can we restrain individual efforts on his behalf.
>
> We have therefore decided not to allow new expeditions to leave from the ports of Genoa and Leghorn, but not to prevent the sending of arms and munitions so long as this is done with some discretion. I am aware of the inconvenience of the ill defined line we are following, but I do not know how to define another line with less grave and dangerous inconveniences.[11]

On June 27, 1860, Francesco II, who had most to fear from the general, belatedly sent a mission to Turin to negotiate a treaty of alliance. Although Cavour received the Neapolitans graciously, he did not favor the proposed customs union and commercial league nor did he accept the conditions of the mission's memorandum, which called upon the Piedmontese to cease their expeditions to Sicily. "Today a unitary Italy is possible," he explained to friends, "tomorrow it may no longer be so." In August, 1860, when all of Sicily was in Garibaldi's hands and it appeared that neither the English nor the French would prevent the guerrillas from crossing the straits to the mainland, Cavour explicitly acknowledged the role of his Ministry in the affair. He admitted that without his treaty of cession of Nice and Savoy, the expedition would have been impossible and Garibaldi would have remained on the island of Caprera instead of completing the work assigned to him by providence for Italy. Without the help of the Piedmontese government, Cavour continued, Garibaldi would not have left Genoa, the ships that brought him medicine and supplies would never have reached him, and the venture would have been doomed to failure as had so many others.

On the other hand, Cavour did not underestimate or denigrate the contribution of Garibaldi; he rejected Nigra's suggestion that he openly oppose the general. He even recognized that it had been for the best that Garibaldi had refused his requests for the immediate annexation of Sicily to Piedmont. In this manner the Turin cabinet could continue to gamble upon great gains if Garibaldi were successful on the mainland while subject neither to the pressure of foreign diplomacy nor by the prospects of failure. At the end of August, 1860, the Minister wrote Garibaldi hoping to reestablish the trust that had earlier existed between them, but to no avail. Not having convinced the general, Cavour then pressed Depretis for a plebiscite approving the annexation of Sicily.[12]

Cavour's greatest concern was that Garibaldi would continue to march northward attacking the Papal States next, thus provoking the intervention of France. To prevent such an eventuality and protect Sardinia's interests in the South, Cavour sent Giuseppe Finzi and Emilio Visconti Venosta to Naples, where some days before Admiral Persano had arrived with a warship. The latest scheme concocted by the Count called for a revolution in Naples or the deposition of Francesco by the Neapolitan army which would remain intact and serve as a barrier to the advancing Garibaldi. Unfortunately the state seemed to crumble like cardboard, removing one of the last buffers between Garibaldi and Pio Nono, who was protected by the French.

Garibaldi's rapid march toward Naples and his well-known determination to proclaim Vittorio Emanuele King of Italy in Rome pushed Cavour to take steps to avert a confrontation between the guerrillas and the French forces. "If we are not at La Cattolica before Garibaldi we will be lost—the revolution will overcome the whole of Italy," he told Napoleon's representatives at Turin. "We are forced act." Having heard of Cavour's need to stop Garibaldi from spreading his revolution throughout Italy and to avoid a possible clash of French and Italian arms, the Emperor gave him a qualified assent to occupy the Marches and Umbria. "If Piedmont," he observed, "thinks this move absolutely necessary to save herself from the abyss be it so; but it must be taken at her own risk and peril."[13] Cavour's conduct was such that Napoleon did not know whether to blame him or be grateful to him.

The Count saw no other alternative following the flight of

Francesco from Naples on September 6 and the entry of Garibaldi the following day. On that same September 7, Cavour issued an ultimatum to the papal government, calling upon it to dissolve its mercenary corps immediately. When on September 11, he received Antonelli's rejection, he issued orders to the army to cross the frontier. The situation was critical, for the French Foreign Minister warned Cavour that if the assurances that his government had given to Cardinal Antonelli—that the Sardinian army would not attack the pontifical troops—were not honored, the French would break relations with the Turin government. Likewise the Emperor warned Vittorio Emanuele that if his troops violated the papal frontier, the French government would have to oppose this aggression.[14] For this reason Cavour regarded the mission as more political than military and called upon his commanders to conduct themselves so that their actions could be justified before the tribunal of public opinion. Above all, Cavour cautioned the military to avoid any collision with the French force protecting Rome and Lazio. Although the Emperor had once again pledged his support to the Pope, Cavour informed General Fanti that if the Piedmontese scrupulously avoided French-held positions, the French would not place any obstacles in their way.

Once again the Count proved correct in his assessment, for once his soldiers had observed the limits he placed upon them, though Napoleon withdrew his ambassador from Turin, he did little else to protect the bulk of the Pope's territory from them. Scandalized by this development, on September 28 Pio Nono issued a protest against the "unjust, hostile, and horrendous" occupation of the Papal States by the Piedmontese King and his government. The Holy Father raised his voice against this spoliation and condemned all the "nefarious and sacrilegious" actions of said monarch and his government, declaring all their actions absolutely null and void. Despite his condemnation, a new Italy was being formed as if under a spell.

The Piedmontese movement southward which appalled the Pope, did not discourage Garibaldi who still spoke of marching to Rome. Indeed, he wrote to Vittorio Emanuele and invited him to dissolve the ministry, push out Cavour, and proclaim himself King of Italy on the *Campidoglio*. The King replied by assuming personal command of the Piedmontese troops in the papal provinces, thus blocking Garibaldi's passage north.

It was clear to the diplomatic community that a wide chasm separated the Machiavellian minister from the Liberator of the

South. "Garibaldi declares that he wishes to complete his work of conquest and to form a new Kingdom with Victor Emmanuel at its head while the Government of Sardinia evidently wishes to have the states annexed to Sardinia as they are conquered and then to deliberate upon the formation of a new Kingdom," wrote Joseph Chandler, the United States Minister to the Kingdom of the Two Sicilies, "and behind all awaiting their opportunity are the friends of a [sic] 'Italian Republic,' " he warned. "They are too well known to be overlooked and too powerful to be neglected, so that it seems probable that before the work of liberating Italy can be accomplished, she will again be made the scene of wild uproar and bloodshed by foreign intervention."[15]

This was averted by Cavour who achieved two successes: first he secured sanction from Parliament authorizing his government to accept the annexation of the lands they occupied, provided that the people of these regions indicated that such was their will by plebiscite. Secondly, he persuaded Garibaldi not to heed Mazzini's suggestion to call an assembly to discuss a constitution for the new Italy. Finally in mid-October, 1860, Garibaldi agreed to a plebiscite in the former Bourbon kingdom at the end of the month, at which time both Naples and Sicily voted overwhelmingly for inclusion in the new state.

Although Cavour did not approve of Garibaldi's request that he be appointed the King's lieutenant in the South for a year, he was otherwise prepared to show himself magnanimous to the redshirts. For this reason he disagreed with General Manfredo Fanti who wanted to send all the volunteers home with a simple thank-you, preferring to resign rather than be responsible for such an act of ingratitude. He could not show himself ungrateful to the man who conquered a kingdom of nine million people for Italy. Nonetheless, the promises were better than the performance of the government, and in November Garibaldi left Naples for his home on the island of Caprera, refusing all offers of rewards, titles, and money. The Count could now mold the state that Garibaldi had helped to create.

CHAPTER XI

So Many Problems, So Little Time

CAVOUR HAD PROMISED HIS ASSOCIATES AND COUNTRYMEN THAT HE did not intend to impose a preconceived political system upon Southern Italy, but would allow its people to shape their own future. This was easier said than done. Some of his advisers who did not understand the mentality of the people of this region complained that it was not Italy but Africa, and that civil virtue was almost unknown. Even the Prime Minister, who had made a number of studies of English political and economic institutions and was acquainted with the political, philosophical, and literary achievements of the French, had never understood Rome, let alone Naples or Palermo. The South was for him and most of his associates a virtual *terra incognita*. Small wonder that he was susceptible to the stories and exaggerated accounts transmitted to him by the score of all-too-partial, self-appointed, southern spokesmen.

Alarmed by the reports of dangerous disorders and social chaos, the perplexed Cavour found that the only solution available was to impose Piedmontese codes and procedures as quickly as possible, taking a firm stand against recalcitrants. Thus General Cialdini, commanding the Piedmontese troops in the Abruzzi, issued orders to shoot all peasants carrying arms, disregarding the fact that many needed these firearms for hunting. The volatile Sicilians were carefully watched and not accorded any degree of autonomy, even thought this had been their greatest complaint while part of the Kingdom of the Two Sicilies. Knowing practically nothing about Sicilian life and law, Cavour assumed that the island would best be served by a strict subordination to the North. When southerners resisted this centralization, the determined Minister called for greater firmness on the part of the authorities, initiating a repression which was to last for a decade.

From Paris Emperor Napoleon advised Cavour that it would be impossible to consolidate Italy by parliamentary means, and from Tuscany Ricasoli saw the need for a temporary dictatorship exercised by Vittorio Emanuele. Prepared to take drastic action to bring the South to submission, Cavour shied from the suggestion of even a temporary dictatorship, observing that if this were desired, Garibaldi rather than he was best suited to implement it. Having no confidence in dictatorships, especially those of a civil variety, he stressed that with a parliament it was possible to accomplish things that were impossible to absolute power—a lesson that Depretis and Giolitti were later to learn. Nonetheless, the Count was not one to let constitutional niceties block his plans. Important matters were often decided by decree while parliament was on vacation. Nor did he hesitate to use official pressure to determine the outcome of an election and on at least one occasion his assumption of the Ministry of the Interior was directly related to his desire to organize the elections.

Realizing that parliamentary rule, like other human institutions, possessed flaws, Cavour was not prone to reform those weaknesses that worked to his advantage. Thus he did not remedy the fact that a large number of deputies, perhaps as many as one-third, were in one way or another dependent upon the government and therefore sensitive to its demands. A restricted suffrage which favored those with wealth and education produced the bourgeois, anticlerical majority which supported the Count, if it did not truly represent the will of the people. Despite these flaws, and in part because of them, Cavour considered the parliamentary system superior to other forms of government, and more important, best suited to his own temperament. A convenient instrument to publicize his plans and earn the goodwill of liberal Europe, the parliamentary regime also provided Cavour with the moral means of offsetting the influence of the King, who was far from friendly to him.

Vittorio Emanuele and Cavour had never been on cordial terms and were often at odds due to differences in political and personal values. Blunt in conversation and boorish in some of his ways, the King stood in sharp contrast to the man who served him, whose words were measured and whose manners were refined. No less socially conservative than the King, the Count favored audacious means to achieve his ends and was prepared to sacrifice those institutions and traditions he considered peripheral in order to preserve the rest. Vittorio Emanuele, frightened by the religious and political implications of his Minister's policies, sought to restrain his extreme measures—especially those directed against the Church. Thus the two had clashed over ecclesiastical policy in the 1850s and the King had acquiesced only because he proved unable to find an alternative to the Cavour cabinet.

Vittorio Emanuele resented his Minister's practice of acting first and seeking royal approval later, a procedure which seriously curtailed his initiative and compromised his influence. Determined to preserve his independence, he resented the Count's arrogant approach and attempts to subjugate all to his opinion. Cavour, with his upper-class prejudices and self-confidence, did not hesitate to intervene even in the private affairs of the King by attempting to discredit his favorite mistress, Rosina. The attempt proved abortive and only served to embitter Vittorio Emanuele. His anger against his Minister increased when the latter berated him for accepting the humiliating terms of Villafranca and deserted him at this crucial juncture. Vittorio Emanuele swore he would never forget this treatment and remained true to his promise.[1]

In January, 1860, the King reinstated Cavour, but had not forgiven him. In April, when he arrived in Florence, largely due to the work of the Count, rather than addressing a single word of thanks to him, he launched into a vicious verbal barrage. Cavour confided that had anyone else but his monarch uttered such words, abused him in such manner, a duel would have inevitably ensued. Respecting the principle of monarchy, which he regarded as a symbol of national unity and a safeguard of the social order, Cavour disliked the person occupying the post and wished to keep as far away from him as possible.

No less an obstacle to Cavour's political program was the Pope and his astute Secretary of State. Throughout 1860 the papal government continuously protested the aggression and usurpations of the Piedmontese and appealed to the Catholic powers for assistance. Antonelli addressed a series of circular letters to the European states accusing Cavour's government of violating all law, all sovereign rights without a shadow of remorse. Denouncing Cavour's use of plebiscites as simply another sly maneuver, the Secretary of State asserted that they could not destroy legitimate rights nor justify Turin's illegal actions.[2] Rome was further antagonized by Cavour's declaration of October 11, 1860, in which he termed the establishment of Rome as capital of the Italian kingdom a pressing national concern.

Cavour, however, did realize that force alone could not produce a solution to the Roman Question and favored negotiation to solve what he acknowledged to be the greatest difficulty facing the new state. As early as 1860 he had announced that the only thing that a government such as his could offer the Papacy was a superabundance of freedom: the Church would be accorded complete liberty in the new state. However it was not he but the liberal Catholic Diomede Pantaleoni who coined the phrase, "a free Church in a free state," which was later adopted and popularized by the Count.

In mid-December, 1860, Pantaleoni's memorandum for the solution of the Roman Question was sent to Paris for approval. It proposed to offer the Church full freedom from governmental control in return for its renunciation of the temporal power. Since Napoleon posed no objections, Cavour prepared to open negotiations with Rome on this basis. Both Paris and Turin recognized that the issues involved were delicate and a successful solution required time and patience. Even the Prime Minister's political opponents admitted that he alone had the energy and cunning to deal with the problem, and expressed concern at the end of 1860 when he fell ill. His recovery was rapid if incomplete and served to conceal from many the obvious fact that the Count was abusing his strong constitution. He moved restively, relentlessly forward.

Born to be a conservative, he had moved to the liberal camp in his youth and had recently emerged as a nationalist. The completion of Italian unity was now his top priority, in part because of his patriotism, but even more so because of his realization that if unity were not completed the agitation of the subversive left would not cease. On this issue the King concurred, convinced by his Minister that stability would not be assured until the new state solved the questions of Rome and Venice.

As regards the first and more difficult of the two problems, Cavour believed that the thought of the times worked in favor of his program of the separation of Church and state. Admitting that political figures and the Pope could delay its acceptance, he remained certain that within the next century the principle would triumph everywhere. There would doubtless be difficulties in persuading the Pontiff, but he found this approach the only one likely to succeed. "All transactions based on purely temporal interests are impossible," the Count prophesied early in January, 1861, "because the Holy Father knows that if he surrenders a bit of terrain he will destroy the principle of inalienability which is the sole moral force he possesses." [3] For this reason, among others, Cavour championed a more comprehensive solution.

Pragmatic to the core, Cavour was disposed to sacrifice even his separatism if by so doing he could go to Rome in accord with the Pope. Unfortunately, he had never been serious in his prior attempts to reach an agreement with the Holy See, and the Vatican had a long memory. Nonetheless, in January he was secretly informed that the Holy See was prepared to negotiate. According to his sources at least six cardinals had sanctioned his program while the Pontiff remained undecided—one day he was prepared to accept the terms, the next he flatly rejected them. Unwilling himself to treat with the usurpers, Pius did permit unofficial talks between Cardinal Santucci, who favored an accommodation with Turin, on the one hand, and Father Passaglia and Diomede Pantaleoni, on the other. From the first Pius had misgivings about these meetings.

Despite his skepticism, Cavour had other reasons to be elated. One by one the last remnants of organized Bourbon resistance to Piedmont had fallen and the stability of the state seemed less precarious. Contending that the Chamber elected in March, 1860, was no longer representative due to the enormous extension of territory, it was dissolved. Elections were held at the end of January, 1861, and on February 18, 1861, the King opened the new Chamber which included representatives from Umbria and the Marches as well as the southern provinces. Although this was in fact the first Chamber of united Italy, it was cataloged as the eighth since the granting of the *Statuto* which in modified form became the constitution of the new state. Furthermore, Vittorio Emanuele, who was shortly to be proclaimed the first King of Italy, agreed with Cavour that he should continue to be called Vittorio Emanuele the Second rather than the First. Cavour believed that to do otherwise would impugn the honor of the dynasty and undermine the basis of law and order—developments which he wished to avoid at all costs. He also fought for the use of the term King of Italy instead of King of the Italians as some suggested. The first title he considered the consecration of an immensely important fact—that Italy had finally been constructed. He was to have his way again.

On March 17, 1861, by a unanimous vote the Italian Parliament proclaimed Vittorio Emanuele II, by the grace of God and the will of the nation, King of Italy. He was recognized as such by the British in the same month, followed by Switzerland, Greece, the United States, and Mexico in April. Paris, Vienna, and of course Rome withheld recognition. Alessandro Manzoni, who had traveled from Milan to Turin to witness his prophecy materialize, was warmly received by the Minister. As the two left the Palazzo Madama where Vittorio Emanuele had just been proclaimed King of Italy, the crowd in the *piazza* below broke into applause. "The ovation is for you," Cavour told the startled author, who moved to the side and began to applaud the Minister, provoking the crowd to intensify its applause. "You see, my good Count," Manzoni replied, "whom the crowd applauds."

In Rome there was cause to complain rather than celebrate. The Pope responded in a consistorial allocution the next day in which he proclaimed that civil society was witnessing a war between truth and error. Those who presented themselves as the champions of the new civilization, Pius declared, were prepared to favor any non-Catholic cult, while they struck out against the religious as well as the secular clergy, depriving them of their just possessions. He claimed that the proponents of this "liberal" civilization sought not only to destroy the Pope's temporal power but to weaken if not destroy the spiritual life of the Church. For this reason the Holy See could not negotiate with Cavour's cabinet so long as it continued to occupy the papal provinces and export its anticlerical legislation to the rest of the peninsula.[4] The next day Father Passaglia reported to Cavour that Antonelli had told him the Pope wanted Pantaleoni to leave Rome.

This apparent rebuff did not deter Cavour who sought to convince Pius both of the wisdom and inevitability of his solution to the Roman Question. At the end of March, 1861, the Prime Minister persuaded Parliament to proclaim Rome the capital of the kindom, even though it remained under papal control with the support of French forces. In his famous speech of March 27, 1861, Cavour coupled the Roman Question with the problem of relations between Church and state, and in particular with the program which accorded the Church complete liberty. He deemed it not only prudent to proclaim Rome capital, but the best means of arriving at an accommodation with the Church.

Holy Father, the temporal power is no longer a guarantee of independence for you. Renounce it, and we will provide you with that freedom you have sought in vain for three centuries from all the great Catholic powers: you have sought to secure a part of this freedom by means of concordats for which you, Holy Father, have been constrained to concede privileges and compensations. Even worse, you have been compelled to surrender your spiritual arms to those temporal powers which granted you some small degree of liberty. That which you have never been able to obtain from those powers which boasted that they were your allies and devoted children, we now offer to you in full measure. We are ready to proclaim throughout Italy this great principle: a free Church in a free state.[5]

Cavour, who found it expedient to champion the cause of liberty in the political and economic area, considered it only natural that the same principle be extended to the relations between Church and state. He realized that his plan would provoke some objections and present some difficulties, but interestingly enough he considered only those he would have to confront. Specifically, he feared the resistance of the magistrates, public opinion, and local traditions, especially in Turin, Naples, and Sicily. Recognizing that his policy would necessarily involve some far-reaching changes, he did not feel that it justified the apprehensions it aroused in the schools, Parliament, and even in the intellectual community. At any rate, he found no other feasible alternative, claiming that only on the basis of a free Church in a free state could the kingdom regularize its relations with Rome. Allowing his optimism free reign, he predicted that once the centuries-old antagonism between the Church's temporal power and the national spirit ended, the Pope and even the Curia would fall under the influence of the liberal principles prevailing in the peninsula.

The Holy Father, however, did not share his vision. He was totally alienated as Piedmont's ecclesiastical legislation was progressively applied throughout the peninsula—including the former papal provinces. On April 5, Antonelli explained to the Piedmontese negotiator Father Passaglia that when the Pope considered the anticlerical legislation of the Turin government, the irreligious spirit manifested there, and the license granted to the Protestants, he did not believe that Piedmont really wished to negotiate. Antonelli did not accept Passaglia's assurances that the Piedmontese sincerely sought conciliation, observing that more than words were needed to win the trust of the Holy Father —facts and actions were necessary. For one thing there had to be an end to the hostility and bitterness directed against the Church. Even then, however, the Pope could negotiate only religious matters in the hereditary states of the King of Sardinia —he could not retreat on the subject of his temporal power and was resolutely determined to endure all sacrifices to maintain this principle. The Pope's temporal power was not a social or national question, Antonelli explained, but an international and Catholic one which could be determined only by the decision of all the Catholic powers.[6]

A short while after this discussion there emanated from the Eternal City a formal protest to the proclamation of the Kingdom of Italy; the Pope expressed shock at the manner in which a Catholic King brushed aside all religious scruples and trampled upon all justice in despoiling the august head of the Catholic Church of the greater part of his legitimate possessions. The Holy Father, the protest continued, could never recognize the title of King of Italy which the King of Sardinia had assumed. This theme was repeated in the *Civiltà Cattolica* which denied the allegations that the Pope was an enemy of the Italian people, insisting that he opposed the cupidity of the Piedmontese who wanted to bring the entire peninsula under their control.[7]

The Pontiff was not the only outstanding Italian figure to resist Cavour's solution to the Italian problem. No less a figure than Massimo D'Azeglio, whose government had commenced the campaign against the Church, was not prepared to carry it to Cavour's conclusion. In his *Questioni Urgenti* (Urgent Questions), he came out against making Rome the capital of the kingdom and proposed Florence as an alternative.

A more serious and fundamental opposition was that of Giuseppe Mazzini, the soul of unification, who remained unreconciled to the entire structure created by Cavour. He refused to consider Vittorio Emanuele as the "Gentleman King" D'Azeglio claimed him to be, commenting that his acceptance of Lombardy as a gift from foreign hands and that his bartering away Nice and Savoy and above all his retention of Cavour rendered him suspect. The monarchical state which had emerged from the Count's unification contained too many features that were contrary to Mazzini's vision of a regenerated Italian people. He believed that revolution had to be made by the people and for the people. "You did not unite with the people of Italy, nor did you call them to join you," he reproached Vittorio Emanuele in an open letter. "Seduced by the sorry politics of a minister who preferred the arts of Ludovico Il Moro to the role of regenerator, you refused the arms of our people and, needlessly, in an ill starred moment called in the arms of a foreign despot to help in the enterprise of liberation."[8] Thus Mazzini, the high priest of Italian regeneration, preferred to remain a pariah rather than accept the structure erected by Cavour.

Garibaldi, too, was less than pleased with the work of the Prime Minister. Following his return to Caprera, he refused to become a candidate in the general elections for the first Italian Parliament. When he perceived that his followers were being shabbily treated, he held the Prime Minister responsible and suddenly decided to have his name submitted for a by-election in March, 1861. Toward the end of April, when the general arrived in Turin to represent the Neapolitans in Parliament, word soon spread that he planned to denounce the Prime Minister both for his cession of Nice and Savoy as well as for the poor treatment accorded his redshirts by the army. Sporting his red shirt, which made him a spectacular sight among the formally attired members of the Chamber, Garibaldi accused Cavour of having provoked a fratricidal war.

This accusation produced a commotion in the Chamber and the President of the Council, visibly upset, walked away. Order was only restored by the suspension of the session for a quarter of an hour. Cavour, who had tried to moderate the opposition of the Minister of War, Fanti, to the Garibaldians, was deeply hurt by the patriot's blistering attack upon him, but he did not reveal any bitterness in his response:

I know . . . that between me and the honorable General Garibaldi there exists a fact which divides us like an abyss. I believed that I fulfilled a painful duty—the most painful duty I ever accomplished in my life—in counselling the King and proposing to Parliament to approve the cession of Savoy and Nice to France. By the grief that I then experienced I can understand that which the honorable General Garibaldi must have felt, and if he cannot forgive me this I will not bear him any grudge for it.[9]

The Chamber, which included many men who had voted with Cavour for the cession, naturally took his side against Garibaldi. Nonetheless, the Count was very disturbed by the entire affair and complained that he never felt well again after Garibaldi's attack. Vittorio Emanuele was also disturbed by the rift between the two makers of modern Italy and arranged a meeting in the hope of effecting a reconciliation. Reluctantly Garibaldi complied with the monarch's request, but he refused to shake Cavour's hand or be reconciled with the Count until such time as a program of armament were undertaken and justice be accorded the Army of the South. Actually, much more separated the two men, for Garibaldi suspected that Cavour wanted to establish a constitutional government molded upon that of Napoleon III, which would rely upon the army to protect itself against its own people, while Garibaldi wanted a constitutional government patterned upon that of Queen Victoria, where the army would be used to fight foreigners, not its own citizens.

In part, Garibaldi's criticism was unfair, because it did not take into account that Italy was a new state in the process of formation and did not enjoy the serenity and tranquility to provide for far-reaching social changes. Besides, any attempt to seriously alter the social structure or promote a popular revolution would have aroused the Minister's liberal-noble and bourgeois allies, encouraging them to make common cause with the clerical-conservative opposition, and very possibly would have provoked foreign intervention. Nonetheless, Cavour recognized the importance of social questions such as the relations between capital and labor. He much admired the manner in which the English aristocracy of birth and wealth managed to preserve its influence by working for the amelioration of the lower classes and recognized that eventually the upper classes in Italy would have to follow in their footsteps. "If I were not a Minister I would engross myself in this study, because it is the great problem of the future," he confided to Massari. "It will emerge in Italy also, but our successors will have to deal with it: we can only think about the national question."[10] In point of fact, Cavour had already assumed too many burdens upon his shoulders.

Cavour generally enjoyed excellent health and after 1847 had rarely been sick. He did from time to time suffer from intestinal troubles which brought fever in their wake and once in office had to combat physical exhaustion. In 1852 he had a bad intestinal attack and his physician urged him to relax in the mountains for some twenty days. Following this prescription, Cavour returned to Turin rested and well. Suspicious of medical science, he nevertheless believed that the body had recuperative powers and his own recovery provided him with proof positive. Once home he resumed his hectic pace and forgot the doctor's warning that he needed an occasional respite and should not work after dinner.

Taxing his health, Cavour maintained a rigid work schedule, constantly thinking of the many problems confronting the new state. To compensate for the precious hours he lost while asleep, he eventually gave up going to the theater—one of his few recreations. Lacking a happy home life, the Count found absolutely no diversion from his work. So preoccupied was he with affairs of state that in his last months he was plagued with insomnia, caused by the pressing problems faced by his government and from which he could not find escape or relief, even though he recognized his desperate need for some sleep. "I rise from my bed, and walk about the room," he confided, "but everything is useless; I am no longer the director of my own thoughts."[11] He was overburdened and tired and thus was forced to place the Ministry of Finance in other hands. Since he realizd that his services were essential, he continued his other work, hoping he could get away to Switzerland in the summer.

The evening of May 29, 1861, Cavour, who that very day had been questioned and had spoken in the Chamber, felt feverish. He thought little of it, until that night when pacing in his room, he collapsed. He then ordered his servant Tosco to call Dr. Rossi, who on the thirtieth ordered bleeding. Within the next four days Cavour was bled five times and as before seemed to respond to this treatment. On May 31, the third day of his illness, he summoned Count Nigra to his bedside in order to continue his direction of affairs. The conversation had proceeded barely half an hour when Nigra perceived that Cavour was having difficulty in speaking. In order not to tire the ailing Minister, Nigra indicated he understood what he wanted, urging him to rest. "Yes, I feel very weary," Cavour replied. "I need a long rest, but I have two things yet to do, Venice and Rome. It will be you others who will do the remainder."[12]

Cavour's fever did not subside and other physicians were consulted; they advised such solutions as mustard plasters and ice packs. A consortium of doctors concluded that the fever was pernicious. The chief characteristic of the illness was delirium, and the Count uttered confused phrases, as one talking in tongues. He would begin by asserting that it was necessary that the King know, and then would jump to some other topic. When Vittorio Emanuele went to see the Minister who had served him so well, Cavour called upon him to take steps to assist the Neapolitans and warned that they all had to be washed. Frightened by his erratic behavior, his niece, the Countess Alfieri, decided to call Fra Giacomo of the Parish of Santa Maria degli Angeli, who heard his confession.

Once Brother Giacomo had left, Cavour called Farini. "My niece had me call Father Giacomo. I must prepare myself for that great passage into eternity; I have said confession and received absolution, later I shall receive communion," he told Farini. "I want it to be known. I want the good people of Turin to know, that I die like a good Christian. I am tranquil, I have never done any harm to anyone."[13] Brother Giacomo administered extreme unction at 5 o'clock the morning of June 6. Recognizing the brother, Cavour pressed his hand and muttered,

"Friar, friar, a free Church in a free state!" Shortly afterwards at 6:45 Cavour passed away. The fact that he died a Catholic created a profound impression—precisely as the Count had sought. The sight of his dead body with the crucifix in his hand seemed to suggest that he had ended the conflict with the Church on his terms. Even in death his iron will was seen to prevail.

As soon as the news of Cavour's death was learned in the capital, the city fell into general mourning, of a genuine and not affected nature. Sclopis, who had never been a supporter of the Count and opposed his policy toward the Church, commented that he had never seen such a display of public sorrow in Turin. Elsewhere in the peninsula the loss was not felt to be as great. Nonetheless, in cities such as Milan shops closed in order to express their sympathy. In papal Rome almost all the theaters were closed for three days, the main thoroughfares were little frequented, and a subscription was circulated for a monument to the courageous Minister.

Upon receiving the news Pio Nono cried out that he was not one of the worst enemies of the Church; these would come after him. Despite the heartaches the Count had caused him, the Pope celebrated a funeral mass for his fallen rival. Rome apparently realized that if Cavour had adopted an antiecclesiastical policy, this was more out of convenience than conviction, a tactic he found necessary in order to maintain the *connubio* pact and preserve his influence with the left. Principle did not prevent the Count from bowing to clerical pressure at the expense of the Protestants, when he thought it prudent for his political policies.[14] The acts of Count Cavour, even upon the eve of his death, gave place to the most passionate controversies, commented *L'Osservatore Romano,* concerned about the fate of Italy following his death.

Neither the passage of time nor the availability of new sources have seriously diminished the stature of the Count, or tarnished the luster of his accomplishments. Without the political support provided by a powerful army, this representative of a relatively minor European state used diplomacy to achieve his national objectives while bridling the revolutionaries and thwarting the pressure of Bonapartism. The fact that the religious and political changes he wrought far outweighed the social and economic ones was conditioned in part by the times, and in part by Cavour's own preferences and priorities. He wished to make Italy without throwing it into social conflict or political turmoil—and succeeded. To have accomplished this with Piedmont's limited resources was a task of no small proportion. Even the Austrians were shocked, for they had always supposed that Piedmont's stomach was not large enough to absorb the whole peninsula. What Spain, France, and the Habsburgs had failed to do in their prime, Cavour enabled Piedmont to do. The world watched the spectacle of a small state, under his guidance, envision, attempt, and complete an enterprise that would have been arduous and dangerous even for one of the great powers.

Undeniably Cavour was not without fault and proved himself unscrupulous in removing obstacles that blocked his goal. "If we were to do for ourselves what we are doing for Italy," Cavour admitted, "we should be scoundrels." Cavour attempted to balance nationalism abroad with liberalism at home, but despite the best of intentions, nationalism increasingly took precedence after the Congress of Paris. As the Count's foreign policy reached a critical juncture all of the powers of the state were concentrated in his hands along with most of the cabinet posts. To the disgust of the Catholic "party" as well as the Mazzinians, the Chamber became submissive to the will of Cavour, which became law, and followed the Prime Minister as its master rather than as its leader.

For all his achievements and real services to the *patria*, Cavour also contributed to what was unhealthy in liberal Italy. His antagonism to the Church, his manipulation of the parliamentary system, his willingness to turn to the right or left as the situation warranted, his treatment of a wide range of opponents not as worthy political rivals but as subversives who had to be suppressed, found reflection not only in the subsequent governments of the right but of the left as well. Furthermore, his success was not complete. He was unable to incorporate Venetia and Rome; he burdened the new state with a religious conflict that was to remain an open wound for half a century, failed to respond to the sectional differences in a satisfactory manner, and produced Italy without the participation of the masses who remained excluded and extraneous to his work of art. He made Italy but left to his successors the equally difficult task of making an Italian people.

In the feverish excitement of nation-building or the "aggrandizement of Piedmont," a phrase used both by the Church and Cavour, social and economic questions were increasingly neglected. Parliamentary opposition was either absorbed or discredited and overwhelming votes of confidence were given for fear of endangering the national enterprise. Despite his domination of Parliament, which his critics termed a "moral dictatorship" and which Solaro della Margarita claimed rendered the Prime Minister more absolute than the King had ever been, Cavour made the Parliament a partner in the process of unification. The Chamber played a crucial role in legitimizing the fruits of his diplomacy and converting Metternich's "geographical expression" into a modern nation state. In the process the prestige of Parliament was enhanced and its future position strengthened. Thus Cavour's achievement was twofold: he not only united Italy but did much to assure that it would remain constitutional and parliamentary.

Cavour would have undoubtedly done more but his premature fall from the scaffold prevented the architect from molding his new creation. His death deprived the new Italy of its greatest statesman. Not one of the men around him shared his fertile imagination, iron will, elastic conscience, or showed the unusual union of subtlety and vigor, thought and action which enabled the Count to tower above them. If he had lived longer his unrivaled political genius, his unique understanding of Napoleon III, his intimate knowledge of the diplomatic world, and his cunning and *realpolitik* would have rendered the pressing problems of the post-unification years less perilous. "Whatever may be thought of him by those whose policy he has thwarted and whose views he has defeated," wrote Palmerston, "I can only say that Italy both present and future, will regard him as one of its most distinguished patriots who have adorned the history of any country."[15]

Notes and References

INTRODUCTION

1. *New York Times*, June 18, 1861.
2. Émile Ollivier, *Journal, 1861–1869*, ed. Theodore Zedlin and Anne Troisier de Diaz (Paris: Julliard, 1961), p. 195; Giuseppe Massari, *Diario dalle cento voci* (Bologna: Cappelli, 1959), p. 81; *idem., Il Conte di Cavour. Ricordi biografici* (Turin: Tipografia Eredi Botta, 1873), p. 263.
3. Charles de Mazade, *Le Comte de Cavour* (Paris: Plon, 1877), p. 187.
4. Massari, *Diario dalle cento voci*, p. 494.
5. A. William Salomone (ed.), *Italy from the Risorgimento to Fascism* (Garden City: Doubleday and Co., 1970), p. xii.
6. Antonio Gramsci, *Sul Risorgimento*, edited by Elsa Fubini; introduction by Giorgio Candeloro (Rome: Editori Riuniti, 1959), pp. 114–115.
7. S. J. Woolf (ed.), *The Italian Risorgimento* (New York: Barnes and Noble, Inc., 1969), p. 98.

CHAPTER I

1. Rosario Romeo, *Cavour e il suo tempo. 1810–1842* (Bari: Laterza, 1969), pp. 21–23, 44–45, 59, 72, 80–82.
2. *Ibid.*, pp. 86–87.
3. *Ibid.*, p. 183.
4. Camillo di Cavour, *Epistolario*, edited by the National Commission for the Publication of the Papers of Count Cavour (Bologna: Zanichelli, 1962), I, 1–5.
5. Pasquale Villari, "The Youth of Count Cavour," *Studies Historical and Critical*, trans. Linda Villari (Freeport, N.Y.: Books for Libraries Press, n.d.), p. 121.
6. *Lettere edite ed inedite di Camillo Cavour*, ed. Luigi Chiala (Turin: Roux e Favale, 1886), V, xxi; Villari, p. 122.
7. Francesco Ruffini, *La giovinezza del Conte di Cavour* (Turin: Fratelli Bocca, 1912), I, 331.
8. Camillo di Cavour, *Epistolario*, I, 37–38, 64.
9. Romeo, p. 220.

10. Pietro Orsi, *Cavour and the Making of Modern Italy 1810–1861* (New York: G. P. Putnam's Sons, 1914), p. 54.

11. Ruffini, I, 73.

12. Camillo di Cavour, *Epistolario*, I, 74.

13. *Diario inedite con note autobiografiche del Conte di Cavour*, ed. Domenico Berti (Rome: Voghera, 1888), p. xlii; Arturo Carlo Jemolo, "Libera chiesa in libero stato," *Cavour 1861–1961* (Turin: Bottega d'Erasmo, 1962), pp. 60–61.

14. *Diario inedite con note autobiografiche del Conte di Cavour*, pp. 115–19; Ruffini, I, 78–84.

15. Ruffini, I, 95.

CHAPTER II

1. Nelson Gay, "Cavour e l'Incognita. Corrispondenza inedita d'amore," *Nuovia Antologia, anno* LXI (February, 1926), 292–93; William Roscoe Thayer, *The Life and Times of Cavour* (Boston: Houghton Mifflin, 1911), I, 19; Villari, p. 122; Romeo, pp. 268, 271, 275.

2. Gay, p. 294; Ruffini, p. 119.

3. Orsi, p. 57.

4. Gay, p. 294; Massari, *Il Conte di Cavour*, p. 14.

5. Evelyn Martinengo Cesaresco, *Cavour* (London: Macmillan and Co., 1898), p. 16; Villari, p. 123.

6. Francesco Salata, "Da Carlo Alberto a Vittorio Emanuele II," *Rassegna Storica del Risorgimento, anno* XXII (December, 1935), II, 837.

7. *Lettere edite ed inedite di Camillo Cavour*, V, 21.

8. Villari, p. 123.

9. *Posthumous Papers of Jessie White Mario: The Birth of Modern Italy*, edited with an introduction by Duke Litta-Visconti-Arese (New York: Charles Scribner's Sons, 1909), pp. 13–14; *Diario inedite con note autobiografiche del Conte di Cavour*, pp. 11, 86.

10. *Diario inedite con note autobiografiche del Conte di Cavour*, pp. 93–97.

11. Gay, pp. 298–99; *Ricordi di Michelangelo Castelli 1847–1875*, ed. Luigi Chiala (Turin: L. Roux, 1888), p. 10.

12. Gay, p. 309.

13. Romeo, pp. 384–87.

CHAPTER III

1. *Diario inedite con note autobiografiche del Conte di Cavour*, p. 141.

2. *Lettere edite ed inedite di Camillo Cavour*, V, 40.

3. Villari, p. 127.

4. *Diario inedite con note autobiografiche del Conte di Cavour*, pp. 225–27.

5. Ruffini, *La giovinezza del Conte di Cavour*, p. 333.

6. Salata, *Rassegna Storica del Risorgimento, anno* XXII (December 1935), II, 824.

7. Ernesto Rossi and Gian Paolo Nitti (eds.), *Banche, governo e parlamento negli Stati Sardi. Fonti documentarie (1843–1861)* (Turin: Fondazione Luigi Einaudi, 1968), I, xi–xvi, xxxviii–xliii.

8. *Count Cavour and Madame de Circourt: Some Unpublished Correspondence*, ed. Costantino Nigra, trans. Arthur John Butler (London: Cassell and Co., Ltd., 1894), p. 43.

9. *Diario inedite con note autobiografiche del Conte di Cavour*, p. 100.

10. Denis Mack Smith (ed.), *The Making of Italy, 1796–1870* (New York: Harper and Row, 1968), p. 114.

11. N. Remsen Whitehouse, *A Revolutionary Princess, Christina Belgiojoso-Trivulzio: Her Life and Times, 1801–1871* (New York: E. P. Dutton and Co., 1906), pp. 135, 144; Arturo Carlo Jemolo, *Chiesa e stato in Italia negli ultimi cento anni* (Turin: Giulio Einaudi, 1952), pp. 40–41.

12. Giuseppe Pasolini, *Memorie 1815–1876*, ed. Pietro Desiderio Pasolini (Turin: Fratelli Bocca, 1887), p. 57.

13. Great Britain, *British and Foreign State Papers*, XXXVI (1847–48), 1197.

14. *Posthumous Papers of Jessie White Mario*, p. 101.

CHAPTER IV

1. *British and Foreign State Papers*, XXXVI (1847–48), 1228; G. de Bertier de Sauvigny, *Metternich and his Times*, trans. Peter Ryde (London: Darton, Longman and Todd, 1962), p. 191.

2. *Posthumous Papers of Jessie White Mario*, p. 127.

3. *Il Risorgimento*, December 15, 1847.

4. *British and Foreign State Papers*, XXXVI (1847–48), 1228.

5. *Il Risorgimento*, January 13, 14, 22, 1848.

6. Marco Minghetti, *Miei Ricordi* (3rd ed.; Turin: L. Roux, 1888), I, 327.

7. *Il Risorgimento*, February 7, 9, 12, 23, 1848.

8. Villari, p. 137.

9. *Il Risorgimento*, February 3, 4, 1848; March 1, 1848.

10. *Il Risorgimento*, March 23, 1848.

11. Pasolini, *Memorie*, pp. 91–92; Minghetti, *Miei Ricordi*, I, 366.

12. *Ricordi di Michelangelo Castelli 1847–1875*, ed. Luigi Chiala (Turin: L. Roux, 1888), p. 27.

13. Massari, *Il Conte di Cavour*, p. 35.

14. *Posthumous Papers of Jessie White Mario*, p. 176.

15. Orsi, p. 145.

16. *Il Risorgimento*, April 10, 1849.

CHAPTER V

1. *Ricordi di Michelangelo Castelli*, pp. 133, 136.

2. Denis Mack Smith, *Victor Emanuel, Cavour, and the Risorgimento* (London: Oxford University Press, 1971), pp. 38–40.

3. *Il Risorgimento*, July 27, 1848; November 23, 1848.

4. Angelo Brofferio, *Storia del Parlamento subalpino* (Milan: Battezzeti, 1866–70), II, 583.

5. Jemolo, *Chiesa e stato in Italia negli ultimi cento anni*, p. 140.

6. "Pius PP. IX Ai nostri amatissimi sudditi," Gaeta, January 1, 1849, *Archivio di Stato di Roma, Archivio del Ministro del Interno*, 1849. *busta* 2, *fascicolo* 1.

7. *Archivio Segreto del Vaticano, Segreteria di Stato Esteri, Corrispondenza di Gaeta e Portici*, 1848–1850, *Rubrica* 2,*fascicolo* 2, *sottofascicolo* 105; Alfonso Leonetti and Ottavio Pastore, *Chiesa e Risorgimento* (Milan: Edizioni *Avanti!*, 1963), p. 149.

8. *Archivio Segreto del Vaticano, Segreteria di Stato Esteri, Corrispondenza di Gaeta e Portici*, 1848-1850, *Rubrica* 257, *fascicoli* 8–9; *Rubrica* 267, *sottofascicoli* 60–61.

9. *Il Risorgimento*, May 10, 1849; July 23, 1849; November 29, 1849.

10. Manuscript of Depretis describing the program to be pursued by the Left, *Archivio Centrale dello Stato, Archivio Depretis, Serie* I, *busta* 10, *fascicolo* 29.

11. Cavour's Parliamentary Speech of January 24, 1850, *Atti del Parlamento Subalpino*, session of 1850, I, 339.

12. *Atti del Parlamento Subalpino*, seesion of 1850, I, 891.

13. *Legge Siccardi sull' abolizione del foro e delle immunità ecclesiastiche tornate del Parlamento Subalpino* (Turin: Pomba, 1850), pp. 75, 78.

14. *Ibid.*, p. 77.

15. *Lettere edite ed inedite di Camillo Cavour*, I, 430.

16. William Roscoe Thayer, *The Life and Times of Cavour* (Boston: Houghton Mifflin Co., 1911), I, 126.

CHAPTER VI

1. *Il Risorgimento*, October 17, 1850; Giuseppe Leti, *Roma e lo Stato Pontificio dal 1849 al 1870. Note di storia politica* (2nd ed.; Ascoli Piceno: Giuseppe Cesari Editore, 1911), I, 312.

2. *Diplomatic Relations between the United States and the Kingdom of the Two Sicilies*, ed. Howard R. Marraro (Ragusa: S. F. Vanni, 1951), II, 51.

3. *Count Cavour and Madame de Circourt: Some Unpublished Correspondence*, p. 102.

4. *Archivio Centrale dello Stato, Archivio Depretis, busta* 4, *fascicolo* 11, *sottofascicolo* 21; Brofferio, V, 37.

5. *Discorsi parlamentari di Camillo Benso di Cavour*, ed. A. Omodeo and L. Russo (Florence: Ente Nazionale di Cultura, 1932), IV, 507–12.

6. *Ricordi di Michelangelo Castelli,* p. 145; Brofferio, V, 287.

7. *Ricordi di Michelangelo Castelli,* pp. 72–73.

8. Massari, *Il Conte di Cavour,* pp. 77–78; Carpi, p. 21.

9. Massari, *Il Conte di Cavour,* p. 82.

10. R. De Cesare, *Roma e lo stato del Papa dal ritorno di Pio IX al XX Settembre* (Rome: Forzani, 1907), I, 238.

11. *Ricordi di Michelangelo Castelli,* p. 162.

12. Massimo D'Azeglio, *I miei ricordi,* ed. Ferdinando Carlesi (Rome: Edizioni Cremonese, 1965), p. 384.

13. *Nuove lettere inedite del Conte Camillo di Cavour,* ed. Edmondo Mayor (Turin: L. Roux, 1895), p. 78; Pietro Pirri, *La laicizzazione dello stato sardo, 1848–1856* (Rome: Pontifica Università Gregoriana, 1944), p. 93.

14. *Archivio Segreto del Vaticano, Segreteria di Stato Esteri,* 1853, *Rubrica* 242, *fascicolo* 3, *sottofascoli* 19–20; *Nuove lettere inedite del Conte Camillo di Cavour,* p. 235.

15. Giovanni Visconti Venosta, *Memoirs of Youth: Things Seen and Known, 1847–1860,* trans. from the 3rd ed. by William Prall (Boston and New York: Houghton Mifflin Co., 1914), p. 196.

CHAPTER VII

1. *Nuove lettere inedite del Conte Camillo di Cavour,* p. 78.

2. Vittorio Gorresio, *Risorgimento scomunicato* (Florence: Parenti Editore, 1958), p. 41.

3. *Nuove lettere inedite del Conte Camillo di Cavour,* p. 190; Minghetti, *Miei Ricordi,* III, 404; Pirri, pp. 101–105.

4. Mack Smith, *The Making of Italy, 1796–1870,* p. 197.

5. Leone Carpi (ed.), *Il Risorgimento Italiano. Biografie storico-politico d'illustri Italiani contemporanei* (Milan: Antica Casa Editrice, 1886), II, 37.

6. Leti, I, 334; *Nuove lettere inedite del Conte Camillo di Cavour,* p. 224.

7. Pirri, p. 104.

8. *Lettere edite ed inedite di Camillo Cavour,* II, 108–109.

9. *Nuove lettere inedite del Conte Camillo di Cavour,* pp. 267, 289; Gorresio, p. 50.

10. *Nuove lettere inedite del Conte Camillo di Cavour,* p. 241.

11. Domenico Massè, *Cattolici e Risorgimento* (Rome: Edizioni Paoline, 1961), p. 49; Pirri, p. 141.

12. Bianca Montale, "Gustavo di Cavour e l'Armonia," *Rassegna Storica del Risorgimento,* XVI (1954), 456–66; Claude Leetham, *Rosmini: Priest, Philosopher and Patriot* (Baltimore: Helicon Press, Inc., 1957), p. 442; Jemolo, *Chiesa e stato in Italia negli ultimi cento anni,* pp. 92–95.

13. Princess Caroline Murat, *My Memoirs* (New York: G. P. Putnam's Sons, 1910), pp. 150–56; Octave Aubry, *Eugenie Empress of the*

French, trans. F. M. Atkinson (Philadelphia: Lippincott, 1931), p. 115; Thayer, I, 372; Harold Kurtz, *The Empress Eugenie 1826–1920* (Boston: Houghton Mifflin Co., 1964), pp. 94–95, 100–102.

14. Minghetti, *Miei Ricordi*, III, 96, 110–11; *Nuove lettere inedite del Conte Camillo di Cavour*, pp. 331–32, 335; *Ricordi di Michelangelo Castelli*, p. 189.

15. Minghetti, *Miei Ricordi*, III, 106.

16. *Ricordi di Michelangelo Castelli*, pp. 190–91.

CHAPTER VIII

1. *Nuove lettere inedite del Conte Camillo di Cavour*, p. 552.

2. *The Memoirs of Francesco Crispi*, trans. Mary Prichard-Agnetti, ed. Thomas Palamenghi-Crispi (New York and London: Hodder Stoughton, 1912), I, 70; Mack Smith, *The Making of Italy, 1796–1870*, pp. 215–16; *Ricordi di Michelangelo Castelli*, p. 73.

3. Minghetti, *Miei Ricordi*, III, 136; Massari, *Il Conte di Cavour*, p. 160; *The Memoirs of Francesco Crispi*, I, 71.

4. *Posthumous Papers of Jessie White Mario*, pp. 277–78; Minghetti, III, 125.

5. Thayer, *The Life and Times of Cavour*, I, 439.

6. Visconti Venosta, *Ricordi di gioventù*, pp. 248, 252, 255; Carpi, p. 58. *Nuove lettere inedite del Conte Camillo di Cavour*, p. 476.

7. Mack Walker (ed.), *Plombières: Secret Diplomacy and the Rebirth of Italy* (New York: Oxford University Press, 1968), p. 164.

8. Mack Smith, *Victor Emanuel, Cavour, and the Risorgimento*, p. 60.

9. Camillo di Cavour, *Discorsi Parlamentari*, X, 411.

10. Pasolini, *Memorie*, pp. 213–14; Minghetti, III, 165, 179.

11. *Nuove lettere inedite del Conte Camillo di Cavour*, pp. 298, 523, 527, 531.

12. Walker, p. 171.

13. *Ibid.*, p. 193.

14. *Il Carteggio Cavour-Nigra dal 1858 al 1861*, ed. Commissione dei Carteggi di Camillo Cavour (Bologna: N. Zanichelli, 1961), I, 63.

15. Evelyn Martinengo Cesaresco, *Italian Characters in the Epoch of Unification* (London: T. Fisher Unwin, 1890), p. 225.

CHAPTER IX

1. Mack Smith, *The Making of Italy*, p. 235.

2. Walker, *Plombières*, pp. 213–16, 221–23.

3. *Ricordi di Michelangelo Castelli*, p. 77.

4. Walker, p. 229.

5. Mack Smith, *The Making of Italy*, p. 251.

6. *Il Carteggio Antonelli-Sacconi (1858–1860)*, ed. Mariano Gabriele (Rome: Istituto per la storia del *Risorgimento*, 1962), I, 7; Massari, *Diario dalle cento voci*, p. 2.

7. *Archivio di Stato di Roma, Miscellanea di Carte Politiche o Riservate, busta 131, fascicolo 4665.*

8. Massari, *Il Conte di Cavour*, pp. 301–303.

9. *Le Moniteur Universel. Journal Officiel de l'Empire Français,* March 5, 1859.

10. *Il Carteggio Antonelli-Sacconi*, I, 54.

11. Massari, *Il Conte di Cavour*, p. 310.

12. *Ricordi di Michelangelo Castelli*, p. 83.

13. *Archivio Centrale dello Stato, Archivio Depretis, serie I, busta 1, fascicolo 6.*

14. *Archivio Segregato del Vaticano, Segreteria di Stato Esteri*, 1860, *Rubrica 165, fascicolo 79.*

15. Massari, *Diario dalle cento voci*, p. 118.

CHAPTER X

1. Mack Smith, *The Making of Italy*, p. 290.

2. Walker, p. 244.

3. Federigo Sclopis di Salerano, *Diario segreto (1859–1878)*, ed. P. Pietro Pirri (Turin: Deputazione subalpina di storia patria, 1959), p. 166; Massari, *Diario dalle cento voci*, p. 308; *Ricordi di Michelangelo Castelli*, p. 212.

4. *Archivio di Stato di Roma, Miscellanea di Carte Politiche o Riservate, busta 137, fascicolo 4789.*

5. Circular Letter of Cardinal Antonelli of December, 1859, *Archivio Segreto del Vaticano, Segreteria di Stato Esteri*, 1860, *Rubrica 165, fascicolo 70, sottofascicoli 9–10.*

6. *Count Cavour and Madame de Circourt*, p. 85.

7. *Archivio Centrale dello Stato, Archivio Depretis, serie I, busta 3, fascicolo 9, sottofascicolo 9.*

8. *Archivio di Stato di Roma, Miscellanea di Carte Politiche o Riservate, busta 134, fascicolo 4838.*

9. Ettore Passerin D'Entreves, "Appunti sull' impostazione delle ultime trattative del governo cavouriano colla S. Sede, per una soluzione della questione romana (novembre 1860–marzo 1861," *Chiesa e stato nell' Ottocento, Miscellanea in onore di Pietro Pirri*, ed. by R. Aubert, A. M. Ghisalberti and E. Passerin D'Entreves (Padova: Editrice Antinore, 1962), II, 568.

10. *Archivio Segreto del Vaticano, Segreteria di Stato Esteri*, 1860, *Rubrica 165, fascicolo 71; Ricordi di Michelangelo Castelli*, p. 89.

11. Shepard B. Clough and Salvatore Saladino, *A History of Modern Italy: Documents, Readings, and Commentary* (New York: Columbia University Press, 1968), p. 115.

12. *Archivio Centrale dello Stato, Archivio Depretis, serie I, busta 3, fascicolo 9, sottofascicolo 9.*

13. *The Memoirs of Francesco Crispi*, I, 431; Walker, p. 259.

14. *Archivio di Stato di Roma, Miscellanea di Carte Politiche o Riser-*

vate, busta 134, *fascicolo* 4809; *Archivio Centrale dello Stato, Fondo Fanti, scatola* 1, Cavour to Fanti, September 11, 1860.

15. *Diplomatic Relations between the United States and the Kingdom of the Two Sicilies*, II, 571.

CHAPTER XI

1. Massari, *Il Conte di Cavour*, p. 195; *idem.*, *Diario dalle cento voci*, p. 298.

2. *Archivio Segreto del Vaticano, Segreteria di Stato Esteri*, 1860, *Rubrica* 165, *fascicolo* 71, *sottofascicoli* 221–24.

3. Nicola Zanichelli (ed.), *La questione romana negli anni 1860–1861. Carteggio del Conte di Cavour con D. Pantaleoni, O. Passaglia, O. Vimercati* (Bologna: Commissione reale editrice, 1929), I, 168.

4. Allocuzione di N. S. Papa Pio IX. *Sancticcisimi Domini Nostri Pii Divinia Providentia Papae IX Allocutio Habita in Consistorio Secreto Die XVIII Martii MDCCLXI*," *Civiltà Cattolica* (Roma: All' Uffizio della *Civiltà Cattolica*, 1861), Series IV, X, 5–12; Jemolo, *La questione romana*, p. 133; Commissione per la pubblicazione dei documenti, *I documenti diplomatici italiani. Prima serie*, 1861–1870 (Rome: Istituto poligrafico dello stato, 1952), I, 46.

5. Jemolo, *Chiesa e stato in Italia negli ultimi cento anni*, p. 161.

6. *I documenti diplomatici italiani*, I, 79.

7. "La confederazione italiana e l'Unità piemontese," *Civiltà Cattolica*, Series IV, X, 529–55.

8. Luigi Salvatorelli, *The Risorgimento: Thought and Action*, trans. Mario Domandi (New York: Harper and Row, 1970), p. 152.

9. Walker, *Plombières*, p. 261.

10. Massari, *Diario dalle cento voci*, p. 41.

11. *Ricordi di Michelangelo Castelli*, pp. 93–96.

12. *Count Cavour and Madame de Circourt*, p. 15.

13. Massari, *Il Conte di Cavour*, p. 434.

14. Giorgio Spini, *L'Evangelo e il berretto frigio. Storia della Chiesa Libera in Italia 1870–1914* (Turin: Editrice Claudiana, 1971), p. 10.

15. Miriam E. Urban, *British Opinion and the Policy of the Unification of Italy, 1856–1861* (Scottdale, Pa.: Mennonite Press, 1938), p. 418.

Selected Bibliography

ARCHIVAL MATERIAL

Archivio Depretis, Serie I. *Archivio Centrale dello Stato,* Rome.
Archivio Fanti. Archivio Centrale dello Stato, Rome.
Fondo Famiglia Benso di Cavour. Archivio Centrale dello Stato, Rome.
Miscellanea di Carte Politiche o Riservate, 1848–1861. *Archivio di Stato di Roma,* Rome.
Segreteria di Stato Esteri, 1844–1862. *Archivio Segreto del Vaticano,* Vatican City.

PRINTED WORKS OF CAVOUR

Bianchi, Nicomede (ed.). *Il Conte Camillo di Cavour. Documenti editi e inediti.* Turin: Unione Tipografico Editrice, 1863.
Carteggi di Camillo Cavour. La liberazione del Mezzogiorno e la formazione del Regno d'Italia. Edited by the National Commission for the Publication of the Papers of Count Cavour. Bologna: Zanichelli, 1962.
Count Cavour and Madame de Circourt: Some Unpublished Correspondence Edited by Costantino Nigra. Translated by Arthur John Butler. London: Cassell and Co., 1894.
Diario inedite con note autobiografiche del Conte di Cavour. Edited by Domenico Berti. Rome: Voghera, 1888.
Discorsi parlamentari di Camillo Benso di Cavour. Edited by A. Omodeo and Luigi Russo. Florence: Ente Nazionale di Cultura, 1932.
Il Carteggio Cavour-Nigra dal 1856 al 1861. Edited by the National Commission for the Publication of the Papers of Count Cavour. Bologna: Zanichelli, 1961.
Lettere edite ed inedite di Camillo di Cavour. Edited by Luigi Chiala. Turin: Roux e Favale, 1882–87.
Zanichelli, Nicola (ed.). *La questione romana negli anni 1860–61. Carteggio del Conte di Cavour con D. Pantaleoni, C. Passaglia, O. Vimercati.* Bologna: Commissione Reale Editrice, 1929.
———. *Cavour e L'Inghilterra: Carteggio con V. E. D'Azeglio.* Bologna: Commissione Reale Editrice, 1933.

MEMOIRS, DIARIES, AND CORRESPONDENCE OF CONTEMPORARIES

D'Azeglio, Massimo. *I Miei Ricordi.* Edited by Ferdinando Carlesi. Rome: Edizioni Cremonese, 1965.

Epistolario di Luigi Carlo Farini. Edited by Luigi Rava. Bologna: Zanichelli, 1911.

Gay, Nelson H., "Cavour e l'Incognita. Corrispondenza inedite d'Amore," *Nuova Antologia,* anno LXI (February, 1926), 289–311.

Hudry, Marius. "Correspondence de Manfredo Bertone, Conte de Sambuy, Ministre plenipotentiaire du gouvernement sarde après du Saint Seige (Nov. 1851–Nov. 1852) à monseigneur André Charvaz, ancien précepteur du Roi Victor Emmanuel II," in *Chiesa e stato nell' ottocento. Miscellanea in onore di Pietro Pirri.* Edited by R. Aubert *et al.* Padua: Antinore, 1962. I, 327–54.

Manzotti, Fernando. "Il problema italiano nella corrispondenza di Luigi Carlo Farini sulla *Presse,* sulla *Morning Post* e sulla *Continental Review,*" *Rassegna Storica del Risorgimento,* IL (1959), 43–60.

Martini, Ferdinando. *Due dell' estrema, Il Guerrazzi e Il Brofferio. Carteggi inediti (1859–1866)* Florence: Felice Le Monnier, 1920.

Massari, Giuseppe. *Diario dalle cento voci.* Bologna: Cappelli, 1959.

———. *Il Conte di Cavour. Ricordi biografici.* Turin: Eredi Botta, 1873.

Minghetti, Marco, *Miei Ricordi.* 3rd ed. Turin: L. Roux, 1888.

Murat, Princess Caroline. *My Memoirs.* New York: G. P. Putnam's Sons, 1910.

Ollivier, Émile. *Journal, 1861–1869.* Edited by Theodore Zedlin and Anne Troisier de Diaz. Paris: Julliard, 1961.

Pasolini, Giuseppe. *Memorie 1815–1876.* Edited by Pietro Desiderio Pasolini. Turin: Fratelli Bocca, 1887.

Pallavicino, Giorgio. *Memorie di Giorgio Pallavicino. Pubblicate per cura della figlia.* Turin: Roux, Frassati and Co., 1895.

Pio IX da Vescovo a pontifice. Lettere al Card. Luigi Amat (Agosto 1839–Luglio 1848) Edited by Giovanni Maioli. Modena: Società Tipografica Modenese, 1943.

Posthumous Papers of Jessie White Mario: The Birth of Modern Italy. Edited with an introduction by Duke Litta-Visconti-Arese. New York: Charles Scribner's Sons, 1909.

Ricordi di Michelangelo Castelli, 1847–1875 Edited by Luigi Chiala. Turin: L. Roux, 1888.

Sclopis di Salerano, Federigo. *Diario segreto (1859–1878)* Edited by Pietro Pirri. Turin: Deputazione subalpina di storia patria, 1959.

The Memoirs of Francesco Crispi. Edited by Thomas Palamenghi-Crispi. Translated by Mary Prichard-Agnetti. New York: Hodder and Stoughton, 1912.

The Roman Journals of Ferdinand Gregorovius, 1852–1874 Edited by Friedrich Althaus. Translated by Mrs. Gustavus W. Hamilton. London: George Bell and Sons, 1907.

Visconti-Venosta, Giovanni. *Memoirs of Youth: Things Seen and Known, 1847–1860.* Translated from the 3rd ed. by William Prall. Boston: Houghton Mifflin Co., 1914.

————. *Ricordi di gioventù. Cose vedute e sapute, 1847–1860.* Milan: Rizzoli Editore, 1959.

PRINTED PRIMARY SOURCES OF A
PUBLIC NATURE

Atti del Parlamento Subalpino. Discussioni. 1848–1861.

Banche, governo e parlamento negli stati sardi. Fonti documentarie (1843–1861). Edited by Ernesto Rossi and Gian Paolo Nitti. Turin: Fondazione Luigi Einaudi, 1968.

Blakiston, Noel (ed.). *The Roman Question: Extracts from the Despatches of Odo Russell from Rome, 1858–1870.* London: Chapman and Hall, 1962.

Diplomatic Relations between the United States and the Kingdom of the Two Sicilies. Edited by Howard R. Marraro. Ragusa: S. F. Vanni, 1951.

Great Britain. *British and Foreign State Papers,* XXXVI 1847–48).

Il Carteggio Antonelli-Sacconi (1858–1860). Edited by Mariano Gabriele. Rome: Istituto per la storia del *Risorgimento,* 1962.

Italy. I Documenti diplomatici italiani. Prima serie, 1861–1870.

Legge Siccardi sull'abolizione del foro e delle immunità ecclesiastiche tornate del Parlamento Subalpino. Florence: Parenti Editori, 1958.

The Letters of Queen Victoria. First Series. Edited by Arthur C. Benson and Viscount Esher. London: J. Murray, 1907.

United States Ministers to the Papal States: Instructions and Despatches 1848–1868. Edited for the American Catholic Historical Association by Leo Francis Stock. Washington: Catholic University Press, 1933.

NEWSPAPERS AND PERIODICALS

Civiltà Cattolica, 1852–1857, 1859–1861.

Il Giornale di Roma, 1860.

Il Progresso, 1851.

Il Risorgimento, 1847–1853.

L'Armonia della religione colla civiltà, 1848–1854.

Le Moniteur Universel. Journal Officiel de l'Empire Français, 1858–1859.

L'Opinione, 1848–1850.

L'Osservatore Ligure-Subalpino, 1851–1852.

L'Osservatore Romano, 1860–1861.

New York Times, 1861.

GENERAL WORKS ON THE RISORGIMENTO

Berkeley, George F. and Joan Berkeley. *Italy in the Making, 1815–1848.* Cambridge: The University Press, 1932–40.

Bersezio, V. *Il Regno di Vittorio Emanuele II. Trent' anni di vita italiana.* Turin: Roux e Favale, 1878.

Bianchi, Nicomede. *Storia documentata della diplomazia in Italia dall' anno 1814 all' anno 1861.* Turin: Unione-Tipografico-Editrice, 1872.

Brofferio, Angelo. *Storia del Parlamento Subalpino.* Milan: Battezzeti, 1866–1870.

Di Nolfo, Ennio. *Storia del Risorgimento e dell' Unità d'Italia.* Milan: Rizzoli Editore, 1865.

Faldella, Giovanni. *Piemonte e l'Italia.* Turin: S. Lattes and Co., 1911.

Flora, Emanuele. "Lo statuto albertino e l'avvento del regime parlamentare nel regno di Sardegna," *Rassegna Storica del Risorgimento,* XLV (1958), 26–38.

Gay, Nelson H. (ed.), *Scritti sul Risorgimento.* Rome: La Rassegna Italiana, 1937.

Gramsci, Antonio. *Sul Risorgimento.* Edited by Elsa Fubini. Introduction by Giorgio Candeloro. Rome: Editori Riuniti, 1959.

King, Bolton. *A History of Italian Unity.* 4th ed. London: Nisbet and Co., 1934.

Mack Smith, Denis. *The Making of Italy, 1796–1870.* New York: Harper and Row, 1968.

Martin, George. *The Red Shirt and the Cross of Savoy.* Cornwall, N.Y.: Cornwall Press, Inc., 1969.

Salata, Francesco. "Da Carlo Alberto a Vittorio Emanuele II," *Rassegna Storica del Risorgimento, anno* XXII (December, 1935), 819–44.

Salvatorelli, Luigi. *The Risorgimento: Thought and Action.* Translated by Mario Domandi. New York: Harper and Row, 1970.

Walker, Mark (ed.), *Plombières: Secret Diplomacy and the Rebirth of Italy.* New York: Oxford University Press, 1968.

Woolf, S. J. *The Italian Risorgimento.* New York: Barnes and Noble, Inc., 1969.

BIOGRAPHICAL STUDIES OF CAVOUR

De Mazade, Charles. *Le comte de Cavour.* Paris: Plon, 1887.

Ferri, Carlo E. *Il pensiero economico del Conte di Cavour.* Milan: Fratelli Treves, 1921.

Malagodi, Giovanni, *Cavour vivo. 1861–1961.* Florence: Sansoni, 1961.

Massari, Giuseppe. "Camillo di Cavour," in *Il Risorgimento Italiano. Biografie storico-politico d'illustri contemporanei.* Edited by Leone Carpi. Milan: Antica Casa Editrice, 1886.

Martinengo-Cesaresco, Evelyn. *Cavour.* London: Macmillan and Co., Ltd., 1898.

Orsi, Pietro. *Cavour and the Making of Modern Italy 1810–1861.* New York: G. P. Putnam's Sons, 1914.

Romeo, Rosario. *Cavour e il suo tempo, 1810–1842.* Bari: Laterza, 1969.

Ruffini, Francesco. *La giovinezza del Conte di Cavour.* Turin: Bocca, 1912.

——. *Ultimi studi sul Conte di Cavour.* Bari: Laterza, 1936.

Salvadori, Massimo. *Cavour and the Unification of Italy.* Princeton, N.J.: Van Nostrand, 1961.

Thayer, William Roscoe. *Cavour e Bismarck. Un parallelo storico.* Rome: Tipografia E. Voghera, 1906.

——. *The Life and Times of Cavour.* Boston: Houghton Mifflin Co., 1911.

Villari, Pasquale. "The Youth of Count Cavour," in *Studies Historical and Critical.* Translated by Linda Villari. Freeport, N.Y.: Books for Libraries Press, n.d.

Whyte, A. J. *The Political Life and Letters of Cavour, 1848–1861.* London: Milford, 1930.

CHURCH-STATE RELATIONS DURING THE RISORGIMENTO

Berselli, Aldo. "Il problema della libertà religiosa nel pensiero di Marco Minghetti," *Rassegna Storica del Risorgimento,* XLIII (1956), 234–43.

Cadorna, C. *Illustrazione giuridica della formula del Conte di Cavour, Libera Chiesa in Liberto Stato.* Rome: Badoniana, 1882.

Coppa, Frank J. "Realpolitik and Conviction in the Conflict between Piedmont and the Papacy during the *Risorgimento,*" *Catholic Historical Review,* LIV (January, 1969), 579–612.

De Rosa, Gabriele. *Della restaurazione all' età giolittiana. Storia del movimento cattolico in Italia.* Bari: Laterza, 1966.

Fonzi, Fausto. "Correnti di opposizione alla politica piemontese tra i Cattolici di Liguria negli anni 1849–1859," *Rassegna Storica del Risorgimento,* XXXVII (1950), 140–50.

Gorresio, Vittorio. *Risorgimento scomunicato.* Florence: Parenti Editori, 1958.

Guichonnet, Paul. "Les archives de Monseigneur André Charvaz, précepteur de Victor Emmanuel II et leur interêt pour l'histoire du Risorgimento," *Rassegna Storica del Risorgimento,* XLI, 385–90.

Hales, E. E. Y. *Pio Nono.* New York: P. J. Kenedy and Sons, 1954.

Halperin, Samuel William. *The Separation of Church and State in Italian Thought from Cavour to Mussolini.* Chicago: University of Chicago Press, 1937.

Jemolo, Arturo Carlo. *Chiesa e stato in Italia negli ultimi cento anni.* 3rd. ed. Turin: Giulio Einaudi Editore, 1952.

——. "I Cattolici e la formazione dello stato nazionale unitario," in *Partecipazione dei Cattolici alla vita dello stato italiano.* Edited by E. Clerici. Rome: Editrice Studium, 1958.

——. *La questione romana*. Milan: Istituto per gli studi di politica internazionale, 1938.

——. "Libera chiesa in libero stato," in *Cavour, 1861–1961*. Turin: Bottega d'Erasmo, 1962.

Massè, Domenico. *Cattolici e Risorgimento*. Rome: Edizione Paoline, 1961.

Montale, Bianca. "Gustavo di Cavour e *l'Armonia*," *Rassegna Storica del Risorgimento*, XLI (1954), 456–66.

——. "Lineamenti generali per la storica dell' *Armonia* dal 1848 al 1857," *Rassegna Storica del Risorgimento*, XLIII (1956), 475–84.

Palumbo, Beniamino. "Preti del Risorgimento," *Rassegna Storica del Risorgimento*, XLIII (1956), 511–14.

Passerin D'Entreves. "Appunti sull' impostazione delle ultime trattative del governo cavouriano colla S. Sede per una soluzione della questione romana (novembre 1860–marzo 1861)," in *Chiesa e Stato nell' Ottocento*, II, 563–95.

——. "I precedenti della formula cavouriana libera Chiesa in libero Stato," *Rassegna Storica del Risorgimento*, XLI (1954), 494–506.

Pirri, P. Pietro. *La questione romana*. Rome: Pontifica Università Gregoriana, 1951.

Pirri, P. Pietro. *La laicizzazione dello stato sardo, 1848–1856*. Rome: Pontifica Università Gregoriana, 1944.

Quinet, Edgar. *La question romaine devant l'histoire, 1848 à 1867*. Paris: Armand Le Chevalier, 1868.

Salvatorelli, Luigi. "Il problema religioso nel Risorgimento," *Rassegna Storica del Risorgimento*, XLIII (1956), 193–216.

Spini, Giorgio. *L'Evangelo e il berretto frigio. Storia della Chiesa Libera in Italia 1870–1914* Turin: Editrice Claudiana, 1971.

ROLE OF OTHER STATES AND FIGURES IN THE RISORGIMENTO

Acton, Harold. *The last Bourbons of Naples (1825–1861)*. New York: St. Martin's Press, Inc., 1961.

Coppa, Frank J. "The Religious Basis of Giuseppe Mazzini's Political Thought," *Journal of Church and State*, XII (Spring, 1970), 237–53.

De Bertier de Sauvigny, G. *Metternich and his Times*. Translated by Peter Ryde. London: Darton, Longman and Todd, 1962.

De Cesare, R. *Roma e lo stato del Papa dal ritorno di Pio IX al XX Settembre*. Rome: Forzani, 1907.

Eyck, Erich. *Gladstone*. Translated by B. Miall. New York: A. M. Kelley Publishers, 1968.

Farini, Luigi Carlo. *Lo stato romano dall anno 1815 al 1850*. 3rd. ed. Florence: Felice Le Monnier, 1853.

Ghisalberti, Carlo. "Il consiglio di stato di Pio IX," *Studi Romani*, anno II (1954), 55–68.

Grew, Raymond. *A Sterner Plan for Italian Unity.* Princeton: Princeton University Press, 1963.

Hearder, Harry. "La politica di Lord Malmesbury verso l'Italia nella primavera del 1859," *Rassegna Storica del Risorgimento, anno* XLIII (January–March, 1956), 35–58.

Kurtz, Harold. *The Empress Eugenie, 1826–1920.* Boston: Houghton Mifflin Co., 1964.

Leetham, Claude. *Rosmini: Priest, Philosopher and Patriot.* Baltimore: Helicon Press, Inc., 1957.

Leonetti, Alfonso, and Ottavio Pastore. *Chiesa e Risorgimento.* Milan: Edizioni *Avanti!,* 1963.

Leti, Giuseppe. *Roma e lo stato pontificio dal 1849 al 1870.* 2nd ed. Ascoli Piceno: Giuseppe Cesari Editore, 1911.

Lodolini, Armando. *Mazzini: Maestro Italiano.* Milan: Dall' Oglio, 1963.

Mack Smith, Denis (ed.). *Garibaldi.* Englewood Cliffs, N.J.: Prentice-Hall, Inc., 1969.

————. *Victor Emanuel, Cavour, and the Risorgimento.* London: Oxford University Press, 1971.

Monaco, Michele. *Clemente Solaro della Margarita. Pensiere ed azione di un Cattolico di fronte al Risorgimento.* Turin: Mariett, 1955.

Monti, Antonio. *La politica degli stati italiani durante il Risorgimento.* Milan: Casa Editrice Vallardi, 1948.

Simon, Alois. "Palmerston et les Etats Pontificaux en 1849," *Rassegna Storica del Risorgimento, anno* XLIII (July–September, 1956), 539–46.

Urban, Miriam B. *British Opinion and Policy on the Unification of Italy, 1856–1861.* Scottdale, Pa.: Mennonite Press, 1938.

Wallace, Lillian Parker. "Pius IX and Lord Palmerston, 1846–1849," in *Power, Public Opinion and Diplomacy.* Edited by L. P. Wallace and William C. Askew. Durham: Duke University Press, 1959.

OTHER WORKS

Clough, Shepard B., and Salvatore Saladino. *A History of Modern Italy: Documents, Readings and Commentary.* New York: Columbia University Press, 1968.

Collodi, C. *Biografie del Risorgimento.* Florence: Casa Editrice Marzocco, 1941.

Mastellone, Salvo. *Victor Cousin e il Risorgimento italiano.* Florence: Felice Le Monnier, 1955.

Saint-Armand, Imbert de. *France and Italy.* Translated by Elizabeth Gilbert Martin. New York: Charles Scribner's Sons, 1899.

Salomone, A. William (ed.). *Italy from the Risorgimento to Fascism.* Garden City: Doubleday and Co., 1970.

Whyte, Arthur James. *The Evolution of Modern Italy.* Oxford: Basil Blackwell, 1950.

Index